MIRRORS OF THE ECONOMY

A volume in the series
Cornell Studies in Political Economy
edited by Peter J. Katzenstein

A list of titles in this series is available at
www.cornellpress.cornell.edu.

MIRRORS OF THE ECONOMY

National Accounts and International Norms in Russia and Beyond

Yoshiko M. Herrera

CORNELL UNIVERSITY PRESS ITHACA AND LONDON

First published 2010 by Cornell University Press
Printed in the United States of America

Library of Congress Cataloging-in-Publication Data

Herrera, Yoshiko M., 1970–
Mirrors of the economy : national accounts and international norms in Russia and beyond / Yoshiko M. Herrera.
p. cm. — (Cornell studies in political economy)
Includes bibliographical references and index.
ISBN 978-0-8014-4585-9 (cloth : alk. paper)
1. National income—Russia (Federation)—Accounting. 2. Russia (Federation)—Economic conditions—1991—Statistics. 3. Russia (Federation)—Statistical services. I. Title. II. Series: Cornell studies in political economy.
HC340.I5H47 2010
339.347—dc22 2010025716

Cornell University Press strives to use environmentally responsible suppliers and materials to the fullest extent possible in the publishing of its books. Such materials include vegetable-based, low-VOC inks and acid-free papers that are recycled, totally chlorine-free, or partly composed of nonwood fibers. For further information, visit our website at www.cornellpress.cornell.edu.

Cloth printing 10 9 8 7 6 5 4 3 2 1

For G. Shizuko Herrera
and Agnes MacDougall Herrera

Contents

Tables and Figures

Tables

Figures

Preface

National accounting is not the most glamorous topic, nor even one that most people have heard of. Yet the System of National Accounts (SNA) is the framework for most of our information about the economic activity of countries around the globe. Although national statisticians usually work behind the scenes, we see the fruits of their labors every day in news about unemployment, gross domestic product (GDP), analysis of when the recession might end, and so on. Politicians, policy makers, and firms regularly make consequential decisions based on economic information provided by the SNA.

The SNA, however, is a relatively new institution. It was developed at the conceptual level in the mid-twentieth century, but even thereafter, a variety of distinct national practices dominated. And why would countries not want to measure their economies in different ways—why should Russia, Fiji, Nigeria, and Canada use the same set of indicators and oblige themselves to follow the same set of rules for measuring economic activity? The scope of the SNA as an international institution and the level of cooperation and coordination that it demands are nothing short of heroic.

A turning point for the SNA as the global norm for national accounting came in the early 1990s, when adherents of an alternative system, the newly postcommunist countries, dropped their Material Product System and enthusiastically embraced the SNA. Their decision is the story of this book. Why did Russia and other postcommunist states abandon a system they had developed and worked with for decades to adopt a competing international institution? Was the SNA good and efficient and, from a Western perspective, the right thing? Absolutely. The general history of postcommunist institutional reform, however, has taken a different path. The story behind the decision requires analysis of what went on in the Russian national statistical office, Goskomstat, in the early 1990s.

To understand the decisions of Goskomstat statisticians, we have to consider their identities and shared norms, their interests, and the political, economic, and ideational context in which they worked. The research for this book, therefore, has taken me to many meetings with statisticians from Goskomstat. I conducted extensive interviews in 2003–5 with Goskomstat officials in Moscow and in ten regions across Russia.[1] To get at the historical development of identity and norms at Goskomstat, I did a systematic content analysis of Goskomstat's monthly journal *Vestnik statistiki* from 1950 to 2000.[2] *Vestnik statistiki,* the in-house journal of Goskomstat, details internal organizational and methodological debates.

But this is an international story as well, or more specifically an examination of how the SNA became an international norm. Hence I have relied heavily on documentation by national statisticians working at the international level and on primary documents published by the UN, OECD, IMF, and the International Bank for Reconstruction and Development (World Bank). I also did interviews with statisticians in Washington, D.C., and officials in the United States and at international organizations who worked with Goskomstat. Overall, the fieldwork yielded over seventy-five interviews with a range of people who worked in or with Goskomstat on the SNA.

Research for this book was made possible by generous funding from several sources. The National Council for Eurasian and East European Research (NCEEER) provided resources for fieldwork in Russia. The International Research and Exchanges Board also supported a research trip for interviews. The Kennan Institute at the Woodrow Wilson Center in Washington, D.C., provided a short-term grant and was a valuable base for D.C interviews. I also received funding from the Project on Russian Governance headed by Timothy Colton and Stephen Holmes. Much of the research leave time for this project was provided by the Davis Center for Russian and Eurasian Studies and the Weatherhead Center for International Affairs at Harvard University. I am also grateful to the University of Wisconsin, Madison, and in particular the Graduate School, the International Institute, and the Center for Russia, East Europe, and Central Asia for research support in the final stages.

The Institute of Ethnology and Anthropology (IEA) of the Russian Academy of Sciences, directed by Valery A. Tishkov, provided valuable logistical support in Russia. In particular, Sergey Sokolovskiy of the IEA did much of the organizational work and accompanied me on interviews; I thank him for his help as well as his engaging conversation and commentary. Everyone should be so lucky to travel across Russia and into the state bureaucracy with one of the country's leading anthropologists.

1. To protect officials from possible punishment for disclosure of information, I use coded numbers, e.g. "GKS24," in attributing quotations from Goskomstat officials. Exceptions include the highest officials: Vladimir Sokolin, the former chairman of Goskomstat; and Irina Masakova, the head of the SNA department. I also refer to independent analysts by name.

2. This journal was renamed *Voprosy statistiki* in 1994.

Dominique Arel organized an international observation project on the 2002 Russian census, which allowed me to meet firsthand with census enumerators at Goskomstat and other Goskomstat officials. Although this book focuses on the economic statistics of Goskomstat rather than the census and demographic data, that opportunity to see how Goskomstat worked from the inside was invaluable.

I am also grateful to the leadership of Goskomstat for opening its doors to interviews and observation. I did not vet any part of this book with Goskomstat officials, and I am not sure they would agree with all my conclusions, but I could not have written such a book without the interviews. I sincerely thank the staff of Goskomstat for making time for me as well as for their professional and courteous reception. Although there are surely some grounds for criticizing the organization, which I discuss in the book, after meeting with Goskomstat statisticians one cannot fail to respect and admire their professionalism and dedication to their work.

Interviews with Russian and international experts who have worked with Goskomstat were enormously helpful as well. In particular, I thank Timothy Heleniak, Andrei Kosarev, Valentin Kudrov, and Vladimir Treml. I also thank Victor Gabor of the World Bank, who not only shared his firsthand knowledge of the Material Product System but also provided me with hundreds of pages of documents. Misha Belkindas of the World Bank has worked very closely with Goskomstat since the 1990s and is one of the most knowledgeable people in the world on national accounts in postcommunist countries and efforts to implement the SNA; I thank him for sharing his insight in interviews and for valuable comments on the entire manuscript.

Two conferences dedicated to the work of the late Abram Bergson at the Davis Center at Harvard in 2000 and 2003, organized by Marshall Goldman and others, brought together academics who have been personally engaged with the debates about the Soviet economy discussed in this book. I learned a tremendous amount from these conferences, and I thank the organizers for including me.

With research assistance on this project, I have been unusually lucky. On the content analysis of *Vestnik statistiki,* George Georgiev, Darya Nachinkina, Kuanysh Batyrbekov, Ana Sirbu, and Evgeny Finkel all did outstanding work, and I thank them for their consistent dedication. Louisa McClintock, Nicole B. Kraus, and Yulia Woodruff provided additional research support. I was also fortunate to have Darya Nachinkina assist in interviews in Moscow.

At Harvard University, the Davis Center was my intellectual base through most of this project, and I am very grateful to the entire staff, especially Executive Director Lisbeth Tarlow for supporting my research. I benefited greatly from the intellectual atmosphere at the Davis Center, beginning with the collegial and engaging tone set by the director, Timothy Colton—no one could ask for a better colleague. I also thank several other colleagues from the Harvard Government Department for their comments and support of this project, including Daniel Carpenter, Jorge Domínguez, Grzegorz Ekiert, Peter Hall, Jennifer Hochschild, Alastair Iain Johnston, Roderick MacFarquhar, Elizabeth Perry, and especially Susan Pharr, who has given me detailed comments on parts of this manuscript as well as astute advice over the years.

The Department of Political Science at the University of Wisconsin, Madison, has become a wonderful new home for me, not least because of the Center for Russia, East Europe, and Central Asia (CREECA) and many excellent faculty and students. I thank my colleagues in the department for making it such a friendly, productive, and engaging place to work.

Parts of this manuscript were presented at professional conferences and academic workshops, too numerous to name. At these conferences and presentations I received valuable feedback from many people, but in particular I thank Regina Abrami, Stephen Deets, Elise Giuliano, Stephen E. Hanson, Stephen Holmes, Ward Kingkade, Pauline Jones Luong, Mark Kramer, John LeDonne, Stanislav Markus, Maria Popova, Mikhail Pryadilnikov, Adam Sheingate, Oxana Shevel, Tom Simons, Hillel Soifer, Richard Snyder, Konstantin Sonin, Kathleen Thelen, Elina Treyger, Susan Webb-Yackee, and David Woodruff.

Several colleagues read an earlier version of the book in its entirety and provided helpful commentary—so helpful that I was convinced to rewrite most of the book and take it in a different direction. I thank Rawi Abdelal for his generous comments and consistently good advice over the years and for convincing me to focus on norms at an early stage. Anna Grzymala-Busse not only provided excellent commentary on my book and papers but organized conferences and panels where I obtained feedback. She has provided friendly support and positive energy throughout. I also thank sincerely Martin Dimitrov, Gerald Easter, Juliet Johnson, Alena Ledeneva, and Theodore Hopf. I have learned a great deal from their work and found their comments on my book extremely helpful. It is asking a lot of someone to read a whole book; I hope I have put the advice to good use.

Some people have commented in detail on specific chapters, even more than once: Hilary Appel, Dawn Brancati, Bear Braumoeller, Timothy Colton, Venelin Ganev, Gary Herrigel, Jacques E. C. Hymans, Andrew Kydd, David Laitin, Jeff Strabone, and Sogomon Tarontsi. All of them went out of their way for me, sometimes far out of the way, and I am very grateful. I am particularly indebted to Gary Herrigel for getting me to think about institutions beyond the idea of rules and constraints. I hope I have done justice to his pragmatist approach to institutions. In addition, I thank Jacques Hymans and Dawn Brancati for reading (and re-reading) drafts at a moment's notice.

I thank Lewis Bateman for his support on this project over the years and for urging me to take a historical perspective. Valerie Bunce suggested that I investigate what was happening with the SNA not just in Russia but in Eastern Europe as well; fortunately, I had the sense to follow up on this idea, which changed the project and led me to appreciate the collaborative nature of the development of the MPS among the East European and Soviet states. I thank Rory MacFarquhar for early and helpful comments when I had barely begun to contemplate the idea of economic information and the state. At the time, Rory warned me that the topic was huge and "full of stultifying technicalities." He turned out to be right. I hope I have been able to move beyond the details to convey some of the real excitement and importance of Russia's move to the SNA.

I thank Peter Katzenstein and Roger Haydon of Cornell University Press. They took a chance on me at an early stage, then were patient when various life events intervened and delayed my revisions. They have both offered excellent commentary and advice on the manuscript. I could not ask for a better editorial team.

For friendship and good cheer over the course of writing the book I thank Margarita Estevez-Abe, Pushpita Casey, Farnaz Fardad, Alevtina Gavrilova, Rose McDermott, Michelle Sieff, and Yulia Woodruff.

Last but not least, I am grateful to my family, and especially Andy for his patience and support. I thank Amelia and Tommy for being the fun part of every day. I have special thanks for my mother, G. Shizuko Herrera, and my grandmother, Agnes MacDougall Herrera. My mother has helped me my entire life, but never more so than in the last few years as she has enthusiastically embraced her role as *bachan*. Her extended visits have sustained us in a chaotic and busy time. My grandmother has similarly helped me in critical ways, and it is because of her that I first was able to visit Eastern Europe in the spring of 1990—the trip that sparked my fascination with Russia and the postcommunist states. Just as important, she continues to be a close confidante and sage adviser. I thank them both for their love and support and encouragement, and I dedicate this book to them.

Acronyms

CEEC	Central and Eastern European country
CIS	Commonwealth of Independent States
CES	Conference of European Statisticians
CMEA/Comecon	Council for Mutual Economic Assistance
Goskomstat	*Gosudarstvennyi komitet po statistike* (State Committee for Statistics)
Gosplan	*Gosudarstvennaia planovaia komissiia* (State Planning Commission)
EBRD	European Bank for Reconstruction and Development
ESA	European System of Integrated Economic Accounts
IARIW	International Association for Research in Income and Wealth
ICP	International Comparison Program
ILO	International Labour Organisation
IMF	International Monetary Fund
ISWGNA	Inter-Secretariat Working Group on National Accounts
MPS	Material Product System
NSO	National statistical office
NMP	Net Material Product
OECD	Organisation for Economic Co-operation and Development
OEEC	Organisation for European Economic Co-operation, precursor to the OECD
PPP	Purchasing Price Parity
Rosstat	*Federal'naia sluzhba gosudarstvennoi statistiki* (Federal Service for State Statistics)
RSFSR	Russian Republic (Russian Soviet Federated Socialist Republic)
SNA	System of National Accounts
Statkom CIS	*Statisticheskii komitet sodruzhestva nezavisimykh gosudarstv* (Statistical Committee of the Commonwealth of Independent States)
TsSU	*Tsentral'noe statisticheskoe upravlenie SSSR* (Central Statistical Administration of the USSR)
UN	United Nations
UNSD	United Nations Statistical Division, formerly UNSO
UNSO	United Nations Statistical Office, precursor to UNSD
USSR	Union of Soviet Socialist Republics
WWII	World War II

Note on Translation and Transliteration

For transliteration of Russian words, I use the Library of Congress (LOC) system with a few exceptions. I adhere to conventional transliterations of words in the text (for example, "Yeltsin" instead of "El'tsin" and "soviet" instead of "sovet") but not in citations of Russian titles. Russian words in English-language publications are rendered as in the work cited, and for consistency, names of Russian authors who have published in English-language sources are rendered as in the existing transliteration. For example, "Youri" Ivanov instead of "Iurii" Ivanov because he has published in English as Youri Ivanov.

For national accounts in the USSR, Russian sources use the term "Balans narodnogo khoziaistva" or its acronym BNKh; it is literally "Balance of the national economy," but I translate it as Material Product System or MPS throughout, because MPS is the conventional term used in international publications.

The title of Russia's national statistical office is somewhat troublesome. The office has had many names over the years, but the four primary ones are:

- TsSU (*Tsentral'noe statisticheskoe upravlenie SSSR,* Central Statistical Administration of the USSR), for much of the Soviet period;
- Goskomstat USSR (*Gosudarstvennyi komitet po statistike SSSR,* State Committee for Statistics of the USSR), 1987–91;
- Goskomstat Russia (*Gosudarstvennyi komitet po statistike Rossiiskoi Federatsii,* State Committee for Statistics of the Russian Federation), 1991–2004; and
- Rosstat (*Federal'naia sluzhba gosudarstvennoi statistiki,* Federal Service for State Statistics), 2004 to the present.

Because most of this book examines institutional changes that occurred when the organization was called Goskomstat USSR and Goskomstat Russia, I call it simply Goskomstat, unless the specific historical name is necessary.

All translations were done by the author or research assistants unless otherwise noted.

INTRODUCTION

We live in an era of globalization—and of resistance to globalization. Although international institutions are multiplying in number, and ever more governments are committing to standardized norms of legal and economic organization, there is wide variation in compliance with international rules. Even as compliance with international norms and rules seems to be relentlessly increasing, seemingly good and efficient "best practices" find detractors all over the world—states, organizations, and bureaucrats who repudiate rules, resist or delay their implementation, subvert their intention, or just plain ignore them.

Nowhere is the puzzle of compliance and rejection of international rules starker than in the postcommunist world. Some of the newly independent countries have rushed to comply with as many international rules as they can find and have sought, as a reward for their efforts, the opportunity to follow thousands more rules embodied in the European Union *acquis.* At the same time, the Eurasian region has become famous for its people's ability to subvert rules. From privatization to democracy to everyday transactions, ingenuity in getting around rules is almost a way of life in the region.[1] This is not a new phenomenon: in many ways, survival under communism required "working the system," not

1. On adaptation and subversion of formal institutions of privatization and economic reform, see Stark and Bruszt 1998 and Woodruff 2000; on democracy, see Wilson 2005; on everyday practices, see Ledeneva 2006; and on corruption, see Karklins 2005.

blind adherence to rules. Yet postcommunist states have taken the lead on compliance with certain important international institutions.

In explaining variation in the implementation of international institutions, the international relations literature has focused on factors at the international or state level: the global balance of power, material interests of states, state-level identities, and international norms. But international outcomes may be the result of actions by actors *within* states, rather than states per se. To address this we must delve more deeply into states, not treating them as unitary actors, and examine contestation in their politics, institutions, and organizational identities.

Because the real work of implementing international rules typically takes place within state bureaucracies, we must look at those responsible for implementation, bureaucrats in particular state agencies. By going *inside* the state, we can understand the processes by which international norms and institutions are embraced, rejected, amended, or partially implemented and assess the reasons why some international norms or rules take hold and others do not.

This approach also yields new insights about the effect of international factors on domestic politics. How do factors such as international norms and institutions explain the variation in state-related outcomes at the domestic level—changes in state capacity across organizations, orientation toward democratic governance and transparency, economic reform, and so on?

One case that exemplifies the interaction of variables at the international and domestic levels is the System of National Accounts (SNA). The SNA structures almost all national economic data. It is the basis for virtually every comparative economic indicator used today, including Gross Domestic Product. The SNA provides information about economies, but it is also the informational basis for public policy and assessments of policy, as well as for private economic decisions including investment choices. It is therefore a critical institution for economic development. Yet the SNA is also relatively new—a mid-twentieth-century innovation—and until recently, not the only choice available to states. Until the 1990s, the USSR and other centrally planned economies used the Material Product System (MPS). Today there is near unanimous agreement on the appropriateness of the SNA for all states, but actual implementation of the SNA across states still varies quite significantly.

In this book I examine one important component of the variation in implementation of the SNA, namely the about-face in support for the SNA by some of the states that most strongly opposed it in the past, postcommunist countries in Eastern Europe and especially Russia and the other states of the former USSR. According to a range of quantitative measures developed by the UN and IMF, postcommunist countries including Russia have gone well beyond a symbolic agreement to implement the SNA, and beyond even what their structural capacities might have predicted. In a radical institutional break with the past, postcommunist states exhibited great enthusiasm for the SNA in the early 1990s, fully abandoning the MPS and ushering in the global hegemony of the SNA today.

To explain this more general phenomenon and its specific manifestation in the USSR/Russia, I analyze the work of Goskomstat, which was the bureaucratic agency responsible for national accounts.[2] The fundamental puzzle is why Russia abandoned a system of national accounts developed over decades—the MPS—for rapid implementation of the SNA. Why did the seemingly gray Soviet bureaucrats of Goskomstat, working for less than $50 a month, amid an unprecedented economic crisis and an incompletely reformed political system, embark on comprehensive institutional reorganization of their statistical system when they might reasonably have taken a much slower, less substantive approach?

My argument centers on norms, in particular a type that I call a "conditional norm." Norms are defined as behavioral prescriptions for a given identity group; they suggest appropriate action for members of the group. A *conditional norm* is one that limits the appropriateness of a given action by specific conditions. It specifies action for certain types of actors or under certain conditions rather than for all members of the group at all times. If conditions change, then we can expect a change in shared understandings of what constitutes appropriate behavior.

I argue that Soviet statisticians' dedication to the MPS was supported by a conditional norm that the SNA was appropriate for capitalist economies and the MPS for centrally planned economies. The appropriateness of a particular statistical system—SNA or MPS—depended on the type of economy. This conditionality provided Soviet statisticians with a legitimate exception to using the SNA in their own country and was consistent with their Marxist view that economic structure should determine statistical institutions.

As economies in Eastern Europe and the USSR became more market-oriented in the late 1980s, national statisticians' regard for the SNA changed and support for the SNA quickly replaced support for the MPS. For actors tasked with implementing the SNA, the Soviet-era conditional norm provided the conceptual link between structural economic change and institutional change.

Clarifying what happened in Russia and the postcommunist experience with the SNA in the early 1990s speaks to the broader questions of how domestic factors affect international outcomes, including norm development and implementation, and how international factors affect domestic institutional change.

---

2. Goskomstat is an acronym derived from the full name of the organization. See the Note on Translation and Transliteration.

The System of National Accounts

To govern, states must gather information about society and the economy. Social and economic actors depend on information to make choices. National accounts shape the content and meaning of this information, making economies "legible" to governments, firms, citizens, and external observers and informing the development of policy and policy assessment.

The System of National Accounts—first formalized in 1953 and updated in 1968, 1993, and 2008—structures the content, categorization, definition, collection, and dissemination of information about the economy throughout most of the world.[3] As a national accounting system, it

- defines what counts as productive activity and what does not (household labor, environmental costs, etc.);
- categorizes that activity in ways that connect to theoretical constructs of the economy, including institutional sectors such as governments, households, firms, and their activities (spending, consumption, investment);
- defines specific indicators and how they are measured; and
- sets out rules for how to assemble and provide access to data.

The SNA provides the basis for aggregate macroeconomic indicators such as GDP, which allow us to make instant economic comparisons across countries and over time. Thanks to decades of institutionalized cooperation across countries on standards of data content, reliability, and accessibility, we see not only the final figures but also the methods by which those figures have been produced—a truly remarkable achievement in transparency.

Even though nearly all countries today, with varying degrees of success, are in the process of implementing the SNA, the development of a single system of national accounts was no easy feat. For centuries, there was no agreement on how to count people, goods, and services, either within or across countries.

The theoretical and technical hurdles in national accounting are daunting. In addition to advances in statistics and the social sciences,[4] the formalization of the SNA depended on theoretical contributions from leading economic thinkers—including John Maynard Keynes, Colin Clark, Morris Copeland, Ragnar Frisch, Simon Kuznets, Wassily Leontief, Jan Tinbergen, and Richard Stone.

---

3. Although the SNA was first formalized at the United Nations and much of the organizational work is still directed by UN agencies, since the 1993 update it has been the joint project of several international organizations and is now formally published by the ISWGNA, which comprises members from the OECD, Eurostat, the IMF, the UN, and the World Bank.

4. On statistics and the development of social science, see Desrosières 1991.

Stone developed the first version of the SNA for the UN in 1953, work for which he received a Nobel Prize in Economics in 1984.[5]

But the theoretical and technical challenges are only part of the story of the development of the SNA. Political coordination across states was equally, if not more, difficult to achieve. States and societies have long differed in what kinds of information they consider necessary to collect and how they process information. That national accounts are a mirror of the economy, as is often said in Russia, is only a metaphor; in practice, capturing the economy in a set of figures requires many decisions. Consequently, there are myriad possibilities for differences in national accounting systems: the economy alone does not determine the statistical system. Rather, as Alonso and Starr (1987) have argued, statistical systems reflect the societies that develop them; they reflect the values or "presuppositions" of time and place.

Moreover, because national statistics not only measure the economy but allow for judgment on the progress, or not, of public policies, states—as well as political factions within states—have a keen interest in the way that economic activity is measured. For example, in debates over the superiority of capitalism versus socialism in the early to mid-twentieth century, growth rates were the key criteria that analysts used to measure success, and those growth rates depended significantly on the system of national accounting in use. Debates over the allocation of resources within countries, such as the United States or European states after WWII, were framed in terms of the Keynesian conceptual apparatus of macroeconomics and the SNA. Hence the SNA did not just reflect the economy but helped shaped economic policy: what one measures will be what one devotes oneself to. A different national accounting system might have resulted in different economic policies.[6]

Although decisions about national accounts always had to balance competing interests within states, the difficulty of cooperation was magnified at the international level. The development of a single global system of national accounts is thus an example of tremendous cooperation in the face of huge obstacles.

Despite consensus on the SNA in theory, there is tremendous variation in states' levels of implementation. Some countries have made only shallow commitments to the SNA and have done the minimum to produce basic data, whereas others have embraced the SNA in its entirety. The reasons for this variation

5. For a discussion of these intellectual influences, see Kenessey 1994a. Simon Kuznets, Wassily Leontief, and Jan Tinbergen were also Nobel Prize winners, though primarily for other contributions.

6. This is one reason that the current debates over GDP are so contentious. To include environmental costs, for example, in a major national aggregate indicator could have significant consequences for subsequent policy decisions.

demand our attention. In speaking of gaps in national accounts data, Michael Ward noted: "These gaps are not value neutral. They occur because there is a conceptual, managerial, budgetary, or political reason why some national data are simply not collected" (2004, 101). Indeed, the point of this book is to investigate this variation in an important set of cases, in order to provide a more systematic explanation of the patterns in implementation that we observe.

The SNA in Postcommunist States

There are two puzzles regarding the current hegemony of the SNA. First, how was this hegemony achieved? How did the SNA beat out all alternative systems, including the MPS, to become the single internationally recognized system for national accounts? To answer that, we have to address the second, related question: What explains variation in the level of implementation of the SNA across countries? These questions are interrelated because implementation is an indication of authentic state support for the SNA, and the development and consolidation of the SNA as an international norm depends precisely on that state support. The process of contestation between states over the SNA versus alternatives informs the pattern of variation in SNA implementation, and likewise understanding variation in implementation of the SNA is a window into the process of the development of the SNA as an international norm.

Using a range of quantitative and qualitative measures, the UN and the IMF have documented the progress of all countries in implementing the 1993 SNA.[7] As one might expect, the richest countries with the most efficient and capable state bureaucracies have advanced the furthest. The poorest, most unstable, incapacitated states generally have the lowest level of implementation. The SNA requires enormous organizational infrastructure, and it is not surprising that at the extremes resources might be determinative—the wealthiest can do more, and the poorest have trouble meeting even the minimum standards for implementation. But resources and capacity do not explain the tremendous variation across countries with similar levels of wealth.

Postcommunist countries as a group have gone further in implementing the SNA than any other geographic region or group of states except North America and Western Europe.[8] They surpass other countries at similar levels of income. This pattern is especially noteworthy given the significant differences among

7. It is too early to assess implementation of the 2008 SNA. It was formally approved only in 2009.

8. I document this point in detail in chapter 1.

postcommunist states, such as Kyrgyzstan and the Czech Republic.[9] Why are some states—newly capitalist and not very rich or capable—so much more able or willing than others to measure their economies according to capitalist principles?

At first glance, the answer may seem obvious. Given the extraordinary events of 1989 and 1991, when so many other political and economic institutions were in flux, perhaps this was just another Western institution introduced to replace the old, less efficient communist ones. But the transition from communism, especially in the states of the former Soviet Union, was not simply the adoption of "best practices"—a victory of rational, efficient, Western institutions over Soviet failures.

Such a triumphalist view of the transition is inaccurate. It also masks the enduring legacy of past practices and institutions that have made the development of markets and democracy very difficult to achieve in some postcommunist states. If postcommunist countries abandoned their commitment to their own statistical system and embraced the SNA owing simply to its superior efficiency, transparency, and material advantages for a market economy, why did they not also adopt other market-enhancing institutions such as stable property rights, functioning taxation institutions, and regulatory oversight? Many postcommunist states adopted the SNA but not other international institutions common to SNA countries. The euphoria of 1989 and 1991 was soon followed by profound disappointment in postcommunist states' willingness or ability to implement a range of institutional reforms. The retreat from democracy in Russia is one of the biggest disappointments of all. That the implementation of the SNA promoted markets and efficiency is not a reason to ignore it. Instead, we should figure out why, given the background of some dramatic failures, implementation of international institutions has succeeded in some areas.

Among the postcommunist countries, Russia did surprisingly well on the implementation of the 1993 SNA and it is a theoretically interesting case. The USSR opposed the SNA from its inception and instead favored its own statistical system; the decision to change to the SNA was abrupt, making it a case of discontinuous, rapid institutional change. Because the USSR was one of the strongest critics of the SNA, understanding its turnaround provides some insight into the broader postcommunist experience. Moreover, Russia inherited the core of the Soviet statistical organization, so any legacy of the Soviet statistical experience was most concentrated in Russia.

9. For the level of SNA implementation on the Milestone assessment, see UN Statistical Commission (1999).

The establishment of the SNA in Russia was also a significant step toward bringing the content and quality of Soviet economic statistics into line with international standards. Goskomstat had to completely reorganize its work and address some of its worst shortcomings, including politically circumscribed content, lack of methodological transparency and related reliability problems, and severe limitations on data accessibility. So the question becomes not just why Russia decided to move to the SNA but how Goskomstat—a conservative, resource-poor, Soviet organization—achieved a relatively high degree of implementation of this particular reform so quickly. Finally, it is also noteworthy that many of the positive international assessments of Russian national accounts continue into the era of Vladimir Putin and Dmitry Medvedev, where, given the shift to authoritarianism, one might expect much less of a commitment to the economic transparency of the SNA.

Russia's past practices, state institutional environment, level of economic development, and resources available for reform, as well as its state identity and position toward international norms and rules, make it an unlikely case for this type of institutional change. Goskomstat's move to the SNA in the early 1990s is an improbable and remarkable story. Explaining what made institutional change possible in these seemingly inhospitable circumstances informs our understanding of domestic institutional change in the context of global institutions and provides insight into the implementation of international institutions from a domestic standpoint, shedding light on why global norms and rules seem to be so strong in some contexts but not in others.

Explanations

What explains the unusual experience of Goskomstat in Russia? What caused Soviet bureaucrats to drop their opposition to the SNA? And what made them adopt this institutional reform but not others? To explain implementation, it is helpful to disaggregate two components of institutional change in favor of the SNA: the direction of change, or the decision to support the SNA; and the magnitude of change, or level of implementation. Although these are interrelated questions, they may have different explanations.

Structural explanations focusing on efficiency, structural changes in the global or domestic economy, and resources (material and human capital) available to states and organizations are incomplete. As I show in chapter 4, the move to the SNA enhanced efficiency in Russia and other postcommunist states, economic reforms did require changes to statistical systems, and the availability of certain resources did boost implementation. But structural factors cannot explain the persistent variation across countries with similar structural conditions and the better-than-expected success of postcommunist countries. For that, we need to examine the motivation of actors in national statistics offices, in particular the development of internal interest in the SNA among postcommunist statisticians. I examine theories that address actors and interests in chapter 5.

For a variety of reasons, the Russian state, societal actors, and international organizations were too weak to force change at Goskomstat. Instead, Goskomstat had an unprecedented level of autonomy from the government, which was then quite weak. As a result, the interests of Goskomstat statisticians themselves proved critical. Goskomstat statisticians strongly favored the move to the SNA. But why, when the same people had strongly rejected the SNA as appropriate for the USSR or Russia only a few years earlier? Material incentives do not explain this shift. There was no added pay or bonuses for implementing the SNA. Instead, the move halved the organization's staff.

A third set of theories considers constructivist approaches to identities and norms. Institutional change in these theories comes from a change in social identities or norms, both of which usually involve long-term processes. The shift in support for the SNA happened very quickly, and I found no radical change in organizational identity at Goskomstat. Thus the move to the SNA is not explained by a change in organizational identity from the Soviet to the post-Soviet period.

Identity theories also ignore an important reality. Although all states are now expected to use the SNA, this norm became global and unconditional only after the USSR and Eastern Europe abandoned the MPS. The ascendancy of the SNA as a norm thus depends on its adoption by postcommunist states; it does not explain those decisions.

Conditional Norms

Norms are important in understanding Russia's move to the SNA, but we have to look at them from a different angle, beginning with a constructivist approach to institutions. The primary contribution of constructivist approaches to institutions, as articulated by Herrigel (2005, 2010), is to take seriously the issue of mutual constitution between agents and structures. Herrigel problematizes the relationship between actors and rules and treats institutions as products or outcomes, rather than as exogenous constraints on actors' behavior. Based on this pragmatic view of institutions, he charts a middle path, explaining actors' choices with regard to institutions between interests and structures, rejecting both the determinism of efficiency and of material interests and the excessive structuralism of some approaches to historical institutionalism and identity. Pragmatism opens the door to a more agent-centered treatment of identities and norms. It corrects the prior focus in the existing literature on the effect of structures (international norms) on agents (states), which overlooks how states affect norms (Checkel 1998).

In the case of the SNA, the Herrigel approach yields uncommon insight for understanding the interaction between national statisticians at the domestic level and the development of an international norm. As I discuss in chapter 3, material incentives and efficiency concerns vied with ideas, rooted in identity, about how to structure national accounts. The result was a messy array of practices across states allowed to choose between two primary systems emerging in the 1970s, the SNA and the MPS. There were also significant national exceptions such as the National Income and Product Accounts System in the United States and the system developed in France by the Service des études économiques et financières (SEEF), as well as other regional adaptations of the SNA such as the European System of Integrated Economic Accounts.

To understand why postcommunist states, especially the USSR, decided to implement the SNA and not some other system, we need a firm grasp of the institutional alternatives available at different times and the opportunities for creativity. We can reach that understanding by taking a pragmatic approach to institutions. In particular, we must consider the ways in which local actors understand rules and norms, how they decide which rules to follow, and how they attempt to change rules and norms.

I depart from Herrigel, however, in arguing for the need to redirect our attention primarily back to identity. Focusing squarely on contestation within identity groups—including norm contestation—reveals the mutual constitution of structures and agents where structures affect agents, but agents *also* affect structures. Mutual constitution is an enduring gap in the literature. Identities should not be seen as simply structural constraints. Actors within identity groups can creatively respond to norms—or even norms in formation, as the SNA was for much of the 1950s through the 1980s—by formulating new norms.

One response is to formulate *conditional norms* that limit the appropriateness of a given action. Norms are held by identity groups, but the subjects of a norm, the actors to whom the norm should apply, can differ from the holders of the norm. For example, an ethnic group may hold a norm about military service, but the obligation to fight for the group may apply only to men. In this case the holders of the norm include both men and women, but only men are the subjects. Thus, we can define conditional norms as those norms for which subjects are limited; that is, there are some conditions on the type of actor for whom the norm should apply.

To give another example, one nation may believe that democracy is always an appropriate form of government. This is an unconditional norm: not everyone accepts it, but those who do recognize no legitimate exceptions. In contrast, a conditional norm might state that democracy is appropriate only for societies that have reached a certain level of economic development. Here the condition is level of economic development. Similarly, the idea that free trade should take place everywhere is an unconditional norm, whereas limiting free trade to certain states is a conditional norm.

Conditions matter because they provide a different mechanism for understanding the possibilities for norm-based institutional change. A conditional norm can be an original formulation or a stage in norm formation, but it can also be a strategic response to existing norms, promoted by actors who care about community legitimacy but seek exemptions from particular norms. Such norms can be weapons of the weak as well as of the powerful. Conditionality is an option for those who want to maintain community standing while creating an exemption for themselves or others. But conditional norms are not just surface-level rationalizations. If we examine the iterative rounds of norm formation, contestation, and compliance, we see that conditional norms may start out as creative contextual strategies, but their evolution into widely accepted norms means that the initially contingent conditions have unforeseen consequences. Conditional norms, like all norms, have deeper ideational effects.

Conditional norms can explain the rapid institutional change at Goskomstat in the 1990s. In the 1960s and 1970s, the SNA was gaining adherents internationally. Although not yet a consolidated or uncontested norm, it attracted more support as it underwent revision and statisticians around the world were focusing attention on the SNA as a means of coordinating national accounts. In addition, the development of the SNA and comparison with the alternatives spurred the formalization of the MPS. The MPS grew out of interaction among the Council for Mutual Economic Assistance (CMEA) states and was based on the Soviet system of statistics developed in the late 1920s, one of the earliest systems of national accounts.[10] Soviet statisticians were conflicted: they cared deeply about maintaining legitimacy in the international community of statisticians, but they were also committed to the Soviet state. The Soviet response to the emerging support for the SNA was to suggest conditions for its appropriateness. They argued that the SNA was appropriate for capitalist economies and the MPS for centrally planned, socialist economies. They insisted on the legitimacy of both systems under appropriate conditions. The norm's condition was the structure of the economy: market-based or centrally planned. This condition

10. The CMEA included most East European states (except Albania and Yugoslavia) and the USSR as well as Cuba, Mongolia, and Vietnam.

was consistent with Marxist-Leninist ideology, which linked economic structure to particular political and social institutions.

So long as the two economic systems coexisted, this conditional norm promoted institutional stability by rationalizing the gap between international and Soviet statisticians' work. Was there a strategic element to this conditional norm, which served Soviet interests? Probably, but it also reflected identity-based understandings of differences between states. Regardless of the motivations, the conditional norm was institutionalized by publication of both systems by the UN in 1971 and further work such as the International Comparison Program in the 1970s and 1980s, which was undertaken by the USSR, CMEA, UN, and other Western countries and which formally recognized and reinforced the structural economic basis for the two systems. Thus the conditional norm became widely accepted among Soviet statisticians, and somewhat reluctantly tolerated, though not necessarily accepted by Western statisticians.

When the economy of the USSR changed, however, Goskomstat statisticians also changed their views on which statistical system was appropriate. For Soviet and Russian statisticians, the economic reforms of the perestroika era (1987–91) sounded the death knell for the MPS and heralded the SNA. These structural economic changes conceptually necessitated adoption of the SNA, thus accounting for the quick change in interests in favor of SNA reform among Soviet and Russian statisticians. Yet, the norm itself did not change: with market reforms the SNA was suddenly appropriate, and the MPS, as in the past, went the way of central planning.

The same argument can be applied to other postcommunist countries. With the end of the Soviet Union and the end of Soviet domination of Eastern European economies, the command economy largely disappeared as an alternative economic system in the region. With this structural change, the conditions legitimating the Soviet alternative to the SNA for CMEA statisticians also disappeared.

A conditional norm was not the only variable necessary for the implementation of the SNA by postcommunist countries. Structural changes in the economy were critical, but not because they changed material incentives. The conceptual link between economic structures and statistical systems mandated the shift. Certain resources—highly educated staff and technical assistance from international organizations—also greatly aided implementation, although they do not explain the decision to move to the SNA nor the internal support for the SNA in postcommunist national statistical offices (NSOs). Likewise, the interests in support of the SNA by the Russian government and international organizations were necessary but not sufficient to explain the actions of Goskomstat. Finally, identities and norms were critical factors, but a conditional norm based on a relatively stable identity proved to be the key variable.

Table 0.1 Key variables in explanations of institutional change and implementation of international institutions

<table>
<tr><th rowspan="2">EXPLANATORY APPROACH</th><th colspan="4">VARIABLES AND LEVEL WHERE VARIATION MIGHT OCCUR</th></tr>
<tr><th>INTERNATIONAL</th><th>STATE</th><th>ORGANIZATION (OR FIRM)</th><th>INDIVIDUAL</th></tr>
<tr><td>Constructivist institutions (chapter 3)</td><td colspan="4">Mutual constitution and contestation: interactive development and revision of actors and rules</td></tr>
<tr><td rowspan="5">Structural factors (chapter 4)</td><td>Efficiency of institution</td><td></td><td></td><td></td></tr>
<tr><td colspan="2">Structural change in the economy</td><td></td><td></td></tr>
<tr><td></td><td>GDP per capita</td><td></td><td></td></tr>
<tr><td></td><td>State capacity</td><td>Resources</td><td></td></tr>
<tr><td></td><td>Education</td><td>Human capital</td><td></td></tr>
<tr><td rowspan="2">Actors and material interests (chapter 5)</td><td colspan="4">Imposition of others' interests (politicians, society, international actors) using material incentives</td></tr>
<tr><td></td><td></td><td colspan="2">Arrival of new change-oriented actors</td></tr>
<tr><td rowspan="2">Identities and norms (chapter 6)</td><td colspan="3">Identity change or new norm development</td><td></td></tr>
<tr><td colspan="3">Socialization into existing identity/norms</td><td></td></tr>
<tr><td>Conditional norms (chapter 7)</td><td colspan="3">Change in conditions specifying norm appropriateness</td><td></td></tr>
</table>

This explanation also sheds light on the development of the SNA as a global norm. The SNA did not achieve dominance, then win acceptance among postcommunist states. Rather, the opposite occurred. The CMEA's decision to abandon the MPS in favor of the SNA was critical to the development of the SNA as a hegemonic norm today.

Table 0.1 summarizes how conditional norms fit with other theoretical approaches to the implementation of international institutions. The table lists the major approaches and explanatory variables associated with each approach, and notes the level (international, state, organization/firm, or individual) where variation might occur. From the table we can see clearly where empirical evidence for each variable might be located. I examine these approaches, one by one as noted on the table, in the chapters that follow.

Implications

The concept of conditional norms has several theoretical implications. First, it specifies the circumstances under which behavioral prescriptions apply, clarifying the logic of norms and the limitations placed on them.

Second, it recognizes the agency of actors in the constitution and amendment of norms. By examining the responses and innovations of actors within identity groups during multiple phases of norm development, we can uncover the mutual constitution between norms and actors. The concept of conditional norms does not regard identities and norms simply as constraints on actors' behavior. Actors can create or reformulate norms and identities by imposing conditions to delimit the appropriateness of rules for the group. Conditionality allows actors to respond to established norms or norms in formation and to adapt norms to fit changing circumstances. Actors can actively change and affect norms rather than simply being constrained by them.

Third, conditional norms provide an alternative model of institutional change, including change in the conditions themselves.[11] In this case, institutional change is a response to changing conditions of appropriateness for certain actions, not to changes in the underlying norms or the identities in which they may be situated. Constructivists often argue that a change in actors' identities or the development of a new identity or norm explains institutional change. This can happen, but the concept of conditional norms reveals a different approach to norm-based institutional change. A change in conditions—even exogenous ones such as structural economic transformation or regime transformation—can alter views on the appropriateness of a particular institution, even if identities and norms remain stable.

Fourth, conditional norms allow for a constructivist incorporation of structural factors into norm-based theories, where structural conditions are linked to appropriate kinds of action via norms. One important example of this concerns the economy: if the structure of the economy is a condition on which norms are contingent, economic change affects institutional choices through the conceptual place of the economy in shared norms rather than its effect on material interests. In this way the concept of conditional norms bridges rationalist and constructivist views of institutional change.

Furthermore, the concept of conditional norms, as it applies to the SNA's adoption by postcommunist states, advances our understanding of state building, bureaucratic reform, and the postcommunist "legacy." Historical legacies allow us to think about how socially constructed experiences affect current approaches to problems. The concept of conditional norms provides a concrete mechanism for how shared norms from the Soviet past shape current institutional choices and practices. In this way, it clarifies the role of culture, historical legacies, and domestic demand in reform (Ekiert and Hanson 2003; Ganev 2007). There is a

11. Conditional norms have always existed but have not been identified as such. What is novel is the theoretical formulation of conditions as a mechanism for norm-based change.

growing literature on general institutional reform in postcommunist countries and on the state but fewer studies of bureaucratic reform.[12] This study of Goskomstat reduces that gap by providing a detailed empirical analysis of the transformation of an important state bureaucracy. Finally, and in conjunction with the effort to bring in international factors, this study of the SNA contributes to the emerging literature on global regulation (Mattli and Woods 2009) by using a more precise definition of norms to get at the relationships among information, interests, and ideas.

---

12. Some notable exceptions include Kornai et al. 2001 and Schimmelfennig and Sedelmeier 2005b on state institutional reform in postcommunist countries; Johnson 2010 on reform of central banks; Easter 2002 on tax collection; and Pryadilnikov 2009 on bureaucratic reform in Russia.

1

A SYSTEM OF NATIONAL ACCOUNTS

The Postcommunist Transformation of Russian Statistics

The System of National Accounts is currently the only internationally recognized framework for national accounts in the world, and nearly all countries are in some stage of implementing it. Yet this has not always been the case. Only a few decades ago the SNA faced a seemingly formidable alternative, the Material Product System, used primarily by communist countries. The SNA itself is a relatively recent institution. Even so, it has no competition at present.

In this chapter, I discuss the concept of national accounts, the SNA as a particular form of national accounting, and the MPS. I also examine key issues that made data from the MPS and SNA difficult to reconcile. Next I outline differing levels of implementation of the 1993 SNA throughout the world, using measures from the United Nations and International Monetary Fund.[1] This analysis sets up the key puzzle in this book: why postcommunist countries, including Russia, have gone remarkably far in implementing the SNA.

In addition, this chapter details Russia's implementation of the SNA. I outline the direction and magnitude of the change away from the Soviet system by reviewing the work of Goskomstat in the 1990s. Finally, I return to the UN and IMF data to consider their assessment of Russia's implementation of the 1993 SNA.

1. The 2008 version of the SNA was not formally approved until 2009, so existing assessments are only for the 1993 version.

National Accounts

In brief, national accounts tackle the question of aggregate economic activity and processes within countries. An everyday understanding of the wealth of nations, per capita income, or comparisons of national productivity across years are examples of issues that can only be addressed by national accounting systems. Because national accounts make economies "legible," they are of great interest to governments, firms, and citizens alike.[2] Yet national accounting is theoretically, politically, and technically enormously complex.

There are myriad ways to define national accounts, but in general they must tackle four fundamental questions:

1. What counts as productive economic activity?
2. How should activity be generally categorized and aggregated?
3. How should activity be defined and measured?
4. How should or how might the necessary data be collected and disseminated?

None of these are easy questions, and none has a single answer, leaving quite a bit of room for debate.

The first question addresses what is called the "production boundary," what should or should not be included in measures of economic activity. A seemingly easy answer might be, count everything! Or count all production for which money (or a substitute) is exchanged. Current debates, however, reveal that drawing the production boundary line entails conceptual decisions that have serious consequences. For example, consider a current debate in national accounting, environmental costs. Should pollution and other environmental factors be counted in national accounts (so called "green GDP")? If these costs were subtracted from current values of production estimates, then our understanding of which countries actually have high growth rates might be very different. Similarly, if a person cleans his or her own house and takes care of children without pay, that activity is not currently within the SNA production boundary; it does not count as productive activity. If that same person paid someone else to clean and take care of children, then those activities would count. This issue of household labor obviously has enormous consequences for the documented level of contribution of women to national output. A final example: should illegal activity be included in national output? Unlike household labor this is often a case where money changes hands, but should legal status determine inclusion

2. On the concept of making society legible, see Scott 1999.

as productive activity? As these examples suggest, there is no obvious answer. In resolving such questions, any national accounting system is likely to be influenced by ideas and interests of the day.

The second question on categorization and aggregation, which is aimed at identifying economic actors and organizing types of activity, can be related to the first. A specific conception of the production boundary can influence the categorization scheme and resulting aggregates (such as GDP). If one considers only *material* output in the production boundary—steel, timber, cloth, wine, and so on—then the type of categorization will reflect industrial sectors. But categorization is also theoretically informed and tied to the goals for which information is to be used. A follower of John Maynard Keynes, who was interested in the relationship between government spending and unemployment, would categorize information differently from the materialist scheme above. This question of classification schemes impinges on the issue of "sectorization" in national accounts, that is, the main types of actors in an economy. At the moment, a Keynesian approach based on "institutional sectors" (government, public and private corporations, households, etc.), and their activity (consumption, savings, investment, etc.) reigns, but for much of the history of national accounting before the mid-twentieth century that was not the case. Similarly, the most widely used method of calculating GDP today relies on these Keynesian-influenced sectors and associated activity (e.g. private consumption, gross investment, government spending, and net exports).

Once we have decided what counts as economic activity and how to categorize and aggregate it, we have to figure out how to connect the national accounting framework to data. Here we move from concepts to indicators and reach the potentially mind-numbing technical minutiae of how, theoretically, to count things we agree should be counted. For example, if we did add pollution, housework, or illegal activity to the production boundary, how would we count them? What kind of pollution (air, water, ground) should be measured? What should its value be? What if the cost of air pollution by a factory equaled the output of the factory, zeroing out the total? Would that situation really be equivalent to no factory existing at all? Even for seemingly noncontroversial issues the question of measurement is not easy. How do we count something like "free checking" from a bank, or distinguish between gardening and subsistence agricultural production? And with illegal activity, measurement is difficult for several reasons. Although illegal activity falls within the production boundary for the SNA, if it is not measured well, it is not actually included in output figures. For data to be reliable and comparable, all these measurement issues have to be worked through and agreed upon.

Even if we can agree on the production boundary, the classification scheme, and measurement schemes for all the data, we then have to tackle the actual collection and dissemination of data. Although this may seem like the easy part, data collection is also rather complicated. Data are typically collected by a national statistical office (NSO) in three ways (UN Statistical Division 2003, 118): by requesting administrative records from other government agencies; through censuses (full enumeration) or surveys (samples) of relevant actors such as firms and households; and through estimation methods carried out by NSOs or affiliates. All three methods require resources, both material and human capital, and the first two methods require a great deal of cooperation among firms, household, individuals, and other government agencies. If a country has limited resources, it may not be able to put theoretically sophisticated measurement schemes into place, even if they have been agreed on. If a government fears the consequences of certain kinds of data, it may not want them collected, much less analyzed and published, and that brings up the question of dissemination, which is also subject to resource and political constraints. Hence collection and dissemination of data do not automatically follow from agreement on the principles of a national accounting system by NSOs and governments. As a result, there is significant variation in implementation of the SNA.

This brief sketch of the fundamental questions in setting up a national accounting system illustrates that there is a significant ideological or ideational component to national accounts—they are not simply a mechanical reflection of the economy. The production boundary and sectorization and aggregation schemes are deeply theoretical, ideological, and political. The way in which national accounts treat these questions is connected to economic theory, to ideas about what matters, and to interests. The measurement, collection, and dissemination approaches are also theoretically informed, but they involve more practical issues, including resources and political calculations.

If one is trying to set up national accounting standards across countries, this discussion of the key issues suggests why cross-national coordination might be difficult to achieve. Countries could (and did) have profound disagreements on theoretical issues that might preclude coordination on less theoretical, practical issues of data collection. Other countries accepted the theory but lacked the resources or political will to implement the agreed-upon framework for national accounts. Some countries opposed the national accounting framework for multiple reasons.

Although the West and the Soviet bloc were not unitary in either theory or practice, the CMEA states disagreed with the West regarding the SNA on all four fundamental questions.[3] The Soviet bloc used a different production boundary

---

3. I use term CMEA to denote the USSR and the states that were part of the Soviet "bloc" or sphere of influence. Albania and Yugoslavia left the CMEA, so it is not an ideal term, but it is consistent with the literature on the MPS and SNA.

restricted to material production, whereas the production boundary (or boundaries) in Western states were broader and included services. Sectorization and aggregation schemes also differed significantly, with a Keynesian-inspired GNP or GDP being dominant in the West and a completely different set of components and aggregate indicators in the East. Soviet statisticians usually counted things using different methodology that they did not share, so that many indicators with similar names were not equivalent to those in the West. Finally, data collection and dissemination in Soviet bloc countries relied almost exclusively on full enumeration (censuses) of firm-level data and eschewed the use of sample surveys and estimation techniques used in the West. Minimal publication of both components and underlying data was another hallmark of Soviet-bloc statistics.[4]

Adoption of the SNA by the Soviet bloc thus required fundamental change in all these principles and practices: the need to agree on a new production boundary, new classification or sectorization schemes and related aggregates, new methods for constructing indicators and variables, and new practices for data collection and dissemination. Abandoning the MPS for the SNA meant a thorough revision of the conceptual as well as the physical apparatus of state statistics—something far beyond buying new computers or retraining staff, though that was important too.

SNA vs. MPS

The System of National Accounts is a comprehensive and detailed framework for understanding economic activity, broadly construed. According to UN documents, the SNA,

> consists of a coherent, consistent, and integrated set of macroeconomic accounts, balance sheets, and tables based on a set of internationally agreed concepts, definitions, classifications, and accounting rules. . . . It provides a comprehensive and detailed record of the complex economic activities taking place within an economy and the interaction between different economic agents and groups of agents that takes place in markets or elsewhere. (UN Statistical Division 2003, 1)

Based on the SNA, we are able to measure critical economic variables such as "the level of economic development and the rate of economic growth, the change in

4. All of the above assumes that the underlying data are of high quality and not subject to errors or falsification; that was a problem in some cases but is different from the issue of coordination.

consumption, saving, investment, debts, and wealth (or net worth) for not only the total economy but also each of its institutional sectors (such as government, public and private corporations, households and non-profit institutions serving households)" (UN Statistical Division 2003, 1). These kinds of data allow for economic forecasting as well as analysis of government polices on various sectors of the economy, or the economy as a whole. In addition, because the system has been standardized, it allows for comparisons across time and space.

As this description suggests, the SNA is a framework for all the building blocks of economic analysis. By implementing the SNA, a tremendous degree of transparency is achieved; governments and other actors will be able to calculate not only a final GDP figure but all the components that go into it. Similarly, with the SNA we see not only changes in aggregate production over time but also the allocation of resources.

The first formal version of the SNA in 1953 was developed by Richard Stone and primarily geared toward measurement of national income. It was composed of three sectors (or economic actors) and six accounts (or types of economic activity). The accounts included domestic product (final expenditure for GDP), national income, domestic capital formation, current and capital reconciliation for households and private non-profit institutions (disposable income and net borrowing of households), current and capital reconciliation for general government, and the external account. There was also a standardized set of tables for countries to fill in and send to the UN. This 1953 document contained forty-six pages of explanation and a two-page description of the accounts (UN Statistical Office 1953; Lequiller and Blades 2006, 399). The production boundary in 1953 did theoretically include illegal activity (no legal distinction was made for productive output; however, for a variety of reasons, in practice large OECD countries have yet to include this) but not household labor such as cooking, cleaning, and child care.

Within about ten years of its publication, approximately sixty countries were using the 1953 SNA, but there were significant other developments by individual countries in national accounts that were not reflected in the 1953 version. A major revision was published in 1968 that was longer (250 pages, with 12 pages for the accounts). One important aspect of the SNA that did not change from 1953 to 1968 was the production boundary. However, the 1968 SNA added to the institutional sectors financial and non-financial corporations as well as nonprofit institutions (Lequiller and Blades 2006, 401). In addition, four accounts for these sectors were expanded to include a production account, an income and outlay account, a capital finance account, and a financial account. Another significant change with the 1968 SNA was the distinction between market and nonmarket producers (and "commodities" vs. "other goods and services"). The 1968 SNA also incorporated other approaches to national accounting—input-output tables, flow-of-funds, and balance sheets—which had existed before the 1953 version but were not integrated into it (Lequiller and Blades 2006, 401).

The second major revision of the SNA was published in 1993. Regarding the production boundary, despite vigorous debates, the 1993 version made only minor adjustments to the production boundary in relation to expenditures on software, mineral exploration, and valuables (art, antiques, etc.). The 1993 SNA did not alter the institutional sectors from the 1968 version but expanded the accounts from four to sixteen. In addition, balance sheets for each sector are fully integrated into the system, and the 1993 SNA has much greater integration with the OECD's Guidelines on Foreign Direct Investment, the IMF's Balance of Payment and Government Financial Statistics, and other international institutions for economic data (Lequiller and Blades 2006, 402–3).

The 1993 SNA was designed eventually to apply to all countries and was therefore much more detailed than previous versions (it is over seven hundred pages). Some countries, such as the United States, depart from the 1993 SNA in certain ways, but the underlying framework is compatible. It is fair to say that the SNA has become a dominant, even hegemonic, international institution.

In 2009 the UN Statistical Commission formally approved a revised SNA, called the 2008 SNA.[5] The 2008 version retains the basic framework of the 1993 version but includes some important clarifications.[6] Implementation of the 2008 changes is just beginning and is expected to take several years even for OECD countries. But the two versions share enough similarities that implementation of the 1993 version is a step toward implementation of the 2008 version. Hence I focus here on the development and implementation of the 1993 SNA.

Gross Domestic Product

The primary aggregate economic indicator of the 1993 SNA is GDP, which measures the value of a country's output in a given period of time. As its critics point out, GDP is not a general measure of social welfare or quality of life; it does not tell us directly about health, happiness, equality, or environmental or other

5. The UN Statistical Commission is a Functional Commission of the UN Economic and Social Council and is made up of twenty-four rotating member countries elected on the basis of geographical representation. The commission oversees the work of the UN Statistical Division (UNSD), which before 1989 was known as the UN Statistical Office (UNSO).

6. As a sign of the closeness of the versions, the 2008 version was originally called "1993 SNA, revision 1" but the title was later simplified to "2008 SNA" the year it was completed.

conditions.[7] It is nonetheless a critically important variable for understanding certain economic processes such as growth. The data used to compute GDP are the result of the painstaking labor that goes into compiling national accounts according to the 1993 rules.

A measure of national output, however, has to adequately account for inflation (so as to not equate a rise in prices with greater productivity) and has to avoid multiple counting of the same output at different stages of production (the wheat, the flour, and the final cookie). Taking these issues into account, three equivalent approaches to compiling GDP have been developed (UN Statistical Division 2003, 1).

The first approach to GDP is the "output" (also called the "production" or "value-added") approach, which as the name suggests treats GDP as output minus intermediate consumption plus taxes minus subsidies. A second is the income approach, which treats GDP as the sum of employee compensation and taxes minus subsides and gross operating surplus and mixed income. Finally, there is the "expenditure" or "final demand" approach, which treats GDP as final consumption plus gross capital formation plus net exports. This last approach is the most commonly applied of the three. These different formulas for GDP remind us that the SNA is more than a single aggregate figure. Rather it is a framework that allows for the calculation of a multitude of variables and is integrally tied to macroeconomic theory.

Material Product System

The MPS was used by the USSR for several decades and by fifteen other centrally planned economies for twenty to thirty years.[8] Although based on Soviet input-output analysis first published in 1926 (for the years 1923–24) (Popov 1926), the MPS was formalized only in 1969 and published as an international standard in 1971 (UN Statistical Office 1971). Like the SNA, the MPS was a comprehensive framework for national accounts aiming to make legible (at least to the state) all productive economic activity. However, the MPS differed from the SNA in some fundamental ways.[9]

First, the production boundary for the MPS was limited to *material* production, meaning it did not include services. According to János Árvay (1994), a

7. For a recent, comprehensive critique of GDP, see Stiglitz et al. 2009.

8. According to János Árvay, the countries using the MPS "for some period" were the USSR, Albania, Bulgaria, China, Cuba, Czechoslovakia, the German Democratic Republic, Hungary, Cambodia, the Korean Democratic Republic, Laos, Mongolia, Poland, Romania, Vietnam, and Yugoslavia (1994, 236).

9. For a comparison of the MPS and the SNA, see Ponomarenko 2002; Vanoli 2005.

Hungarian expert on national accounts, the MPS followed Adam Smith (1976 [1776]) and Karl Marx as well as most of the history of national accounts up to the mid-twentieth century in drawing the production boundary around material goods only; this was largely based on Marx's labor theory of value.[10] Even in this strict materialist view of output, however, there was some ambiguity. For example, freight transport was supposed to count toward material production, but not passenger transportation; household telephone service theoretically was not supposed to be included, but some countries included it anyway.[11] It is important to note that activity outside the production boundary of the MPS, such as services, did exist in centrally planned economies; but, as with debates over the SNA production boundary, certain activities were not included in the national accounting system as productive output for conceptual, ideological, and political reasons.[12]

Second, beyond the production boundary, the classificatory scheme and related macroeconomic indicators of the MPS were fundamentally different from the SNA. Whereas the SNA drew on Keynesian categories of economic analysis, the MPS divided the economy into three sectors: productive enterprises, the nonproductive sphere, and households. The system was based primarily on detailed tracking of material production. Its Russian name can be translated as "Balance of the National Economy." The 1969 version reflects this, setting out four "balances": material balance (production, consumption, accumulation); financial balance (production, distribution, redistribution, and final disposition of income); balance of manpower; and balance of national wealth and fixed assets (Árvay 1994, 225). The MPS had no concepts like operating surplus (gross profit income), disposable income (gross income minus income tax), or savings (Árvay 1994, 227), all of which are part of GDP calculations.

Instead of GNP/GDP, the MPS gave rise to two alternative macroeconomic indicators: "global social product" and "national income" (*natsional'nyi dokhod*). Global social product in SNA terminology would approximate gross material production. National income could be understood as net material production. National income was global social product minus intermediate consumption and depreciation of fixed assets. In English the Soviet concept of "national income"

---

10. In contrast, a Keynesian or Tinbergenian concept of output includes more than material goods.

11. Both were listed in the 1971 MPS guidelines, although in practice the USSR and Czechoslovakia did not include them. For more discussion of this, see UN Statistical Office 1971, para. 1.13; Árvay 1994, 230.

12. Furthermore, some politically sensitive activities, such as those related to the military-industrial complex, were in practice excluded or only partially included.

was rendered "net material product" (NMP), which made it more consistent with the SNA terminology (Árvay 1994).[13]

In considering the two systems from a theoretical position, it is clear they had different goals and hence produced different kinds of information. In *Quantifying the World: UN Ideas and Statistics*, Michael Ward ends his first introductory chapter on ideas and statistics with a short comparison of the SNA and MPS, arguing that both systems had laudable aspects:

> Although GNP provides an important means of quantifying the world, it provides essentially a singular dimension that relates to production and to net, not gross, output and to a gross, but not more economically meaningful, concept of net value added. The Soviet Material Product System (MPS), though similarly linked to a detailed structure of production balances generated from the establishment level within their respective industry sectors, automatically generates measures of gross material output. These have the virtuous property that, at the industry and enterprise level, they can be associated directly and perhaps more meaningfully to employment and overall productivity and to statistics about occupational status. *Each of the two systems has value.* (2004, 61, emphasis added)

As Ward does, one could make the argument that at the level of the production boundary and classificatory scheme, both systems were equally legitimate but different ways of organizing national accounts.

If we further consider the issues of definitions and measurement of indicators and collection and dissemination of data, however, then we see that the two systems were not equal in the reliability and accessibility of data that they produced. The SNA was consistently superior in reliability of data, and data from the SNA countries were also more accessible. Combined with the theoretical differences, the result was that there were several serious incongruities between the SNA and MPS, which rendered the data from the two systems not easily comparable.

A key structural issue that made comparison between the SNA and MPS difficult was the difference in prices in centrally planned and market economies. While there was some variation in price systems in CMEA countries, in the USSR most prices were set by central planners and did not reflect supply and demand. In technical terms, prices did not "equate marginal productivities in the production of goods and services with the marginal utilities of those who

13. The terminological differences between NMP (or "national income") and GDP are only the first hint of difficulties to overcome before comparing countries using the two systems.

purchase them" as they are assumed to do in market economies (Lequiller and Blades 2006, 406). In terms of their role in aggregate output, Western economists raised concerns about planned prices: they understated inflation (a critical issue for accurate estimation of GDP); they were generally higher on consumer goods than on capital goods; and many goods were exchanged outside formal markets, making their actual prices higher than those reflected in official statistics. "Turnover" or sales taxes and subsidies were not even across commodities, leading to further price distortions, and there were discrepancies with the way profits and depreciation were calculated (Pitzer 1990, 3).[14] It was not possible simply to add services and subtract depreciation from NMP to arrive at GNP (or vice versa).[15]

Arguably, the structural difference in prices and the discrepancies in associated variables might have been overcome by greater methodological transparency and efforts to bridge the gaps between the systems.[16] Instead, certain practices of CMEA NSOs exacerbated the incommensurability of data from the two systems.[17] Because of the variation in CMEA countries, let us consider the USSR on the question of transparency, the relationship of the NSO and the state, the use of methodological deceits, and limitations on data accessibility.

The Soviet government, dominated by the Communist Party, had no interest in promoting transparency in economic statistics or legibility of the economy to outsiders or to its own citizens. The control of information was a hallmark of communist rule. As the early Soviet secret police, the Cheka, ominously noted, "information is the alpha and omega of our work."[18] The Party had to meticulously monitor the economy for central planning purposes—Lenin famously remarked, "Socialism is accounting!"—but the state did not want to share that information.[19] Keeping people in the dark about the shortcomings and deficiencies of socialism and hiding the truth about successes in noncommunist systems were means of controlling the population.

In CMEA countries, NSOs had a different relationship with the state from their counterparts in the West. In centrally planned economies, NSOs were not

---

14. Profits reflected the current cost of production because they did not take the volume of capital stock employed into account. Depreciation reflected the historical cost of capital rather than the current cost because it was based on an exaggerated service life for equipment. See Pitzer 1990.

15. This was done both ways to estimate NMP and GNP, but the results were not very satisfying.

16. For example, Abram Bergson's Adjusted Factor Cost Standard (Bergson 1953a, 1961) was a methodological attempt to adjust Soviet prices for GNP calculations.

17. For a summary of the problems with Soviet statistics, see Schroeder 1995; Treml 2001, 32–34.

18. Cheka circulars, 1920–21, as cited in Holquist 1997, 415.

19. There were not, however, two sets of books: one set of high-quality data on which central planners relied, and a second set of shoddy and incomplete data released to the public. The planners used the same data as everyone else.

considered independent of the government but viewed as the state's eyes and ears with respect to plan monitoring. For example, the Central Statistical Administration of the USSR was responsible for monitoring fulfillment of state five-year plans, and for a good part of its history, it was actually part of Gosplan, the central planning apparatus. Blades and Harrison argue that this "auditing role" had methodological implications for the way statistics were organized (1992, 102). Because plans were written in volume terms, as physical units, most data were collected by NSOs that way as well, rather than as prices or the value of goods produced (or associated costs). Most data were published in these volume terms as well, or by using problematic price indices to convert the volumes to values. Every firm had a plan target, so NSOs collected data from every enterprise, meaning they did full censuses for all their data collection.[20] In contrast, market economies used sample surveys to collect firm-level data. Finally, because enterprise-level data was used to gauge plan fulfillment, there were well-known incentives for firms to overestimate production to meet plan targets (Kudrov 1993, 124–26; Treml 1994, 22).[21] This went beyond the usual problems with respondent error or bias in the West.

Although there was a general perception that the Soviet Union falsified data, such an oversimplification ignores the complex methodological maneuvers that were used to achieve statistical results.[22] It was the fact that Soviet statisticians did not just invent numbers that made analysis of Soviet statistics such a difficult but potentially tractable enterprise; analysts pored over published data trying to figure out what was behind the figures and where they came from. One of the leaders in this field, Abram Bergson, wrote: "While there are many harassing deficiencies, it seems clear that the Soviet government does not falsify those statistics which it elects to publish. If it were not for this fact, of course, research on the Soviet economy today would be entirely out of the question" (1947, 234–35). Similarly, in explaining the "numerous and puzzling inconsistencies," in Soviet statistics Vladimir Treml concluded, "as a general case, I believe that these puzzles are the product of archaic and often conflicting methodologies and conventions, faulty and biased price and output indexes and formulae, and poorly designed classifications and not of outright *ad hoc* manipulation and deliberate falsification of data" (1989, 96).[23] Among these "harassing deficiencies" there are two

20. The reason for not using sample surveys goes beyond the connection to plans; there was also an ideological proscription against surveys and sampling.

21. This is a type of falsification (*pripiski*) that Goskomstat itself constantly monitored and tried to circumvent.

22. On falsification claims, see Vanous 1987, 13; Kirichenko 1990; Belkin 1992, 97; Kudrov 1993, 130.

23. For a similar assessment, see Bergson 1947, 1953b.

cases that made comparisons between the SNA and the MPS especially difficult: the so-called "comparable" price indices and what Gregory Grossman called "descriptive distortions" (Grossman 1960).

A great deal of intellectual effort in the SNA is devoted to distinguishing between changes in volume versus changes in prices (because with inflation prices may rise without a corresponding rise in output). In the SNA output is valued in "current" and "constant" prices; constant prices essentially factor in inflation (often using a fixed-base Laspeyres formula). In the Soviet Union, much information was collected in physical units or volume; these data were then converted into "comparable price" indices using price lists that ignored unofficial transactions and did not take inflation into account. Noren writes, "Essentially, the price deflators—whether for retail or wholesale trade—were based on the prices in official price lists.... The problem with the resulting price indexes, as decades of discussion in the USSR and abroad brought out, was that the price lists ignored transactions outside official channels and failed to capture the inflation embodied in the pricing of new products in the Soviet Union" (1994, 14).[24] Similarly, Blades and Harrison noted that "comparable" price indices did not reflect product improvements or deterioration and that while these indices may "at first glance" seem like OECD price indices, they "significantly understate inflation as measured in the West" (1992, 104).

A more general way to understand why what were called "comparable" prices were not easily comparable with Western prices is Gregory Grossman's concept of "descriptive distortions," where indicators are said to mean one thing, when they really mean something else (Grossman 1960).[25] For example, Treml noted that the number of "doctors" might include dentists; "grain weight" might include dirt, water, and other matter not initially separated during the harvest; "meat" might include lard and other inedible animal parts, and so on (2001, 10). A higher-profile example of this obscurantism concerns the category of "defense expenditures," which turned out to mean only pay and current material expenses, not research, construction, or weapons purchases, which together are estimated to have represented 70 percent of the actual defense budget (Treml 2001, 10).

"Descriptive distortions" could arise from terminological disagreements: Soviet statistics used similar terms but different content for some indicators ("national income"). But "descriptive distortions" also came about because CMEA

24. For more on problems with Soviet price indices, see Kudrov 1993, 123–24; 1994.

25. This concept is cited in Treml 2001, 9. See also Kirichenko 1990. Descriptive distortions occur in other countries as well, but they were a key mechanism used by Goskomstat to hide information.

NSOs rarely published methodological descriptions of their indicators, so users could not easily figure out what the indicators contained. Agreement on standards or norms for defining particular measures varied over time, and the Soviet government had no interest in clearing up misunderstandings. Hence Soviet statisticians explained neither the content of their indicators or categories nor changes to or problems with their published data.

Another way in which CMEA NSOs diverged from international experience and exacerbated the incommensurability of MPS data concerned accessibility, both the dissemination of data and transparency in data collection and processing. Many of the theoretical differences between the MPS and the SNA and problems with the reliability of Soviet statistics could have been addressed if more data had been released and the methodology used to obtain data had been more open. Instead, inaccessibility was a prevailing feature of Soviet statistics. The government released a fraction of what was available in Western countries—limiting the scope of data collected, publishing aggregates rather than detailed data sets, limiting the number of copies of works published, and then limiting access to those publications (Schroeder 1995, 200).[26]

Why the Use of the MPS vs. SNA Mattered

National accounting systems provide a comprehensive way of understanding economic processes and a metric to assess economic policy and economic systems. The differing ways of evaluating economies—and countries—were a crucial aspect of the competition between communism and capitalism as economic systems. It is hard to overstate the importance given to figuring out which system was more productive, especially in the wake of the Great Depression in the West and apparently stunning growth in the USSR, as well as the trajectories of WWII and the Cold War.

In 1947 Seymour Harris, an economist at Harvard, convened a symposium of prominent economists aimed at improving understanding of Soviet statistics and the Soviet Union.[27] The papers were later published in *The Review of*

---

26. For more on data restrictions, see Heleniak and Motivans 1991; Kudrov 1993, 124–26.

27. Other authors attending the symposium were Paul Baran, Abram Bergson, Colin Clark, and Alexander Gerschenkron. Gerschenkron and Bergson were prominent Harvard and Columbia University economists; Baran was a well-known Marxist economist; and Clark was the first person to compile national income accounts for the United Kingdom. Seymour Harris was a professor and chair of the economics department at Harvard, as well as economic adviser to several politicians, including Adlai Stevenson, Douglas Dillon, and Presidents Kennedy and Johnson.

Economic Statistics, also edited by Harris. In explaining the reasons for the 1947 symposium, Harris wrote,

> Russian economic advance is a matter of great interest to economists, statisticians, and others. We want to measure the achievements of a planned economy against those of an unplanned and free economy. We want to know how much the U.S.S.R. produces in peace, and how much she can produce for war. Glowing reports come from Russia about the large gains in output and income. Writers on the Russian economy are frequently too disposed to accept the Russian statistics uncritically. . . .
>
> This symposium will reveal, it is hoped, the need of devoting greater resources in this country to the study of Russian statistics. Contributors to this symposium throw a penetrating light on important statistical series which will undoubtedly contribute to a realistic approach to Russian achievements on the economic front. (1947, 213)

In later decades, hundreds of people in the governments of the West, the USSR, and international organizations were devoted to trying to understand and compare economic processes around the world, especially in the post-WWII major powers.[28] Had the Soviets used the SNA that was developing in the West instead of the MPS, they would have provided a tremendous amount of information about the Soviet economy both to the outside world and to their own citizens, and it would have been much harder to hide the country's postwar economic decline. There is a voluminous literature on the difficulties in comprehending the economies of the USSR and CMEA countries. I have highlighted here only a few major issues to illustrate what made Soviet statistics so problematic from a Western standpoint and why the shift to the SNA by postcommunist states was such a dramatic development, with important political and economic consequences.

Given the history of Soviet and CMEA statistics, a move to the SNA would require fundamental changes in every aspect of national accounting: a different production boundary, different classificatory schemes, different methodology

---

28. For an overview of economic Sovietology and the achievements as well as shortcomings in Western economists' attempts to understand the Soviet economy, see Schroeder 1995. On CIA attempts to estimate Soviet GNP, see CIA 1990. Pitzer (1990) evaluates Abram Bergson's (1953a, 1961) Adjusted Factor Cost Standard in light of changes to Soviet statistics during perestroika. On growth for the USSR up to 1990, see Kostinsky and Belkindas 1990, 186–89; Bergson 1991. For critical Soviet analysis of NMP vs. GDP, see Khanin 1988; Belkin 1992; Kudrov 1993, 1994, 1995. For recent work on the Soviet economy, see Mark Harrison's website on Research in Former Soviet Archives on Issues of Historical Political Economy, www2.warwick.ac.uk/fac/soc/economics/staff/academic/harrison/archive/, accessed December 2, 2009.

and data collection and dissemination. This would be a matter of political will at the top but also of fundamental conceptual changes in approaches to national accounting as well as a transformation of long-established practices on the ground. The implementation of the SNA would constitute a radical institutional break with the past.

Implementation of the 1993 SNA: The Postcommunist Puzzle

The UN and IMF have documented the progress of all countries in the world on the SNA, using a range of quantitative and qualitative measures.[29] In its first assessment of compliance with the 1993 SNA, the UN rated all member states based on how much completed economic data countries had submitted. This index, called the "SNA milestone assessment," took the form of a seven-point scale (0 to 6), corresponding to six "milestones" in data provision to the UN.[30] The milestone assessment was carried out for 1990–95, 1992–97, and 1993–98, but individual country scores were published only for the first two assessments, making the 1992–97 period the latest one for which country data are available (UN Statistical Commission 1999, 2000).

The mean score for all 185 countries was 1.6, while the average for the former Soviet (FSU) and East European (EE) states was 1.89, putting it ahead of all other regions of the world, save North America and Western Europe (UN Statistical Commission 1999).[31] The median response was one in which a country compiled the most basic data, such as GDP at current and constant prices, but not more specific data on institutional sector accounts. However, many countries (48 out of 185, or 26 percent) were not even able to compile basic data (UN Statistical Commission 1999). Figure 1.1 shows the milestone assessment for 1992–97.

International organizations continually update their frameworks for assessment of SNA implementation. In response to concerns that the milestones were too narrow a measure, the UN decided in 2001 to expand assessment along three dimensions: conceptual compliance, scope of accounts in compliance, and quality.

---

29. It is important to note that many of these assessments are for the 1993 SNA, not the 1968 SNA. Although there is a certain amount of overlap, some assessments were aimed at measuring this transition, not at measuring compliance with the SNA in general.

30. See appendix for definitions of each milestone and additional notes on the assessment.

31. These data (UN Statistical Commission 1999) have been adjusted according to notes in the document. The average for countries in the CMEA is 2.0. The average for CMEA states excluding Vietnam and Cuba, which are still nominally communist, is 2.09.

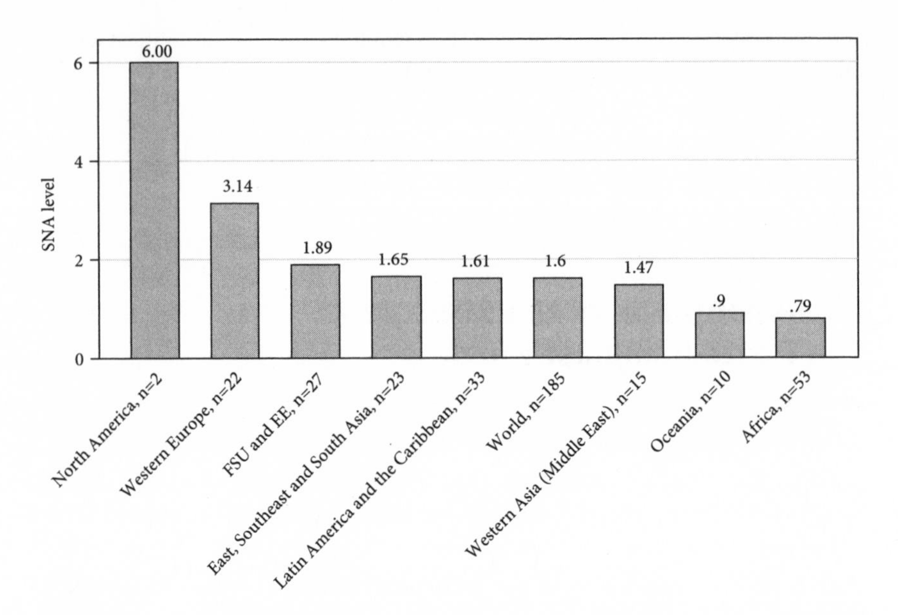

FIGURE 1.1. Average SNA milestone level by world region, 1992–97

Conceptual compliance refers to whether the concepts of the 1993 SNA have been implemented for the data that are most important to a country's economy. This conceptual implementation was measured by a set of questionnaires that were sent to all national statistical agencies. According to the UN, the objective of these surveys was "to determine to what extent important concepts in the 1993 SNA affecting the level of GDP, gross capital formation, or gross national income (GNI) have been implemented" (UN Statistical Commission 2002, 8). Based on the survey responses, the UN decided whether a country adhered to the 1993 SNA (UN Statistical Commission 2001, 2002, 2004b).[32]

Beginning in 2003, the UN changed the regional categories it used in SNA assessment from strictly geographic regions (as in the milestone assessments) to categories based on economic status—"developed" and "developing" countries. It also added the category of "transition" countries for the FSU and Eastern Europe. This new category suggests recognition of these countries' specific trajectory in terms of SNA achievement.[33] The alternative measurements of SNA achievement—conceptual implementation, the "minimum required data set"

32. The lack of compliance here can indicate adherence to the 1968 SNA as well as noncompliance in general with the SNA.

33. "Developed" countries include North America, Western Europe, Japan, and Australia. "Developing" countries include Africa, Asia, Latin America, Middle East, and Oceania, minus Japan and Australia. In addition, over the course of 1999–2002, six new states joined the UN: Kiribati, Nauru,

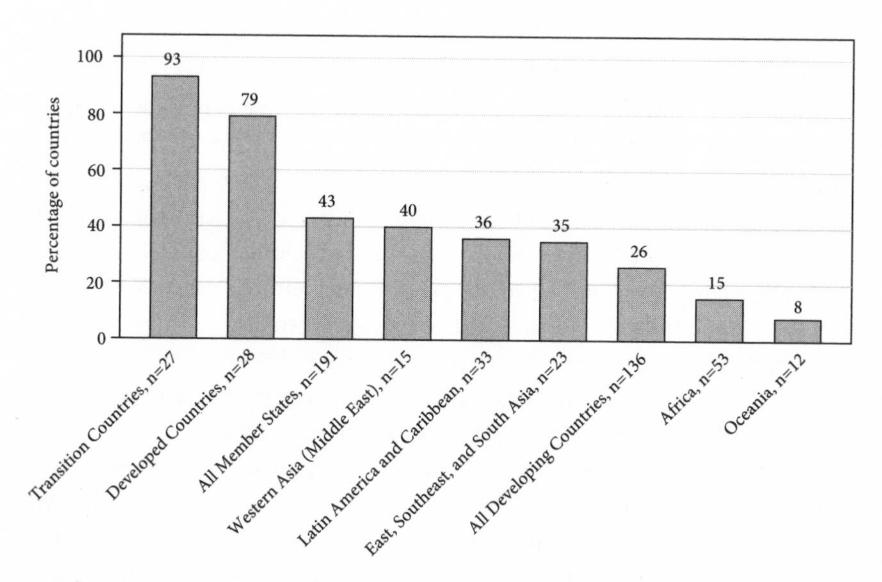

FIGURE 1.2. Conceptual implementation of the 1993 SNA, 2002 assessment

benchmark, and dissemination standards—also reflect the distinctiveness of transition countries.

Figure 1.2 shows the results from the conceptual implementation assessment by region (UN Statistical Commission 2004b). Transition countries have the highest level of conceptual compliance to the 1993 SNA: 93 percent, at a time when only 43 percent of all countries and 26 percent of developing countries had met this standard. This figure is even ahead of that for developed countries. Transition countries may have done so well on this indicator in part because most did not adopt the SNA prior to the late 1980s, so they follow the 1993 SNA, as opposed to the earlier 1968 version. Nevertheless, the level of compliance for transition countries in comparison to other regions is striking.

The UN also constructed a new benchmark, the "Minimum Requirement Data Set" (MRDS) which consists of seven tables of data essential to the 1993 SNA (UN Statistical Commission 2000, 2001, 2004b, 2005). The MRDS is roughly equivalent to the content of milestones 1 and 2, plus one additional table (on value-added components by industry). The MRDS turned out to be a higher standard than milestone 2: by 1998, 44 percent of countries had reached milestone 2, but only 13 percent had met the MRDS standard. The MRDS was

Tonga, Tuvalu, Switzerland, and Timor-Leste. The first four of these states were added to the category of Oceania; Switzerland was added to developed countries, and Timor-Leste was added to Asia.

assessed three times: in 2000 for the 1993–98 period, in 2003 for the 1996–2001 period, and in 2004 for the 1997–2002 period.

Figure 1.3 shows the trajectories of 1993 SNA implementation using the minimum required data set (MRDS) for three groups of states: developed, transition, and developing countries (UN Statistical Commission 2005).[34] Although transition countries started out with the lowest percent of compliance in the first assessment, by 2004 they had far surpassed developing countries. In addition, although neither developed nor developing countries improved between the second and third assessments, the percentage of transition countries meeting this standard went from 19 percent to 41 percent. For all member states, the percentage meeting the MRDS standard in the three periods was 13 percent, 25 percent, and 27 percent, respectively (UN Statistical Commission 2005).

The third change in the SNA implementation assessment was a focus on data quality and accessibility. Quality is difficult to measure quantitatively. The IMF and other international organizations interested in data quality offer longer qualitative reports rather than quantitative assessments of data quality (Laliberté et al. 2004). The IMF has developed a Data Quality Assessment Framework (DQAF), which "provides an integrated and flexible framework in which data quality is assessed using a six-part structure that spans institutional environments, statistical processes, and characteristics of the statistical products" (IMF 2009b). Using this framework, the IMF has produced Reports on the Observance of Standards and Codes (ROSCs). The ROSCs cover a range of topics of interest to the IMF and World Bank relating to transparency, governance, and data, including "data dissemination and quality." As of 2009, the IMF had published 103 reports on 82 countries (IMF 2009c).

In addition, the IMF has standardized measurement of data *dissemination* through the Special Data Dissemination Standard (SDDS) and the General Data Dissemination System (GDDS) (IMF 2009e). These standards are based on a broad view of "dissemination," which includes four dimensions: data characteristics (namely the coverage, periodicity, and timeliness of data), access, integrity, and quality. The SDDS is the higher standard. Countries subscribe to one or the other depending on the amount, type, and timeliness of data released to the IMF. The SDDS is primarily for countries that want to borrow on international capital markets. To date, only 64 of 186 IMF member states have subscribed to the SDDS. Although not a substitute for qualitative assessments of accuracy, the data dissemination standards are another indicator of statistical capacity and compliance with the 1993 SNA.

34. Individual country-level data for the MRDS are not available.

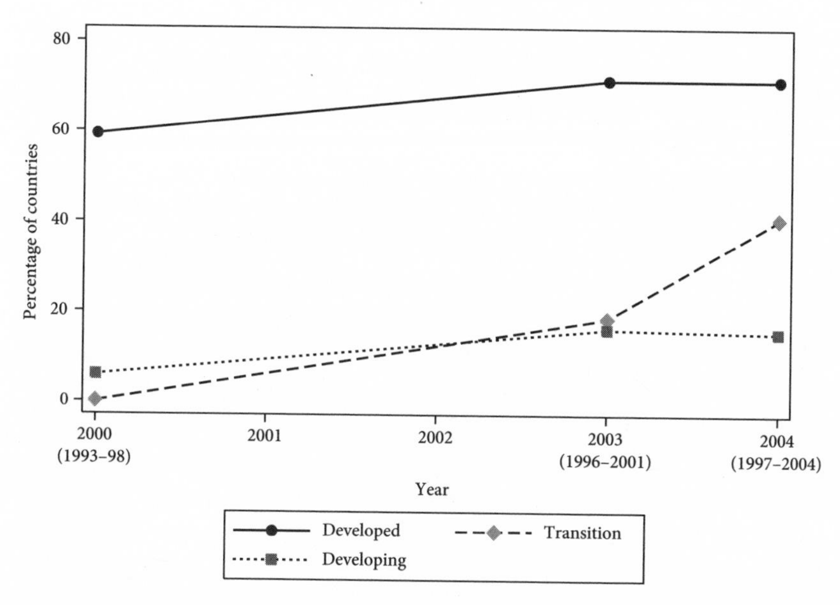

FIGURE 1.3. SNA minimum requirement data set, 2000–2004 assessments (years reviewed given in parentheses)

While most transition countries meet the SDDS, many countries work with the GDDS, and some do not comply with either standard. To compare regions of the world, I compiled a dissemination standards index based on 2005 data (IMF 2009d), by giving countries a 0 for meeting no standards, a 1 for meeting the GDDS, and a 2 for meeting the SDDS. Figure 1.4 shows the average score on this index for all countries, according to region. Here again transition countries do very well. Figure 1.4 shows that they are the second highest achieving region and are closer to developed countries in this respect than to other regions of the world.

A more interesting finding, however, is the type of data dissemination standard by region, shown in figure 1.5. The darkest bar shows compliance with the SDDS. Both developed and transition countries are likely to meet the highest standard rather than the intermediate GDDS standard. This is not the case for other regions of the world. Once again, transition states as a group have done very well. Moreover, given the past level of secrecy in CMEA statistics, their progress on this dissemination standard is remarkable.

An additional cross-national measure of statistical capacity that is related to SNA implementation is the World Bank's Statistical Capacity Indicator (World Bank 2010). This index is based on assessment of three areas: methodology, data sources, and periodicity and timeliness of data. Countries are given individual scores ranging from 0 to 100 in each of these three areas as well as an

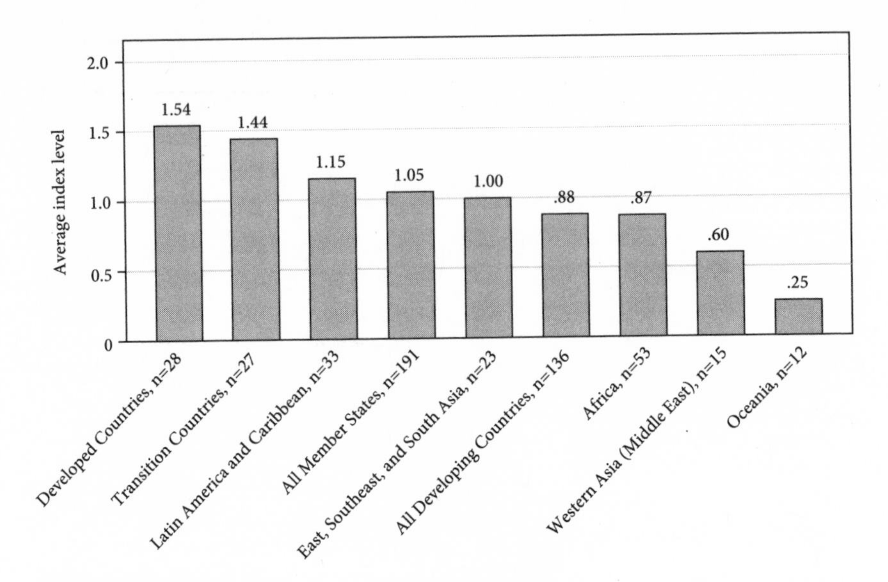

FIGURE 1.4. IMF dissemination standards index, 2005

aggregate score. While the Statistical Capacity Indicator is not a measure of SNA implementation, its assessment criteria are in areas that would be directly and positively affected by SNA implementation. It is therefore suggestive of institutional changes in NSOs in the direction of SNA implementation, and has the advantage of being more up-to-date than existing SNA assessments.

The Statistical Capacity Indicator is primarily aimed at developing countries, excluding most OECD countries. It contains assessments of 145 countries over six years, 2004–09. As shown in figure 1.6, the average score for all countries in 2009 was 65, but the score for transition countries was 79, making that the highest scoring region.[35] CMEA countries were slightly higher at 81. The same pattern exists for all previous years.

Taken together, these findings on postcommunist versus other countries suggest that the experience of East European and FSU states in SNA implementation is distinctive. On a range of indicators, these states have achieved a greater level of implementation than all other regions except developed Western countries. The question is how to explain this regional pattern of success in SNA implementation.

---

35. The Czech Republic, Slovenia, and Cuba are not included in this data set. Inclusion of Czech Republic and Slovenia would raise the average for FSU/EE and CMEA countries; likewise exclusion of some outliers like Turkmenistan, which scores 43, would also raise the averages. The mode for CMEA countries is 85.

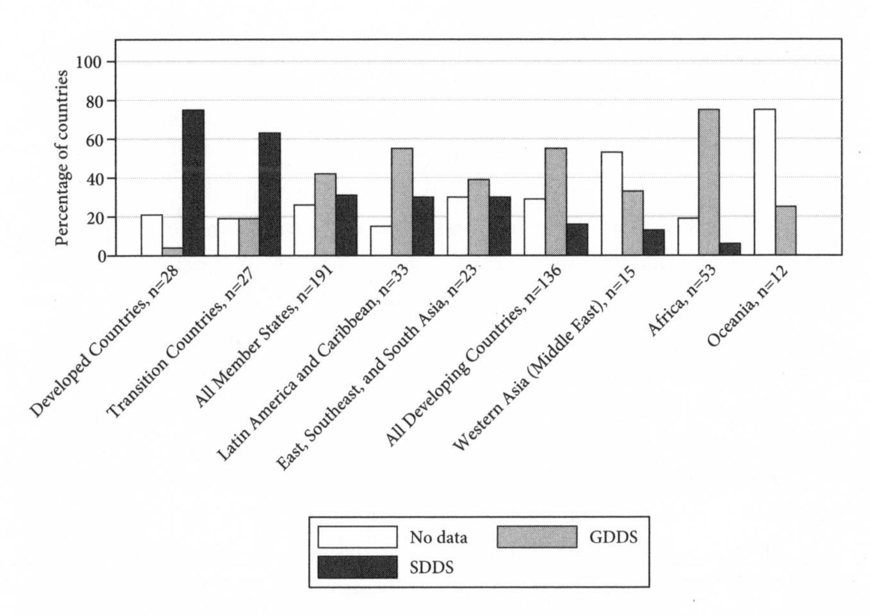

FIGURE 1.5. IMF dissemination standards, SDDS and GDDS, 2005

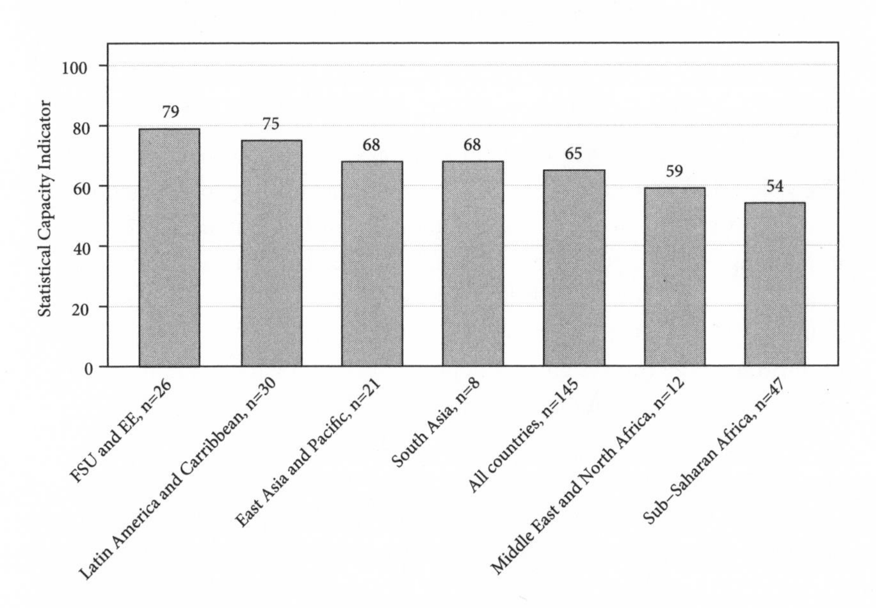

FIGURE 1.6. World Bank Statistical Capacity Indicator, 2009, by region

Russian Economic Statistics after 1991

As the most powerful member of the CMEA, the USSR led the way in promoting the MPS as an alternative to the SNA. Unlike some other communist countries, the USSR had no obligation to accept the MPS and no incentive to abandon it as an unwanted imposition from outside. Moreover, adoption of the SNA by Goskomstat required a commitment to overhaul its previous methodology and practices. If we understand how this happened in Russia, we will be better prepared to study institutional change in other transition countries.

After the fall of communism, Goskomstat underwent complete reorganization and methodological restructuring. It lost most of its functions related to state-socialist goals, such as monitoring plan fulfillment (because there were no more central plans), and gained new responsibilities related to collecting and compiling information according to the SNA. During this time, departments were reorganized and renamed; new tasks were added, and entire categories of work that had been done in the Soviet period were halted.

A joint report on national accounts cowritten by Goskomstat and the World Bank (1995) elucidates the scope of institutional change at Goskomstat in the early 1990s. The report is a comprehensive analysis of national accounts in Russia for 1991–94 that examines methods and sources of data. It details the transition to the SNA through analysis of the entire range of statistical data being collected by Goskomstat and it lays out the challenges facing national accounting at Goskomstat in the early 1990s. Notably, the report is written from the perspective that Russia is in the midst of implementing the SNA; despite significant difficulties, there is no hint of a return to the MPS.

Systematic content analysis of Goskomstat's in-house journal, *Vestnik statistiki,* yields clear conclusions about the commitment to systems of national accounting over time in the USSR and the Russian Federation: that the change in thinking regarding the appropriateness of different systems happened fairly quickly between 1988 and 1992. Whereas before 1988 there was a solid commitment to two systems in the world, that was challenged in 1989–91 in favor of integrating the two systems. In published articles by mid-1992 the MPS was abandoned and there was total commitment to the SNA alone, including detailed plans on the conversion to the SNA written by senior Goskomstat officials.

The first phase in implementing the SNA took place from 1992 to 1996.[36] In that period Goskomstat worked toward compiling the basic components of GDP in current and constant prices. By 1993, in conjunction with Statkom CIS,[37] GDP

36. For further details on specific steps in SNA development in the early 1990s, see Guzhvin 1993; Noren 1993; Pogosov 1993; Noren 1994; Kudrov 1995; Tabata 1996; Nesterov 1997. Ivanov and Homenko detailed the variation in progress on national accounts in all postcommunist countries as of 1992 (Ivanov and Homenko 1996, 319–22).

37. Statkom CIS was the statistical agency set up in 1992 for the Commonwealth of Independent States, which included most of the former Soviet republics except the Baltic states. Its primary task was to coordinate efforts to implement the SNA in the CIS.

for Russia was calculated according to the SNA methodology going back to 1989.[38] In 1995 Goskomstat began to revise input-output tables in accordance with the SNA (Guzhvin 1993, 81–82). According to Nesterov, a second phase of implementation began in 1997, which entailed full and systematic standardization of all Goskomstat economic data according to SNA principles (1997, 1473).

The move to the SNA introduced a multitude of internationally recommended standards for collecting and processing the underlying data that comprise the *system* of national accounts. Among other changes, industries had to be organized according to the International Standard Industrial Classification (ISIC), labor statistics according to International Labour Organization (ILO) standards, government expenditures according to the Classification of the Functions of the Government (COFOG), and goods and services according to the Central Product Classification (CPC).

To comply with these standards, Goskomstat had to alter the type of data included in its national accounts, in particular its primary focus on industrial production. New data series on prices, capital investment, and foreign trade were begun. There was reorganization and reform of accounting, financial, and banking data, including moving to International Bookkeeping Standards (IBS) (Guzhvin 1993, 8–12). Goskomstat also began collecting and publishing data on previously ignored areas such as the military, the informal economy, and the environment. From the 1990s on, it collected "moral" statistics—crime, arrests, alcoholism, divorce, abortion. By 1996 Goskomstat had switched to international standards for assessing economic asset values.[39] In areas such as the informal economy and foreign trade, data were still insufficient in the early 1990s.[40] The lack of adequate data on the informal economy was particularly troublesome owing to its record-breaking rate of growth during that time (Noren 1994, 23–24).[41] Whatever Goskomstat's flaws, however, the decision to engage in new types of data coverage marked a significant break with the past.

Goskomstat had to revamp its general methodology, moving away from full enumeration censuses of firms to sample surveys (something which the organization had long opposed). By 1993 Goskomstat was already working on a registry of enterprises to be used for future sampling purposes (Noren 1994, 33)

---

38. There were a number of criticisms of these early GDP estimates; see Noren 1994, 31. His overall assessment was that FSU statistics for production, consumption, and foreign trade were understated.

39. This new methodology, which was consistent with the 1993 SNA, was explained in Goskomstat Russia 1996a, 331–39.

40. Foreign trade statistics in the early years of transition to the SNA were difficult to decipher due to methodological questions and lack of coverage; see Noren 1993, 422; Tabata 1994; Belkindas and Ivanova 1995.

41. On gaps in data coverage, see also Kudrov 1993, 126–29.

and had initiated surveys of enterprises to supplement employment and wage data; household surveys to collect on data on poverty; an employment survey of households and individuals in accordance with ILO standards; and in conjunction with the World Bank, a public health survey (Guzhvin 1993, 8–9).

Sample surveys and the implementation of international standards in turn required increased cooperation from firms and other respondents.[42] For financial statistics Goskomstat relied on other state organizations such as the Ministry of Finance and Central Bank, which did not always cooperate in the early years of the transition, if only because they too were undergoing reorganization. After 1990–91 the consumers of statistics in Russia and other CMEA countries changed as government bodies, private-sector firms, and international organizations demanded various kinds of data (Blades and Harrison 1992, 103). At the same time, the physical presence of staff from the IMF, the World Bank, the European Community, the OECD, and the UN in statistical offices throughout the postcommunist region, led to further internationalization of the process.

In implementing the 1993 SNA, Goskomstat had to address one of the most criticized areas of Soviet statistics, price indices. The methodology of these indices had to be changed to conform to international standards and to account for inflation, no easy task during a period of hyperinflation.[43] The agency needed monthly and quarterly as well as annual data (Blades and Harrison 1992, 102–3). By 1993 Goskomstat had developed weekly price indices. In cooperation with the UN Statistical Commission and the OECD, Goskomstat attempted to develop PPP (purchasing price parity) data for 1993 in accordance with the European International Comparison Program (Guzhvin 1993, 11). These efforts were not entirely successful; despite help from the IMF and the World Bank in improving the methodology behind price indices in the early 1990s, harsh criticism of Russian price indices continued during the first few years of the transition (Noren 1994, 27).

Goskomstat's publications, the agency's most visible output, were completely transformed in the 1990s, illustrating the trajectory of international standardization. Already by 1994 the form and content of Goskomstat's publications bore little resemblance to those of the Soviet period. The statistical yearbooks titled *Narodnoe khoziaistvo SSSR* (The national economy of the USSR) reverted to their prerevolutionary name, *Rossiiskii statisticheskii ezhegodnik* (Russian statistical

42. On lack of cooperation with firms and other government organizations, see Noren 1994, 34; Goskomstat Russia and World Bank 1995.

43. For elaboration on the accuracy of deflators during 1992, see Noren 1993, 421. See also Nesterov 1997, 1476–83, on the problems with price deflators.

yearbook). Similarly, Goskomstat's main in-house journal lost its Soviet title, *Vestnik statistiki* (Herald of statistics), and was renamed *Voprosy statistiki* (Questions of statistics) in 1994. In both cases the organization of the content of the publications changed significantly to reflect that of Western publications.

Perhaps the biggest change in Russian statistics (and statistics in all other CMEA countries) in the early post-Soviet period was the rapid increase in the volume and type of data published.[44] In addition to its new data series, since 1996 Goskomstat has published five volumes of methodological notes (Goskomstat Russia 1996a, 1998, 2000, 2003; Rosstat 2005), as well as extensive methodological commentary in *Voprosy statistiki,* a major departure from Soviet practices.[45] In another shift from the Soviet era, when almost no regional (sub-republican level) data were published, by the end of the 1990s Goskomstat was publishing almost all of its data disaggregated to at least the regional level. These data were made available in various outlets—as free online content as well as via phone and Internet sales, in regional offices, and in retail bookstores.

International Assessments of Russian Statistics

Given this flurry of activity at Goskomstat in the 1990s, what can we say systematically about the implementation of the 1993 SNA? If we go back to the UN and IMF comparative standards and assessments we see that Russia fared very well. On the "SNA milestone assessment," which rated all UN member states on the basis of how much completed economic data countries had submitted in accordance with the 1993 SNA (UN Statistical Commission 1999), Russia scored a 2, meaning that out of 185 countries, it was at the same level as 55 others, worse than 33, and better than 94 (the mean score for all countries was 1.6).

On the UN's three assessments of conceptual compliance (UN Statistical Commission 2001, 2002, 2004b), aimed at measuring whether the concepts of the 1993 had been implemented for important economic data, Russia was deemed to be in compliance as of 2002. The percentage of all countries that had conceptually implemented the SNA at this time was 43 percent (UN Statistical Commission 2004b).

---

44. For discussion of lists of available publications in the early 1990s, see Heleniak and Motivans 1991; Noren 1994.

45. Commentary on specific methodological questions as opposed to general methodological policies was not as forthcoming.

On the "Minimum Requirement Data Set" benchmark (UN Statistical Commission 2000, 2001, 2004b, 2005), Russia met the standard in 2004 (which assessed the 1997–2002 period). At that time, only 27 percent of all member states had met the MRDS standard (UN Statistical Commission 2005).

Finally, for assessments of data quality or accuracy, we can consider the IMF's Report on the Observance of Standards and Codes for Russia for 2004 (IMF 2004). The assessment of Russian statistics was generally positive. For example, in discussing agencies responsible for statistics in Russia, the report concluded that "all agencies evidence professionalism, transparency, and provide guidelines on ethical conduct of their staff" and "all datasets get high marks for accuracy and reliability" (IMF 2004, 4).

On the IMF's measurement of data accessibility, based on its data dissemination standards, Russia met the highest standard, the SDDS, in January 2005. In comparison, only 32 percent of all member states (60 out of 185) during the same period met the SDDS (IMF 2009d).

For 2009, Russia scored an 80 out of 100 on the World Bank's Statistical Capacity Indicator overall, as well as in methodology, source data, and periodicity and timeliness. In comparison, the world averages in those categories, respectively were 65, 56, 63, and 77 (World Bank 2010). Again, while this is not a direct measure of implementation of the 1993 SNA, it does suggest that the statistical capacity of Goskomstat remained relatively high compared to other non-OECD countries.

To review, using UN and IMF sources that compare Russia's progress on the 1993 SNA to other countries of the world, Russia achieved above-average levels of implementation at all stages of review, and on all dimensions of measurement. Combined with qualitative accounts of what has happened at Goskomstat, a picture emerges of a fairly comprehensive, as well as rapid, move from the Soviet MPS to the SNA in the early to mid-1990s.

Vladimir Sokolin, the former chairman of Goskomstat, summarized the change:

> It is recognized that we have implemented international standards. We did it quickly and well. The first program on the transition to international standards was signed in early 1992 and this program was actually realized, which rarely happens in this country. (2004)

Similarly, the economist Vladimir Treml, a long time analyst of Soviet statistics, summed up change at Goskomstat:

> By and large, we can conclude that the Goskomstat Russia has done relatively well since the declaration of Russia's independence, particularly given the weight of the Soviet past, immensely complex tasks which

> faced Russian statisticians, the chaotic state of the Russian economy, special conditions of the transition period, and the widespread corruption of public and private organizations and institutions. (2001, 49)

Despite problems with certain data and delays along the way, and although the work is ongoing, even the strongest critics of Goskomstat would acknowledge that the progress in implementing the SNA has been impressive.

The system of statistics and national accounts used in the USSR for nearly seventy years and in CMEA countries for decades no longer exists. Although in 1988, it still seemed likely that the world would have two internationally recognized national accounting systems, the SNA and the MPS, indefinitely, within a few years the MPS all but disappeared. East European and former Soviet states not only dropped the MPS by 1990–92 but moved speedily to implement the SNA, a process that would take years, but which they remain committed to despite wide variation in political and economic developments of the region since 1989 and the end of the USSR.

How can we understand this move to the SNA by nearly all postcommunist countries? As an institutional change, it was abrupt and discontinuous, to use the language of Streeck and Thelen (2005a, 9). The goal was to put in place, within a short period of time, a complex set of institutionalized rules for tracking all economic activity, most of which replaced the previous rules.

Such a goal could not, however, be fulfilled overnight. Given the differences between the SNA and the MPS in terms of content, organization, methodology, and data collection practices, implementation required years of work and commitment by NSOs like Goskomstat. More than the political decision to move to the SNA (although that is also of interest), it is this sustained commitment and effort from below that warrants further attention. What explains the turnaround in thinking regarding the superiority of the MPS vis-à-vis the SNA? I take up these questions in the chapters that follow, beginning with a discussion of theoretical approaches to institutional change.

2

ACCOUNTING FOR IMPLEMENTATION

A Theory of Conditional Norms

The System of National Accounts (SNA) is a complex set of conventions for collecting, processing, and presenting economic data—an international institution for national accounts that renders economies legible and comparable. Yet implementation of the SNA varies significantly across countries. In developing an explanation for the implementation of the SNA in postcommunist states, we must address head on the question of institutional change in bureaucracies—that is, how to get national statistical offices to embrace and implement a different institution. Moreover, our analysis of the possibilities for institutional change depends on how we define institutions.

I set the stage for explanations of institutional change and SNA implementation, therefore, with a brief discussion of the definition of institutions, and in particular the contribution of constructivist approaches and pragmatism. I then propose a novel concept, *conditional norms*, to suggest how norms can be a source of institutional change.

Constructivist Institutionalism

In what could now be called a "traditional" approach, institutions have two key features: they comprise "rules," which act as "constraints that shape human interaction" (North 1990); and these rules are separate from actors or organizations. Constructivists take issue with both these points by not reducing institutions to "constraints," instead turning the spotlight on the way in which actors decide which rules to follow and how actors attempt to change rules, and by rejecting a sharp distinction between rules and players.[1] In brief, constructivism tries to understand how agency can occur in socially structured contexts. Constructivism posits bureaucrats as both "rule makers" and "rule takers" (Streeck and Thelen 2005b, 13).

Pierre Bourdieu (1990, 1992 [1977]) and John Dewey (2002 [1992]) both contributed to this constructivist approach to institutions by stressing the importance of improvisation and agency, even within normative environments. Dewey focused on distinguishing "habit" from mere repetition, so as not to lose all agency in a structured context (2002 [1922], 42). In much of his work, Bourdieu tried to understand how people who live in among social rules nevertheless innovate and act creatively. Bourdieu wrote that "the rule is not automatically effective by itself" instead, we have to ask, "under what conditions a rule can operate" (1990, 76). He rejected structuralism as well as total individualism, saying "notions like that of habitus (or system of dispositions), practical sense, and strategy, are linked to my effort to escape from structuralist objectivism without relapsing into subjectivism" (1990, 61). Moreover, he explained, "I can say that all my thinking started from this point: how can behaviour be regulated without being the product of obedience to rules?" (1990, 65). In explaining Bourdieu's point, Swartz wrote, "Actors are not rule followers or norm obeyers but strategic improvisers who respond dispositionally to the opportunities and constraints offered by various situations" (1997, 100).

In linking Dewey and Bourdieu's concepts to current theoretical work on institutions, Gary Herrigel outlines a pragmatist theory of institutions and argues that "actors confront considerable uncertainty, which in turn makes the meaning of rules ambiguous, thus making interpretation and creativity an inescapable dimension of social action and institutional change" (2005, 560).[2] Herrigel defines institutions as "provisional solutions to commonly defined problems rather than static systems of constraining rules" (2005, 560).[3] Herrigel's formulation brings

---

1. Historical institutionalism shares some common ground with constructivism on these points, as in the definition of institutions in Streeck and Thelen 2005b, 9–16. See Herrigel 2010 for a critique of historical institutionalism from a pragmatist perspective. There are also other approaches within constructivism, including the concept of "creative syncretism" (Galvan and Sil 2007; Berk and Galvan 2009). On constructivist approaches to institutions in international relations, see Checkel 1998. A constructivist approach is also largely consistent with approaches based on organizational theory (March 1965; Allison 1971, chap. 3; Simon 1976 [1945]; March and Simon 1993 [1958]).

2. This kind of "puzzling through" is similar to that described by Hall in the economic crisis in Britain in the 1970s (1993, 289).

3. The treatment of institutions as creative solutions to problems is consistent with many ideational arguments that crises provide opportunities for institutional change (Heclo 1974, 315–18; Odell 1982, 371; Hall 1993, 278; McDonald 1993; Rose 1993, 50–76; Reiter 1996, 19–21; Checkel 1997; McNamara 1998; Walsh 2000).

agency not only to compliance with institutions and rules but also to their formation. He writes,

> actors allow themselves to be constrained by rules when they believe those rules solve problems. When they do not, creative actors coping with uncertainty and guided by dispositions that are not reducible to specific institutional arrangements either modify the rules or agree simply to ignore them in order to construct new arrangements that address more directly jointly identified problems. (2005, 565).

Herrigel's pragmatic approach is agent-centered and open-ended; in terms of predicting institutional change or the implementation of international institutions, we would expect actors to consider whether a given institution meets their needs and if not, to reformulate a different one that does. What distinguishes Herrigel's approach from much of the rational-choice institutionalism is the idea that there is not necessarily convergence on efficient institutional forms. Rather than treating actors as one-dimensional material interest-maximizers, actors in Herrigel's approach are guided by dispositions and habits in their institutional choices, but they are also not simply constrained by their identities, norms, or previous choices (e.g., path dependency). This is a critical distinction that sets pragmatic approaches like Herrigel's apart from rationalist theories focusing on material interests and efficiency and more structural versions of historical institutionalism (Pierson 2000; Thelen 2003).

A pragmatic theory of institutional change does not directly predict the implementation of a specific institution such as the 1993 SNA. It does, however, suggest that we must look more carefully at institutions' development and the implications for actors' understanding of rules and propensity to implement them. This constructivist approach draws our attention to mutual constitution and agency in the development of institutions and norms. By understanding how rules develop—where they came from, who supported and opposed them, how they became established in particular forms—we take a step toward understanding variation in implementation.

But this is only a first step; pragmatism and constructivist institutionalism suggests a flexible, open-ended process. To explain specific outcomes such as postcommunist countries' move to the SNA in the 1990s, we have to take into account the insights of a constructivist approach and test specific theories of institutional change, those focusing on structural factors, actors and material interests, and identities and norms. But first we need to re-examine theories of identities and norms in light of pragmatism and constructivist institutionalism.

Identities and Norms

Two key theories of institutional change that rest on constructivist principles focus on social identities and norms. The basic argument in these theories is that institutional choices are strongly influenced by a shared social identity or shared norms; and institutional change is the result of socialization into, or the development of, a new identity or norm.

Identities are social categories that vary in content (shared purposes, norms, cognitive worldviews, relational comparisons with other groups) and contestation (Abdelal et al. 2006, 2009). Sharing a social identity means sharing some kind of identity content with others: plans for the future, ways of doing things such as selecting leaders, ways of understanding a past conflict, and views of other groups. It also means contesting that content within the group by debating the group's goals, discussing the best way to choose leaders, considering different interpretations of the impact of a conflict, and reconsidering the group's friends or enemies at any point in time. This definition suggests that norms are a type of identity content, and as such norms and identities are inextricably related.

Norms, according to Jepperson, Wendt, and Katzenstein, can be defined as "collective expectations about proper behavior for a given identity" (1996, 54).[4] In this way, norms provide a theoretical link between shared identities and action and cannot be reduced to either "ideas"[5] or "rules."[6] A shared identity both prescribes and circumscribes norms: individuals who share identities also share norms, but those outside the identity group are not expected to follow the norm.[7] Moreover, norms are constitutive of identities because they partially define the content of an identity group; they lay out a set of informal rules by which all members of the group should abide, and following those informal rules becomes

4. There is a great deal of consensus on this definition. For example, Finnemore defines norms as "collectively held ideas about behavior" (1996a, 23), and Checkel defines them as "collective understandings that make behavioral claims on actors" (1998, 327–28). Tannenwald brings identity and morality into the definition of norms; she defines norms as "a standard of right or wrong, a prescription or proscription for behavior 'for a given identity'" (2005, 8).

5. For a review of ideational approaches, see Blyth 1997; Berman 2001. For arguments on the role of ideas in specific institutional outcomes, see Berman 1998 (the development of political parties); Finnemore 1996b; Boli and Thomas 1999 (the development of international organizations); Bleich 2002, 1055 (race policy in the Britain and France); Knott and Miller 1987; Light 1997 (reform of American bureaucracy); and Peterson 1997; Appel 2000 (economic reform in Eastern Europe).

6. In most rational choice approaches, norms are treated as separate from actors and as exogenous constraints on action, i.e., "rules." For examples see Elster 1989; Hardin 1995, chaps. 4–5; Weingast 1995; Chong 1996, 53–57; Morrow 2002.

7. Identity can be located in different sites. Organizational identities may play the same role as state or national identities in limiting the group of people for which a norm is meaningful.

a criterion for group membership.[8] Kowert and Legro put the case strongly: norms are "behavioral prescriptions for the proper enactment of...identities" (1996, 453).

Normative prescriptions are often based on a logic of appropriateness,[9] in that they structure behavioral choices by providing a set of legitimate and acceptable, as well as unacceptable, actions.[10] But norms are not just external structure, and they do not only constrain choices; they also help define interests. In explaining logics of appropriateness, Checkel writes, "under them, agents ask 'What kind of situation is this?' and 'What should I do now?'—with norms helping to supply the answers. Norms therefore constitute states/agents, providing them with understandings of their interests" (1998, 326). Because identity content, including norms, is always subject to contestation, norms are outcomes as well as part of the social structure in which interests develop and institutional choices are made.[11]

Scholarly literature from several fields supports the idea that norms and identities can influence institutional change.[12] In international relations scholarship on norms, states are motivated to act in ways that are consistent with their identities, and norms provide appropriate guides to action (Katzenstein 1996).[13] Hopf has persuasively argued that the behavior of the USSR in the Sino-Soviet split can best be explained by considering Soviet identities, and the interests that stem from those identities (2002). Similarly, national identities have been used

---

8. There are multiple relationships between norms and formal rules. Norms can be the basis for the development of complementary formal rules, but they can also substitute for formal rules in a subversive way that leads to rejection of formal rules. See Helmke and Levitsky 2004 for a typology of informal institutions in the context of effective or ineffective formal institutions.

9. On logics of appropriateness, see March and Olsen 1989, 1998. Hopf notes that a "logic of appropriateness" does not provide an account of where norm selection originates; for that, Hopf suggests, we need to consider identities, which are the "source for an individual's receptivity to one norm over another" (2002, 13).

10. Norms may also be a subset of "ideas." By definition, however, they are linked to shared social identities and usually entail more specific behavioral prescriptions. Because of this prescriptive element, norms may have a more direct relationship to particular institutional choices than ideas.

11. The level of contestation varies, resulting in a spectrum ranging from the hegemony of certain ideas and actions ("unthinkability") to lack of agreement over what is appropriate. See Hopf's discussion of the "logic of the everyday" and its related logics of "intelligibility," "thinkability," and "imaginablity" (2002, 13–16). In addition, contestation of norms may occur at many levels (international, national, local) and within groups. Contestation takes place first among actors in the formation of norms, then in the face of existing norms, and in the implementation and adaptation of norms.

12. For a broader review of identity as a variable and the wide range of outcomes associated with it, see Abdelal et al. 2006.

13. State identity-based norms are similar to Schimmelfennig's concept of "community norms." According to Schimmelfennig, these community norms "define the collective self by the way 'we do things.'" Schimmelfennig uses the term "specific norms" to refer to norms that "regulate behavior in individual issue areas" and "are not decisive for community membership" (2002, 6).

to explain cross-national differences in domestic institutions, such as the development of bureaucratic organizations (Crozier 1967; Herzfeld 1992) or institutional change in bureaucracies (Peters 2001, chap. 2; 2003).[14]

While international or national-level identities may be critical for some kinds of institutional choices, identities and norms can also be located at the level of bureaucratic organizations and professional networks.[15] In this way, one can use identity to explain variation in outcomes *within* a state. Theories of bureaucracy that focus on building an esprit de corps to motivate employees are examples in which a shared organizational identity has an effect on bureaucratic behavior (Kaufman 1960, 161–200; Simon 1976 [1945], chap. 10; DiIulio 1987, 256).[16] Carpenter (2001) has argued that organizational norms and identities partly explain the emergence of "bureaucratic entrepreneurs," which accounts for variation among U.S. agencies. Barnett and Finnemore (2004) show how organizational and professional norms influenced the development of interests within international organizations.

Based on these theories, we would expect certain identities at the international, national, or organizational level to have a particular orientation toward the SNA. Among actors sharing identities who viewed the SNA positively, we would expect implementation of the SNA. The "view" of the SNA could be measured in various ways depending on the particular theory of identity. To test a given theory, we would examine the identities of international organizations, states, or NSOs and their orientation to the SNA. But we would discover that these identity-based theories would not predict a change in support for the SNA without a change in the relevant identities themselves.

Becoming part of an identity group may result in a change in interests toward a particular institution. This process can work through "epistemic communities" (Haas 1989, 1992) or transnational activists (McAdam and Rucht 1993; Keck and Sikkink 1998; Evangelista 1999). The mechanism here, however, is not the imposition of interests by international actors, but rather social learning (Checkel 2001) or change in actors' identity. Moreover, in contrast to the idea that domestic actors have to be coerced or actively convinced or taught to follow

---

14. In contrast to Crozier (1967), Suleiman has problematized this cultural basis of bureaucracies by noting similarities across countries, especially France and Spain (1974, 277–81). Suleiman does not dispute the role of identity as much as the source of these identities—national culture versus the functional requirements of organizations.

15. On bureaucratic culture and organizational culture, see Vaughan 1996; Alvesson 2002; Martin 2002; Eden 2004. On corporate culture, see Kreps 1990. On organizational identities and preferences in trade unions, see Levi 2003.

16. On organizational culture, see Schein 2004, 52, 70–71. On ways in which organizational identities may negatively affect cooperation with outside interests, including politicians, see Merton 1952, 367.

international norms, Barnett and Finnemore (2004) suggest a more diffuse sense of authority which has been conferred on international institutions and which gives international organizations constitutive effects, i.e. "the ability to create, define, and map social reality" (Barnett and Finnemore 2004, 30–31).

In an application of how international norms influence domestic institutional change, Finnemore examined several cases of norms promoted by international organizations regarding the structure of domestic bureaucracies (1993, 1996a). She argued that international organizations and experts convinced states that they needed particular types of science bureaucracies and showed domestic actors how to develop them (1996a, 12). What drove international organizations as well as domestic actors was the set of international norms about state development and science. For example, in the case of UNESCO, Finnemore demonstrated that the development of organizationally similar scientific bureaucracies within states was largely a function of international norms at the time, rather than a function of resources or domestic political interests (1993; 1996a, chap. 2).

In explaining the implementation of the SNA, these theories of social learning would suggest that statisticians from postcommunist NSOs participated in international organizations and related networks; through this interaction they learned about the SNA and came to value it.[17] If this theory is correct, we should expect increased interaction with international actors in the USSR/Russia to precede the decision to move to the SNA and to be the source of new information about the SNA. Moreover, "learning" suggests that there has to be a change of views; what statisticians in the USSR previously thought should be rejected (at least to some extent) and a new view of the SNA should be evident after the interaction with international actors.

Lacunae in the Norms and Identity Literature

Three issues in the norms literature remain underspecified theoretically and under-researched empirically but have particular relevance in explaining institutional change. These are agency and mutual constitution at the level of local or domestic actors; variation in the power of norms across states or societies; and the role of norms in rapid institutional change.

---

17. This appears to be what happened with the reform and development of central banks in the postcommunist region, according to Juliet Johnson's recent work (2010).

The concept of mutual constitution suggests that identities and norms influence actors, but actors also create and amend norms and identities. Another dimension to this mutual constitution issue is the relationship between the international and domestic levels: mutual constitution means that international norms influence domestic actors but also that domestic actors have some influence on the development and amendment of norms. Much international relations (IR) literature has addressed only the first area of contestation, the effect of global norms on states.[18]

Jeffrey Checkel (1998) has noted that many works that take a constructivist approach have failed to address the question of agency and have sidestepped the important issue of mutual constitution of norms and actors. Checkel wrote, "constructivists, despite their arguments about mutually constituting agents and structures, have advanced a structure-centered approach in their empirical work" (1998, 342). Understanding how norms are contested, challenged, and amended by local actors requires the kind of fieldwork and qualitative evidence that IR scholars have so far mainly amassed only at the international level. For example, in discussing Finnemore's (1996a) book on norms and the development of state interests, Checkel argues, "the agents she should be exploring, especially given her emphasis on global norms as the structures, are groups and individuals in those same states. If Finnemore had focused on these agents, it would have led her to explore several important issues, for example, the feedback effects of state (agent) behavior on the norms themselves" (1998, 332).

Finnemore's focus on international actors is indicative of a more general problem in the IR literature: its focus on international organizations as the source of change. To date, comparativists and Americanists have not filled this empirical gap. A notable exception in sociology is Bockman and Eyal's (2002) analysis of neoliberal ideology in Eastern Europe. They rejected the one-way diffusion model, where Western experts give advice to their novice East European counterparts, and instead considered neoliberalism as a network, a continuation of the economic laboratory for discussion and debate over economic policy that existed in socialist times.[19] Increasingly, more scholarship does attempt to address empirically how norms work (and are contested) in domestic contexts (Cortell

18. This is not to suggest that the literature ignores local actors in the development of global norms. For example, Tannenwald (2005) argues that the nuclear taboo was the result of bottom-up, social pressure against the interests of the powerful. In this case, as in many others, local actors are involved in the initial development of the norm at the international level, rather than at the level of domestic contestation once the norm has been established.

19. On learning and information processing in bureaucratic organizations, see Lindblom 1959; Simon 1976 [1945]; Padgett 1980, 1981; Meyer 1990; Hall 1993; March and Simon 1993 [1958]; Bendor 1995; Carpenter 1996. On learning and institutional change, see Mantzavinos et al. 2004.

and Davis 1996; Gurowitz 1999; Cortell and Davis 2000; Schimmelfennig and Sedelmeier 2005a). Even so, much more remains to be done in addressing the issue of how domestic actors influence global norms, especially after their initial establishment.

A second problem in the norms literature concerns persistent variation across states in the implementation of global norms.[20] This presents a critical challenge for a literature that has only begun systematic analysis of the conditions under which norms "work" in some states and not others.[21] Indeed, much of the norms literature has been oriented toward demonstrating convergence with international norms rather than divergence (Klotz 1995; Finnemore 1996a; Gurowitz 1999). For example, Finnemore (1996a) makes a convincing case for the role of international norms in guiding knowledge about science bureaucracies and affecting the form of certain state bureaucracies. But her argument is explicitly oriented toward explaining the lack of variation across states. Similarly, the diffusion and isomorphism literatures focus on explaining convergence, either within or across states.[22]

There may be convergence on some institutions, but even in those cases, countries may still differ in the magnitude (as opposed to direction) of institutional change. This is the case with the SNA; all countries have agreed to it in principle but implementation varies. One might argue that there is almost always some level of societally specific, creative, partial implementation or adaptation of institutional rules. If we analyze only what appears to be the same across countries, we will miss the story of what makes institutional reform as heterogeneous as it is.

Finally, the locus and timing of institutional change is not addressed by much of the work on norms. To the extent identities and norms are involved in institutional change, that change comes primarily from socialization into an existing identity (identity change among those learning new norms, often domestic-level actors) or development of new social identities or norms themselves (often at the

---

20. There are too many examples here to name. One attempt to systematically test norm compliance concerning educational policy is Hunter and Brown 2000. They argue that there has been less learning by countries than one might expect, despite the research on diffusion of ideas and teaching by international organizations. They examine education policy in Latin America from 1980 to 1992 and show that despite policy pronouncements, there has not been much increase in government spending on education or a shift in government spending to primary education.

21. See the burgeoning literature on socialization and persuasion in a special issue of *International Organization* in 2005; Checkel 2005; Risse and Sikkink 1999; Johnston 2001.

22. Diffusion refers to the spread of policies or institutions across countries, and there are many types of diffusion theories; for an overview, see Elkins and Simmons 2005; Simmons et al. 2008. Isomorphism (DiMaggio and Powell 1991) refers to the process by which organizations around the world are becoming more similar as a result of being structured by their environment (i.e., their organizational fields).

international level). However, identities and norms are very sticky, meaning the prospects for identity or norm-based change are limited and involve slow, long-term processes.[23] This suggests not only that identity or norm-based change is unlikely but that such theories are ill-equipped to explain rapid change. The challenge then is to theorize how we can explain institutional change in the face of relatively stable identities and norms, without excluding norms altogether.

In sum, the literature on norms and identity faces three challenges in reference to institutional change: mutual constitution, especially as concerns the influence of domestic actors on global norms; cross-national variation in implementation; and limited possibilities for norm or identity-based change. One way to address these issues is to return to the question of agency in institutions and the process by which norms are developed, contested, and amended.

Conditional Norms

In addressing implementation of the 1993 SNA by postcommunist states, I argue that we have to look at norms from a different angle, one which takes seriously the issues of mutual constitution and contestation. In particular, we have to consider the ways in which local actors understand norms, decide which to follow, and creatively reformulate or amend them. In this interactive process of norm contestation and development, some norms become *conditional norms,* in which conditions limit the appropriateness of a prescribed behavior for certain actors.[24] Because the triggering conditions are subject to change, they make possible norm-based behavioral change, even in situations where identities and norms remain fairly stable.

As a first step in developing a constructivist, agent-centered approach to norms, we have to distinguish between "holders" and "subjects" of norms. Identity groups are holders of norms. The behavioral prescription in a norm, however, might target a group other than the norm holders, and hence subjects are the specific actors to whom the norm is supposed to apply. For example, a norm among conservative Muslims is that women should cover their hair; in this case the norm holders are conservative Muslims (men and women), but the subjects to whom the norm's behavioral prescription should apply are women only (not men). In this example, both the holders and subjects of the

23. Similarly, theories of bureaucracy that focus on culture or national differences (see Crozier 1967) suggest that bureaucratic change is unlikely.

24. As far as I know, this is the first use of the term "conditional norm" in the social sciences. The term is used in Deontic logic in computer science, but not with the meaning discussed here.

norm are restricted: only conservative Muslims hold the norm, and the subjects are limited on the basis of sex differences, that is, women.

The holders of norms are always limited, because identity groups are limited,[25] but, importantly, the restrictions on subjects vary. When a norm is supposed to apply to all types of actors in all circumstances (subjects are unrestricted or all-encompassing), a norm is *unconditional*, even though the norm may not be universally held across identity groups. For example, the norm against the *use* of first-strike nuclear weapons is unconditional for those who hold it in that no state (or other actor) should be exempt from following the norm (Tannenwald 2005), that is, the subjects of the norm are unrestricted. In contrast, when only certain actors in particular circumstances are supposed to follow the norm, that is, subjects are restricted, we can call such norms, *conditional norms*. For example, the norm on *possession* of nuclear weapons is conditional and is codified in the Nuclear Nonproliferation Treaty: states that had nuclear weapons as of 1968 are allowed to have them, while other states are not (Smith 1987, 257–58).[26]

In other words, conditional norms are those in which the appropriateness of a behavioral prescription for given actors is contingent on specific conditions, restricting the type of actors subject to the norm, and hence providing a legitimate exemption (or forced exclusion) for some actors from following the norm. The conditions that specify the types of actors to whom a norm applies can include structural as well as ideational factors—political or economic conditions, military capabilities, types of identities (race, gender, religion), and so on.

Another set of examples concerns democracies: among some identity groups, the norm regarding democracy as an appropriate form of government is unconditional in that democracy is supposed to be suitable for all people in all states (subjects are all-encompassing). In contrast, in the 19th century among some identity groups, democracy was considered appropriate only for states that were of a certain level of economic and political development, hence subjects were limited and the norm regarding political institutions was conditional.[27]

---

25. If the holders of the norm were unlimited, we could say the norm is "universal." But this would require an all-encompassing identity group. In practice, even norms that seem universal, such as norms against cannibalism, are not held by certain societies and hence are not really universal.

26. This norm, even among its holders, is now being contested. Or, more specifically, the conditions specifying different types of subjects of the norm are being contested.

27. For example, In *On Liberty*, John Stuart Mill argued that liberty was conditional on types of societies. He wrote, "Despotism is a legitimate mode of government in dealing with barbarians.…Liberty, as a principle, has no application to any state of things anterior to the time when mankind have become capable of being improved by free and equal discussion." (Mill 1956 [1859], 14). This argument could also be applied to types of people within countries in the form of limited enfranchisement.

Similarly, "Asian values" proponents claim democracy is appropriate only for some countries, but not all countries, and hence would like to establish conditions (Zakaria 1994).

As an illustration of conditional norms in a domestic context, consider norms regarding voting rights. Ideas and practices regarding who can and should vote differ across political communities. An unconditional norm would suggest that everyone, without restriction, has a right and obligation to vote. In practice, though, the subjects of voting rights norms are almost always restricted in some important ways, making these conditional norms. To take the United States as an example, in norms of previous eras, subjects were limited on the basis of race and sex differences; although those conditions have since dropped out (i.e., members of the political community no longer think women or certain minorities should not be allowed to vote), subjects are still limited by age, formal citizenship status, and sometimes other criteria, such as criminal history, mental competence, and advance registration. By highlighting the specific conditions that limit subjects in these norms, we see clearly whose behavior will be regulated, or the conditions under which the voting norms do and do not apply.

The concept of conditionality clarifies the underlying logic of many norms and reveals how they might be consistent with rapid behavioral change. Conditionality is the source of "norm-based" change. To return to the example of a voting rights norm, if the circumstances of a subject change, for example, a person reaches voting age, the norm would predict an immediate change in the prescribed behavior, namely an obligation to vote by someone who had previously never voted, even though the norm itself and the identity of the holders of the norm do not change. Similarly, if a norm is conditional on specific kinds of states, unexpected regime change, as happened in Eastern Europe in the revolutions of 1989, could transform the conditions of states, bringing them into or out of the set of actors included in a norm (e.g., in regard to EU accession).

The conditions that limit subjects in norms are socially constructed, a product of a particular time and place, but they can be structural factors, such as age or income level, or more subjective criteria, such as "citizen" or race. In norms that apply to states, conditions are varied but often include political or economic criteria, such as the level of economic development (advanced versus developing economies), the type of economic system (capitalist versus communist states), or the type of political system (democratic versus authoritarian states). Whether conditions are changeable depends on the nature of the conditions and social understanding of them (consider the "changeability" of status as an "advanced democracy"; it is obviously possible but rather limited in practice).

Origins of Conditional Norms

There are two sources of conditional norms: like unconditional norms they can be original formulations based on other ideational and structural factors—shared ideas, identities, dispositions, habits, and experiences, as well as the need to coordinate and solve some kind of collective problem. Conditional norms can also be strategic responses to existing norms, promoted by actors who care about community legitimacy but are seeking exemptions to particular norms. Both sources address issues of agency and mutual constitution by treating conditional norms as *outcomes* produced by agents in particular contexts, rather than merely structures that constrain actors.

The first source of norms posits actors as innovative and creative, capable of formulating norms in response to particular problems. For this reason, conditions are historically specific: in the nineteenth century status as a "civilized" country or race were common conditions, but these attributes are no longer common. Unconditional norms are also reflective of changes in shared thinking about the appropriateness of conditions. For example, the ideas that democracy is appropriate for every country of the world or that all people have certain human rights are unconditional norms; previously these prescriptions had been subject to specific conditions, such as types of people, levels of development, or geographic region.

The second source of conditional norms brings contextualized choice to the development of norms. Conditional norms can be strategies by local actors who want to respond to broader norms while maintaining community membership. This source of conditionality reminds us that norms "work" only to the extent that actors care about community legitimacy; those who do not care about their standing in the community that holds a norm can simply reject the norm. But for those who do care, conditions can provide legitimate exemptions from the norm for themselves or others. And the acceptance of conditions can lead to the development of alternative norms. This means that conditional norms can be complementary or subversive for implementation of other norms; they may allow for limited compliance as well as selective noncompliance. In this way, conditional norms can be a weapon of the weak as well as the powerful.

Conditionality emphasizes the need to trace the iterative rounds of norm formation, contestation, and compliance. Conditional norms may start out as creative, contextual, even instrumental, strategies of local actors, but their evolution into norms means that eventually they can have constitutive effects on actors' identities and their sense of what is appropriate.

Such norms may also go beyond their sponsors' initial calculation or vision because the conditions that prescribe exemptions from norms may change in unpredictable ways. If apparently stable conditions change, the appropriateness of particular actions also changes. Conditionality then may affect actions in ways that the initial norm promoters did not foresee.

Conditional Norms in Practice

The concept of conditional norms extends the literature on institutional change and norms in international relations by emphasizing agency in norm development, amendment, and implementation at both the international and domestic levels. Conditions clarify when norms work and the basis for noncompliance and provide a mechanism for norm-based institutional change.

In table 2.1 I list four examples of conditional norms taken from the international relations literature: the use of chemical weapons, the possession and use of nuclear weapons, missile technology transfer, and EU membership. This list is illustrative, not exhaustive. The first two cases show how explicit attention to the conditionality of norms helps us to see how norms developed in response to the concerns of actors. Missile technology involves a norm in development and demonstrates the fluidity of conditions, but the focus on conditions also clarifies the interests at stake. In the EU case, an unexpected change in conditions triggered changes in membership, rather than a change in identities or norms per se.

Table 2.1 Examples of conditional norms

APPROPRIATE ACTION	SUBJECTS OF THE NORM	TYPE OF CONDITION	EMPIRICAL EXAMPLE
Use of chemical weapons	Uncivilized vs. civilized states	Political institutions and identity	For late 19th-century civilized states, the prohibition on the use of chemical weapons only against other civilized states (Price 1995)
Possession of nuclear weapons	Existing nuclear vs. non-nuclear states	Military capabilities	Nuclear weapons for states which had them before 1968, but not for any other state (Smith 1987)
Missile technology transfer	Missile-producing states	Political institutions, identity, and military capabilities	Missile technology for "responsible" missile producers only (Mistry 2003)
EU membership	European states	Political and economic institutions	EU accession for states with liberal democracy and a market economy (Schimmelfennig 2001)

An unconditional norm exists against the possession and use of chemical weapons, and is formalized in the Chemical Weapons Convention (CWC 2006). This norm was not always unconditional. In the late nineteenth century, it opposed the use of chemical weapons against other great powers. As codified in the Hague Treaty of 1899, it reads: "The Contracting Powers agree to abstain from the use of projectiles the sole object of which is the diffusion of asphyxiating or deleterious gases. The present Declaration is only binding on the Contracting Powers in the case of a war between two or more of them. It shall cease to be binding from the time when, in a war between the Contracting Powers, one of the belligerents shall be joined by a non-Contracting Power" (Hague Declaration 2006).[28] Richard Price has argued that the condition of the norm was actually civilizational status: "Those contracting powers were the nations that would count as members of an emerging society of civilized states" (1995, 95). Interestingly, the category of civilized state was not static, and joining the Hague treaty offered one way of attaining that status. In the twentieth century this norm became both unconditional and wider in scope. The subjects expanded from only civilized states to all states, and the restricted action included the possession and production as well as the use of chemical weapons.

With regard to nuclear weapons there is an unconditional norm against a first strike (Tannenwald 2005).[29] The situation surrounding the possession and proliferation of nuclear weapons, however, is a prime example of a conditional norm. States that had nuclear weapons before 1968 are allowed to have them; states that did not have nuclear weapons at that time are not. The condition—level of military capabilities as of 1968–is codified in the Nuclear Nonproliferation Treaty, which was signed in 1968 and came into force in 1970 (NPT 2006). The treaty makes clear distinctions between "nuclear-weapon State Party to the Treaty" and "non-nuclear-weapon State Party to the Treaty" and adjusts the prescribed action accordingly. In explaining the conditionality of the norm, Roger Smith argues:

> [the NPT] explicitly lays out the essence of the "nuclear bargain" between the nuclear "haves" and "have nots" in six operative clauses. The first three articles obligate the signatories not to transfer nuclear weapons to non-nuclear weapons states, not to produce nuclear weapons unless they had already succeeded in doing so, and not to export nuclear materials without international safeguards. The next three clauses establish

---

28. See discussion of this in Price 1995, 83, 95–98.

29. Tannenwald (2005) calls the norm against use of nuclear weapons a "taboo." This distinction is based on the strength of the norm and the serious consequences for breaking the norm. However, not all states hold this norm.

> the "inalienable right" of all parties to develop nuclear energy for peaceful purposes. It also provides that all parties should facilitate, and have [the] right to participate in, the *fullest* possible exchange of equipment, materials, and scientific and technological information for the peaceful uses of nuclear energy. (1987, 257–58)

This conditional norm was clearly in the interest of the five countries defined as nuclear weapons states (Britain, China, France, the USSR, and the United States). These states did not simply assert their power; rather, they worked to legitimate their exception to the norm. This conditional norm was a response to the development of the general norm against the use of nuclear weapons, which had been growing in strength over the postwar period (Tannenwald 2005). In addition, selective denial of nuclear technology developed in stages between the invention of the bomb and the NPT (Smith 1987, 264–66). In 1943, at the Quebec conference, Britain and the United States agreed to not share atomic bomb technology with other states. The United States outlawed export of nuclear technology with the MacMahon Act of 1946. The 1953 Atoms for Peace program also distinguished between nuclear and non-nuclear states, with the idea of maintaining restrictions on other states becoming nuclear by offering incentives to non-nuclear states in the form of peaceful-use technology transfers. Tannenwald argues that "as the [nuclear] taboo emerged the Eisenhower administration sought to resist it and to promote a competing norm of selective use of nuclear weapons" (2005, 14).

The strategy of promoting an alternative conditional norm has been reasonably successful. The idea that there are nuclear and non-nuclear states has become acceptable to many states around the world. Now, however, there are two new nuclear states, India and Pakistan, which have never signed the NPT. Israel has neither signed the NPT nor admits having nuclear weapons. It is too early to predict the outcome, but India and Pakistan could formulate a different conditional norm to attain an exemption and acceptance by the international community, which might favor some kind of new norm, even if conditional, rather than just the breakdown of the NPT and no norm against nuclear proliferation. Proposals for changing or eliminating the condition altogether are also possible.

Norms on missile technology are newer and less established than those against nuclear and chemical weapons. Even so, conditionality gives us a sense of who may be subject to the eventual norm, what possible exceptions there are, and how the norm may influence the actions of different kinds of states.

The emerging global norm presently indicates that missile-producing states should be allowed to have extensive missile technology, whereas some other states should not. This norm developed in the mid- to late 1980s and has not been accepted by all states. It is conditional but not purely dependent on military capabilities. The condition for receiving missile technology is that a state should be responsible and trustworthy, and these criteria are the basis for membership in the exclusive Missile Technology Control Regime (MTCR).[30] The MTCR has grown from a small band of G-7 countries in 1987 to include thirty-four states. But it is not an open organization, and unlike the Nonproliferation Treaty and the Chemical Weapons Convention, it is not a treaty. Its goal is to stop missiles and missile technology from being passed along to untrustworthy states, and it pursues this goal by restricting membership and offering selective benefits.

The first agreement by G-7 countries, in 1985, grew out of talks initiated by the United States (Mistry 2002, 98). Mistry writes, "cooperation was rapidly facilitated by limiting the regime's scope to a small but important part of the problem—that of technology controls—and by limiting its domain to only the G-7" (2002, 99). From the start the members recognized that they could not offer any strong incentives to states to stop their missile programs, because, as an exclusive club of like-minded states, they had little to offer except the distant proposition of membership. After several worrisome events—missile attacks by Iran and Iraq against each other in 1987–88, the revelations that China sold missiles to Saudi Arabia in 1988 and that Argentina was cooperating with Egypt and Iraq in the Condor missile project, and India's 1989 missile test—there was increased motivation to add members beyond the G-7 (Mistry 2002, 99–100). The group began its expansion within Europe, then added other states.

One problem with setting a coherent condition for allowing missile technology is that the same technology is used for many nonmilitary purposes. For example, space launcher technology is used for commercial satellites as well as the most dangerous kind of missiles, intercontinental ballistic missiles. In 1993, a U.S. policy paper first addressed the issue, suggesting that some states but not others should be allowed to keep the technology. Mistry writes: "It allowed new MTCR members to retain their space programs but required them to destroy their offensive ballistic missiles and related technology. In addition, Washington would not encourage new space programs that raised concerns on nonproliferation and economic viability grounds" (2003, 133). This sounds like the nuclear nonproliferation norm, but it is actually much messier. The policy statement listed three conditions for maintaining space launcher technology: age of the program, economic viability, and proliferation concerns. In practice this meant that Brazil, Ukraine, and South Korea could keep their space launcher programs

30. For a history of the MTCR, see Mistry 2002, 2003.

after joining MTCR, but Argentina and South Africa could not keep their dual-use rocket programs, apparently because "they were only in their initial phases (and therefore not economically viable) and because they were based on existing missile programs (which were of proliferation concern)" (Mistry 2003, 136). Thus, age of program mattered for some countries, but more subjective factors mattered for others.

The missile technology issue highlights several important points in institutional and norm formation.[31] First, problem definition—in this case, recognition that proliferation of missile technology is a problem—has to precede institutional solutions (formal or informal). Many actors do not see missile technology as a problem, so they have no interest in institutions seeking to limit the technology. Second, the absence of an established global norm leaves a hole filled by seemingly strategic conditional rules that various states hope to develop into broader norms. Although the development of a norm against missile technology might seem far-fetched, especially since missiles are used by nuclear powers as weapons delivery systems, the idea has been proposed. Mistry writes, some "science and technology expert groups have proposed a global ban on all missiles, and one state—Canada—made a similar proposal at the 1993 MTCR plenary session" (Mistry 2003, 139). In addition, while it seems like powerful countries like the United States would never agree to give up missile programs, as the world's leader in aircraft technology, the United States would be at an enormous advantage in a world without missiles. Norms against missile technology are in flux, and both the powerful and the weak attempt to exploit conditionality as they seek a legitimate way to include or exclude actors.

Instrumental attempts to limit the behavior of certain actors become conditional *norms* when the strategic use of ideas about what constitutes legitimate membership has an effect on the promoting actors themselves. In an analysis of EU enlargement in the late 1990s, Frank Schimmelfennig argues: "strategic behavior is constrained by the constitutive ideas of the community and the actors' prior identification with them. Once caught in the community trap, they can be forced to honor identity- and value-based commitments in order to protect their credibility and reputation as community members" (2001, 77).

---

31. The case of landmines provides another an example of norm formation, see Price 1998; Rutherford 2000. In this case, there is now an unconditional norm against landmine use: all states are supposed to get rid of them. The United States tried but failed to promote two conditional norms as an alterative. The first used the type of mine as a condition ("smart" mines versus "dumb" ones). The second involved certain types of military threats, such as North/South Korea, where landmines are necessary to protect South Korea from a North Korean invasion. This exemption based on the North Korean threat presents an interesting possibility for change. If political and military conditions in North Korea were to change, that would seriously undermine the legitimacy of the U.S. argument for maintaining landmines.

In this case, EU members made certain political and economic conditions the basis for membership in the Union, but they also repeatedly affirmed an ideology that membership should be open to all European states. The first substantive sentence of the preamble of the Treaty of Rome, which established the European Economic Community (EEC), says that the founding heads of state are "determined to lay the foundations of an ever closer union among the peoples of Europe." The treaty calls "upon the other peoples of Europe who share their ideal to join in their efforts" (Schimmelfennig 2001; Treaty of Rome 2006, 67). Schimmelfennig details how European leaders have since repeated this invitation to other European states. The aspect of this case relevant to conditional norms is that what changed in the late 1990s was not the norm but the conditions. When communism fell in Eastern Europe, the European Community suddenly found itself confronted by East European states who had now met the basic political and economic conditions for membership and were armed with the EU's own rhetoric of inclusion. Schimmelfennig argues:

> The Central and Eastern European governments have based their claims to membership on the standard of legitimacy of the European international community: European identity and unity, liberal democracy, and multilateralism. They invoked the community's membership rules and took its ritualized pan-European liberal commitment at face value. They tried to demonstrate that these values and norms obliged the EU to admit them and that failing to do so would be an act of disloyalty to the ideational foundations of the European international community. (2001, 68)

Here institutional change, enlargement of the EU, was not an intended consequence of the original norm conditionality. EEC framers probably did not imagine that, in the span of a few years, several East European countries would meet the structural political and economic conditions for membership. The original norm promoters did not foresee the timing of change in Eastern Europe, but when it came, community legitimacy demanded that they allow expansion in accordance with the membership norm.

Conditionality in norms deserves our attention for four reasons. First, it clarifies the logic of norms: when and for whom a given norm should apply. That determination leaves us better prepared to answer the question why particular norms develop and where they are likely to be accepted or rejected.

Second, a focus on conditionality sheds light on the social construction of norms, how actors adapt norms to their own interests. Conditions suggest multiple phases of innovation in norm development and reveal strategies by local actors, both at the point of norm creation and in response to existing norms. Debates over conditionality open a window on contestation within identities and can account for mutual constitution between norms and actors.

Third, conditions provide a different, potentially much more rapid mechanism for understanding the prospects of norm-based institutional change. Identities and norms may be stable while changing conditions can quickly alter the appropriateness of norm-based action, legitimating abrupt behavioral and institutional changes.

Fourth, the concept of conditional norms encompasses objective (economic structure, military capacity) and subjective factors (identities) and connects these factors to the legitimacy of specific actions within identity groups. Rather than competing with ideational factors such as identities, structural and material factors can be integrated into ideational frameworks and connected to agents' sense of appropriate action. For example, if a normative prescription relied on a state's economic structure as its condition, a change in the economic structure could alter actors' sense of what is appropriate due to their relationship to the norm, rather than due to the effect of economic structural change on material incentives. This is a quite different way of understanding the effect of the economy on political behavior and institutional choice.

By emphasizing agency in the development and evolution of norms, the concept of conditional norms bridges the rationalist and constructivist approaches to institutional change.[32] It posits actors whose institutional choices are contextualized by normative environments, by identities and communities, as well as by material circumstances and power relations. In this way, it builds on previous "integrated" theories.[33]

---

32. On rationalist versus constructivist approaches to institutional change see Lieberman 2002; Blyth 2003; Jupille et al. 2003; Schimmelfennig 2003.

33. Some notable examples of integrated approaches include Hall's notion of "policy paradigms" (1993), Bleich's concept of "frames" (2002), Sabatier's concept of "belief systems" (1987), Berman's concept of "programmatic beliefs" (1998), Marcussen's concept of ideational life-cycles (1999), Swidler's conceptualization of culture in terms of "symbols and strategies" (1986), and Wilsford's integration of Reinhard Bendix and Max Weber (1985).

3

ACCIDENTAL HEGEMONY

How the System of National Accounts Became an International Norm

The SNA is a massively ambitious institutional enterprise that—through a complex and lengthy series of rules on data definitions, classificatory schemes, methodology, and collection—aims to clarify the overall structure and dynamics of a country's economy. As a single standardized system, it makes legible economic activity around the globe. Although countries continue to debate the content of the SNA, there is no alternative system and they no longer question the value of a single, comprehensive international framework for national accounts. The SNA has become an unconditional norm.

Today's ostensible hegemony, however, masks the mutual constitution and contestation that defined the development of the SNA. It is important to uncover those processes to understand the bases for compliance and implementation of the SNA, because while it is one thing to sign on in principle to an international institution, it is another to implement it in practice. Yet the value of the SNA rests on its implementation.

In this chapter I analyze the development of the SNA from a constructivist institutionalist approach. The advance of the SNA can be understood as a gradual institutional development, but following Herrigel (2010) I demonstrate that the development of the SNA was marked by multiple decision points, and a variety of ideas and national interests, which led to the "accidental" hegemony of the SNA.

Mutual Constitution

Mutual constitution refers to the productive and consequential interaction between norms (or rules) and their followers (actors). In studying the SNA there is also a spatial dimension, the interaction between international rules and national actors. The development of the SNA was simultaneously a national and international effort. The SNA emerged as a single framework as the result of countries working through problems and coordinating (or not) with other states and with international organizations.

Moreover, the SNA and its primary rival, the MPS, developed in relation to each other; they were mutually constituting as well. The MPS appeared in association with the revision of the SNA, and the hegemony of the SNA is integrally tied to the demise of the MPS. Neither of these institutions was developed only by international organizations; the contributions of member nations and mutual learning led to the formalization of both institutions.

Finally, the development of the SNA is not a story of exogenous rule development and imposition. The SNA did not appear on the scene as a self-evident set of rules that suddenly constrained or enabled behavior; it was and is a product of discussions about how economic data could and should be compiled. No leviathan oversaw the creation of the SNA. Nor is it a story of West versus East or of powerful states dictating to everyone else how national accounts should be organized. Instead, it grew out of mutually constituting contributions from individuals and countries at the national, regional, and international levels.

Contestation

With so many cooks in the kitchen, there was a great deal of contestation. Debate occurred over every aspect of national accounts, beginning with the production boundary, the overall classificatory scheme, the methodology of indicators, and the specific data collection and dissemination procedures.

There was and still is extensive variation in accounting practices among both individual countries and "types" of states (Western, CMEA, developing, etc.). Some OECD countries fought to include their own practices in the SNA or simply maintained their previous ways of doing things. The United States follows its own system of national accounts (National Income and Product Accounts [NIPA]), which is fully consistent with SNA principles but not exactly the same. France at various points also took an alternative path. Among postcommunist countries there was variation between East European states and some FSU states in not only structural conditions and economic reforms but also in their statistical practices and their familiarity with the SNA; not all participated to the same degree.

Over time, the SNA did not stamp out variation so much as find space for it. The 1993 SNA aims to fit every type of economy. To understand this amalgamation, it is all the more critical to analyze the fierce debates along the way. In many respects, the 1993 SNA integrated and incorporated the debates and is a product of opposition and alternatives.

Given its history, the coherence of the SNA, like many other international institutions, can easily be overstated. The apparent coherence of the SNA is in reality an abstraction. As Herrigel argues, the abstraction of coherence "blends out a great deal of anomalous relationships, habits, dispositions, and institutional practices" (2005, 565). By remaining attentive to contestation, we can detect variation in institutional practice and the causes of that variation.

Compliance

Why people follow rules is closely connected to what they think of rules. There are other factors, but actors' understanding of rules is an important part of compliance. By focusing on mutual constitution and contestation in the development of the SNA, we can see how the statisticians tasked with implementing it perceive the situation. Debates over the development of the SNA reveal clues to the interests that would (or would not) support its implementation.

A specific manifestation of contestation from CMEA countries was the formation of a conditional norm that set out the boundaries of appropriateness for the SNA versus the MPS. Hence, understanding the development of the SNA, and the contestation that produced it and the MPS, is critical for understanding the variation in its implementation.

I explore the development of the SNA and the MPS in tandem. After considering the evolution of the SNA up to 1968, I examine the emergence of the MPS. Then I examine the revision of the SNA between 1968 and 1993 before analyzing the end of the MPS as an international standard. In each discussion I consider the influence of mutual constitution and contestation.

Development of the SNA up to 1968

Sir William Petty undertook the first attempt to measure national income in England in 1665 (Vanoli 2005, 3). The collection of data on populations and the economy coincided with the development of modern states.[1] As states sought to build strong defense capabilities, they needed revenue, which in turn required

1. On the relationship among statistics, governance, and the economy, see Porter 1995; Desrosières 1998; Poovey 1998.

information on trade and populations (Mitchell 1939; Furst 1964; Husein 1964, 40). States and organizations within them developed statistical accounts suited to the conditions of particular economies and the demands of particular governments or organizations. Adam Smith (1976 [1776]) identified the need to compare countries in the *Wealth of Nations*, but he set out a specific conception of economic output, material production, which would dominate understandings of national income for more than a century and a half.

Influences on the Development of Modern National Accounting

Modern national accounting appeared after the Great Depression.[2] According to Kenessey (1994a, 6–8), modern national accounts are distinguished by six features. First and foremost among these is the systematic application of macroeconomic theory to national accounts, especially that of John Maynard Keynes. In 1936 Keynes set out the key theoretical basis for modern national accounts with three equations:[3]

Income = Value of Output = Consumption + Investment
Savings = Income – Consumption
Therefore, Savings = Investment

The critical contribution by Keynes is the move away from an entirely empirical approach to national income focused on aggregation of industrial production and toward the concepts of income, consumption, investment, and savings and the relationships among them.

There were other intellectual influences in the development of modern national accounts as well. Zoltan Kenessey (1994a, 2–5) names Ragnar Frisch, for his early econometric work in Norway; Simon Kuznets in the United States and Colin Clark in the United Kingdom, for their work on national income in the 1930s;[4] Morris Copeland's concept of "money flows" or "flow of funds"; and Jan Tinbergen, for his econometric work at the League of Nations and in the Netherlands.

In addition, according to Kenessey, Wassily Leontief's "input-output statistics and analysis was a crucial invention of the 1920s and 1930s for the presentation and interpretation of macroeconomic relationships in general, and the structure

2. On the history of modern national accounts and the SNA, see Studenski 1958; Kenessey 1994b; Vanoli 2005.

3. Keynes 1936, book 2, chap. 6, cited in Vanoli 2005, 19.

4. See Clark 1940.

of modern economies in particular" (1994a, 5). Approximately a hundred countries began doing input-output on the basis of Leontief's work. One of the influences for Leontief's contribution was the analysis of interindustry tables in the USSR, compiled by Pavel Popov (1926). These tables were the basis of Popov's very early estimation of national accounts for the USSR in the 1920s, which was later the theoretical and empirical basis of the MPS. The work of Popov, therefore, influenced not only the MPS but also, via Leontief, the SNA.

Another innovation necessary to the development of modern national accounting was double-entry bookkeeping. Irving Fisher and Morris Copeland in the United States both advanced the connection between double-entry bookkeeping and national accounts. This may seem like a technical issue, but it was critical to the connections between concepts and indicators. According to Kenessey, "One can say that the discipline of this bookkeeping technique, and the way it permits relating flows of expenditures to incomes, production to consumption, or savings to investments was indispensable for the systematic integration of statistical macro-aggregates" (1994a, 6).

Third, Kenessey noted that modern national accounts were more oriented toward public policy than in the past. Statistics and national accounts have always had some policy relevance and connection to politics and state formation, but the economic problems created by the Great Depression and WWII greatly increased politicians' interest in figuring out ways to affect production and employment. During the Depression, for example, President Hoover and his advisers knew that things were bad, but they had only the roughest guesses about what was going on with regard to investment and unemployment. Keynes wrote a series of newspaper articles, titled "How to Pay for the War" in November 1939, later published as a book (Keynes 1940). These articles applied his *General Theory of Employment, Interest, and Money* to financing WWII in the United Kingdom. Richard Stone and James Meade wrote a "white paper" (Meade and Stone 1941) applying double-entry bookkeeping and national accounts to U.K. data.[5] Stone went on to become the main architect of the SNA.[6] The creation of modern national accounts, based on work by Keynes and Stone, significantly changed both the type of information available to governments and the options for assessing government polices.

The SNA differed from previous estimates of national income in its "statistical portrayal of the whole economic process" (Kenessey 1994a, 7). Comprehensive and extremely detailed, the SNA brought together macro-level institutional

5. James Meade also wrote a secret paper on this topic (1988 [1940]).

6. Stone was a student of Colin Clark's at Cambridge. He was later knighted and awarded a Nobel prize in economics in 1984 for his work on the SNA.

actors (governments, households) and concepts (savings, investment) in a single system. Other national accounting devices, such as input-output and flow of funds statistics, were also detailed, but less comprehensive. These different tools, however, were all brought back together and connected in the 1993 SNA.

Another feature of modern national accounts is the "internationalization of methodological development" (Kenessey 1994a, 7). Before WWII there were international conferences and bilateral interactions, but national income work was conducted separately. With the development of the SNA and MPS, the UN, the OECD (earlier OEEC), and other international organizations played critical roles.

Finally, the technical complexity of national accounts, with their heavy reliance on mathematics and computers, distinguishes the current system from past efforts. This development is concomitant with the changes in statistics and economics as disciplines more generally.[7]

Formalization of the SNA

The League of Nations had a small statistical office. After WWII, the UN Statistical Commission was set up, initially called the Nuclear Statistical Commission (UN Statistical Commission 1946). The Nuclear Statistical Commission met for the first time at Hunter College in New York on May 1–15, 1946. The commission formally included seven members: the United Kingdom, India, France, the United States, Norway, China, and the USSR. The Norway representative could not attend and sent written comments instead. The Chinese representative arrived only on May 13. When the meeting began, the representatives from the USSR and the Ukrainian SSR were not in attendance. A temporary USSR representative (P. I. Fedesimov) arrived on May 14.[8] In addition, Brazil was invited to send a representative, but the person chosen declined for health reasons. Thus most of the work of the meeting was carried out by representatives from the United States, the United Kingdom, India, and France, with the U.S. representative chairing the meeting.

The Nuclear Statistical Commission recommended the establishment of a permanent UN Statistical Commission and a United Nations Statistical Office (UNSO, later the UN Statistics Division, UNSD). Of the Nuclear Statistical Commission, Michael Ward wrote that, "the basic concern, namely, to promote the worldwide compilation and coordinated development of key statistics,

7. On the development of statistics in the twentieth century, see Stigler 1999; Salsburg 2001.

8. Ward (2004, 37) suggests that this was due to visa problems, but no mention of the reasons for the late arrivals of the Chinese and Soviet representatives is noted in the official report.

particularly relating to the economies of each country, and to make such information as comparable as possible, has changed little since that date" (2004, 37).

According to Ward, there was some debate as to whether the UNSO should represent nations or simply statistical expertise; the Soviets and Chinese favored the former and wanted country representatives. As a compromise, it was decided that the UNSO should be staffed by people from NSOs with scientific qualifications, rather than political appointments.

The Nuclear Statistical Commission recommended the establishment of a new international scientific organization for consultation and arbitration of UNSO debates. At the time, the International Statistical Institute and the American Statistical Association were prominent, but the commission decided that neither these nor the former statistical office of the League of Nations could handle postwar economic problems. Hence the International Association for Research in Income and Wealth (IARIW) was formed as an offshoot of the International Statistical Institute (ISI) in September 1947 to work specifically on national income accounting. It became a key contributor to the development of national accounts.

The Nuclear Statistical Commission took action on two important issues early on: national accounts and sampling. The commission's very first report mentioned these issues (UN Statistical Commission 1946, 225–26). According to Ward, the development of a system of national accounts "drove the early UN agenda in statistics" (2004, 45). The idea was for the SNA to give governments information to make "rational macroeconomic policies" and help them avoid the problems that had led up to the two world wars. Ward wrote: "prior to WWII, both probability sampling and national accounting were viewed as somewhat untried and questionable endeavors. Doubts about their relevance and reliability persisted even after the war, despite the successful uses of both approaches by governments in the intervening period" (2004, 40). For this reason he called the UNSO's decision to focus on national accounts "a significant leap of faith" (2004, 77). Nevertheless, the Statistical Commission advanced both right away: It published the work of Richard Stone on national accounts (UN Statistical Office 1947) and set up a Subcommission on Sampling (chaired by P. C. Mahalanobis of India).[9]

The 1947 publication of Stone's work was a milestone in national accounts.[10] Some analysts, such as Frits Bos of Eurostat, considered it the first version of the SNA. The 1947 UN report had two distinguishing features, according to

9. Stone's work was originally written as an appendix in a League of Nations report in 1945 (Stone 1945).

10. For further detailed analysis of the changes over time in formal SNA documentation (1947, 1953, 1968, 1993) see Bos 1994.

Bos: "First, it contained the first fully elaborated and detailed national accounting system. Secondly, it contained, for the first time, *international recommendations on compiling national accounts.*" (1994, 198, emphasis in original). It seems hard to imagine a time before there were international recommendations, but this 1947 document represented a significant step beyond just sharing national data toward *collective* work at the international level.

One of the key goals of the 1947 report was comparability of data—a goal that remains part of the core mission of all international organizations involved in national accounts today. The preface to the 1947 report says: "The Sub-Committee hopes that the guiding principles and recommendations formulated...will be applied to the widest possible extent in each country in the computation of national income and related accounts in order to secure greater international comparability than in the past" (UN Statistical Office 1947, Preface, also cited in Bos 1994, 199).

In addition to the UN Statistical Commission and its newly created UNSO, the OEEC (later, the OECD) played an important role in advancing the SNA. Set up as a temporary organization in 1947 to administer the Marshall Plan, the OEEC became permanent on April 16, 1948.[11] In 1949 it set up a National Accounts Research Unit, directed by Richard Stone, in Cambridge to train statisticians from member countries (Kenessey 1994a, 12). That unit produced two early SNA publications in 1951 and 1952 (National Accounts Research Unit 1951, 1952).

These three publications, the UN's 1947 report and the OEEC reports from 1951 and 1952 (all based on the work of Richard Stone, and James Meade for the 1947 report), gave rise to the first official document on the SNA in 1953 (UN Statistical Office 1953). The 1953 version was concerned almost exclusively with calculation of aggregates (i.e., GNP), although the 1947 report and the 1968 and 1993 SNAs all had broader goals (Bos 1994). The 1953 SNA employed a Keynesian framework that produced macroeconomic aggregates by linking production and factor incomes with household and government consumption and investment (and savings). The core accounts from this system as elaborated in 1953—income, production, and expenditure—remain part of the SNA.

Stone continued to work on the SNA after the 1953 publication. He again played a critical role in producing the revised version published in 1968 (UN Statistical Office 1968). Ward described the 1968 version as "a quantum leap forward" (2004, 78). In particular, the 1968 version incorporated and expanded Leontief's interindustry input-output tables and included flow of funds. It also

11. According to the OECD website, the OEEC "sought to establish a permanent organisation to continue work on a joint recovery programme and in particular to supervise the distribution of aid."

outlined the basis for price indices that would allow for measurement of aggregates in current and constant prices.[12]

One indicator of growing international cooperation on national accounts is the publication of comparative national accounts data (Ward 2004, 79–82). In 1939 the League of Nations published a *World Economic Survey* that considered national accounts data for twenty-six countries for the 1929–38 period; about half were submitted by countries and the other half estimated by experts. In 1950 the UNSO published *National Income Statistics, 1938–1948,* which had data for forty-one countries. In 1958 the UN published the first *Yearbook of National Accounts Statistics,* with data for seventy countries; this became an annual publication (renamed *National Accounts Statistics: Main Aggregates and Detailed Tables* in 1982). It now includes data for almost all states and territories.

Mutual Constitution and Contestation in the Development of the SNA up to 1968

In this early period a great deal of work at the national level influenced the development of the SNA at the UN. The United Kingdom, Norway, Denmark, the Netherlands, the United States, France, Japan, Germany, India, and the USSR were among the countries working on national accounts as well as contributing internationally.[13] Of the USSR, Kenessey writes: "The early efforts regarding the establishment of the national economic balances of Russia for 1923/24 (which included a kind of interindustry [input-output] table) should be recognized when speaking of the wide, sometimes rather indirect, intellectual heritage of contemporary national accounting" (1994a, 5).

It would be premature to characterize this process in terms of mutual constitution of international institutions (e.g. the UNSO and SNA) and domestic actors (NSOs). In the run-up to the 1968 SNA national experiences influenced the international level, but significant variation in national practices remained, and the UN recommendations were just beginning to take hold. In addition, the 1953 and 1968 SNA versions were dominated by the work of Richard Stone and did not reflect, as the 1993 SNA would, a diverse and multinational as well as multi-institutional approach to the drafting of the formal documents.

Nevertheless, contestation or debate over the goals as well as the content and uses of national accounts data took place at every step of SNA development. In *Quantifying the World: UN Ideas and Statistics,* Michael Ward wrote that "statistics is primarily a science of order and classification" but "there is no unique

12. See Ward 2004, 78–83, for a more detailed account of changes from the 1953 to 1968 SNA.

13. For more on national contributions, see individual chapters in Kenessey 1994b.

classification structure that serves all conceivable purposes equally well" (2004). Hence there will always be debate over national accounts.[14]

In the post-WWII era, the UN was initially interested in growth and unemployment, not in poverty and how to end it. The SNA encapsulates these concerns. Although numerous discussions have raised the issues of women's (often unpaid) contributions and the environment,[15] even in 1946,[16] these areas remain largely outside the production boundary of the SNA. Criticism of the SNA also came from the political right: there was controversy in the United States when national income accounting was introduced because of the Hayekian fear that it would enable policy makers to tinker with the economy by manipulating government spending and interest rates, which was in some ways the point from a Keynesian perspective.

A key indicator of the level of contestation is the variety of country practices that accompanied the SNA's development. There were regional differences, exemplified by the later development of the MPS, but there were also the European System of Integrated Economic Accounts (known as ESA),[17] and the National Income and Product Accounts in the United States, to name just two examples. Although largely compatible with the SNA, ESA and NIPA illustrate decisions to deviate from the SNA.

There were also differences within regions. In regard to the OECD countries, Peter Hill (later an author of the 1993 SNA) has written, "No two countries tackle the problem of measuring real product in quite the same way and every country has its own idiosyncrasies" (1971, 42). He detailed differences in national accounts in Norway, the Netherlands, France, Japan, Sweden, Italy, West Germany, Belgium, Canada, and the United States.

Development of the MPS

The development of the MPS differs from the development of the SNA in that an informal statistical system for national accounts existed in the USSR and

---

14. For more on the politics of modern state statistics, see Alonso and Starr 1987; Dorling and Simpson 1999. On controversies and criticisms of GNP, especially in the United States, see Maier and Easton 1999, 97–108. On criticisms of the SNA more generally, see England and Harris 1997.

15. For a critique of SNA for not including data relevant to women and the environment, see Waring 2004.

16. Interestingly, the status of women and how to quantify it was suggested as an agenda item by the Czechoslovak delegation to the UN in April 1946, but there is no record that the topic was taken up (Ward 2004, 285–86).

17. The ESA was an adaptation of the 1968 SNA for Europe, and the European Community published guidelines for the ESA in 1970 (Eurostat 1970). For further discussion of the 1995 ESA, see Jackson 2000.

Eastern European countries before it was formalized in a written document. To a large extent, the development of the MPS formalized and harmonized existing practices.

The formal documentation of the MPS took a rather circuitous route. Pavel I. Popov (1926), the head of TsSU, published a study of national accounts in the USSR for 1923–24. Popov's study, which he called the "Balance of the national economy," made use of inter-industry or input-output tables. The document was in two parts: 350 pages on methodology and data analysis, followed by 275 pages of statistical materials (Árvay 1994, 220).

According to János Árvay,[18] this 1926 document was nearly forgotten. After WWII, when East European countries were setting up their statistical systems using the USSR as a model, they did not have access to Popov's analysis.[19] To learn about the MPS, East Europeans held bilateral meetings, primarily in Moscow, with Soviet statisticians. Árvay writes, "In this situation the compilation of national balances started in the new socialist countries without an overall description of the concepts and methods; *they relied frequently on the principle of 'learning by doing.'*" (Árvay 1994, 220, emphasis added).

The first general description of the MPS was published by the UN Statistical Commission in 1957, with the approval of all CMEA countries. In response to expressions of interest, the UN asked the Conference of European Statisticians to undertake a comparison project between the SNA and the MPS. Árvay states that interest in the comparison of macroeconomic aggregates (i.e., GNP and NMP) was not the only reason for the comparison project. Another motivation was that UN dues were based on national income, and some people suspected that the MPS underestimated CMEA countries' national income by excluding services. In any event, at the Sixth Conference of European Statisticians (CES) in 1958, eight countries, four from the East and four from the West, were invited to undertake a comparison. The participant countries included the USSR, Czechoslovakia, Poland, Hungary, the United States, the United Kingdom, France, and Italy (Conference of European Statisticians 1958).

In preparation for that 1958 CES meeting, Czechoslovakia gave the Secretariat of the conference two documents: one that described the methodology for national income under the MPS and one that presented the system as whole.[20] According to Árvay, these two documents, which together totaled twenty-five

18. János Árvay, a Hungarian statistician, participated in all phases of the MPS.

19. The status of Popov's document changed over time; in its 1996 history of Russian statistics, the Goskomstat leadership highly praised it and even reprinted a diagram of the system (Goskomstat Russia 1996b, 65).

20. Árvay (1994, 221) cites these as "CES/83" and "CES/84."

pages, were translated into three languages, and were the first international presentation of the MPS by the CMEA. Based on these documents and an early version of the SNA, the eight countries were compared (Árvay 1994, 221).[21] Of this work, Árvay says, "Looking back at this period from a sufficiently long historical perspective, it can definitely be stated that the comparison of the two systems exerted a mutual influence which was perceivable later when the development of the two systems proceeded" (1994, 221). He then noted where representatives found shortcomings in both systems: consumption of the population and the treatment of indirect taxes.

Within the USSR, a short formal description of the MPS was not published until 1960 (Sobol 1960), that is, some years after the work on documenting the MPS had begun at the UN. Written by V. A. Sobol, head of national accounts at TsSU, it only briefly mentioned the 1926 work by Popov. The CMEA made extensive use of Sobol's work, both in individual countries' national accounts and in the further development of the MPS (Árvay 1994).

There was another revision of the country comparisons in 1964, when the CES set up the Working Party on National Accounts and Balances at its twelfth plenary session. The Working Party was supposed to represent the CES during the overall SNA revision in the UN Statistical Commission, but it had two additional tasks: (1) to develop a description of the MPS; and (2) to consider "establishing links between a revised and developed SNA and MPS and of drawing up a European statistical program of national accounts and balances" (Árvay 1994, 223). In conjunction with this expanded comparison effort, representatives from all countries of the CES were invited to join the Working Party.

Closely following these efforts in the CES, in 1965 the CMEA countries decided to work toward harmonizing national accounts within the CMEA, and began further documenting the MPS to produce a revised and more detailed account. Initially different countries were to work on different parts, with the USSR coordinating the effort (Árvay 1994, 223). After one round, this proved unworkable and Goskomstat USSR took over, using some country papers as supplements. At the ninth session of CMEA statisticians in November 1967 they agreed on harmonization of input-output tables.[22] The CMEA approved a final document at its eleventh session in November 1968,[23] which appeared in Russian in 1969.[24] This document provided three methods for calculating GDP and NMP

21. They used the 1952 version of the SNA, Series F, No. 2.

22. The document was titled "Basic Methodological Principles and Indicators of the Statistical Input-Output Table" (Árvay 1994, 230).

23. *Vestnik statistiki* reports differences between the SNA and MPS in a November 1968 article on the fifteenth session of the UN Statistical Commission (VS 1968).

24. For a detailed discussion of the 1969 MPS document, see Árvay 1994, 225–29.

from either system. It was later sent to the UN Statistical Commission, which published it in 1971 (UN Statistical Office 1971). With this publication the MPS became officially recognized as "one of the available international recommendations" (Árvay 1994, 224).[25] The 1971 UN document resulted from a combined effort by the CMEA countries, which in turn had been instigated or inspired by the earlier work of the UN.

Despite the publications in 1969 and 1971, statistical practices continued to vary in the CMEA countries. Some countries experimented with limited market-oriented reforms, changes that, according to Árvay, "required more and different statistical indicators from those offered in the CMEA accounting system" (1994, 224). Árvay stated that Hungary and Poland were the most dissatisfied with the MPS, but "after many compromises, a rather restricted and simplified description of the MPS was adopted and published" (1994, 224).

Through the 1970s and 1980s the CMEA countries further revised the MPS. Since the mid-1970s it had sought a method to account for services, and in 1978 the Statistical Division of the CMEA Secretariat published "The System of the Statistical Indicators of Non-Material Services and the Method for Their Calculation" (Árvay 1994, 230). In 1979 the Statistical Standing Commission of the CMEA agreed to a new, more comprehensive set of indicators for income. Some were income related to material production only, called "final income of the population" and defined as the "total value of material goods consumed by the population." Others, called "personal and total income of the population," were closer to the ones used in the SNA. This set of indicators was formally approved by the CMEA in 1979, but Hungary had already been publishing the second set since 1964 (Árvay 1994, 231).

In 1981 the UN revised its comparison of the SNA and the MPS (UN Statistical Office 1981). This time the project involved ten countries: eight SNA countries (the United States, the United Kingdom, Japan, Austria, Finland, Peru, the Philippines, and Zambia) and two MPS countries, Hungary and Yugoslavia.

By 1986, the CMEA Statistical Commission decided to update the MPS. The goal was to produce one document to reflect all the agreed upon changes over the previous twenty years, which would clarify and harmonize the MPS (Árvay 1994, 233). The group working to revise the 1968 SNA had similar goals. In 1987 the CMEA sent its revised document on the MPS to the UN Statistical Commission, which published it in 1989 in two volumes (UN Statistical Office 1989). That was the last major document on the MPS published by the UN.

---

25. The Soviet view of this process is described in a *Vestnik statistiki* article (VS 1971).

Mutual Constitution and Contestation in the Development of the MPS

The MPS developed on three levels: at the UN, within the CMEA, and in individual communist states. Developments at one level directly affected others: a clear case of mutual constitution between rules and actors' practices. It is hard to imagine the development of the MPS in the absence of comparisons between it and the SNA. In discussing the achievements of the UNSO and its goals of "co-ordination, comparability, and consistency of statistical methods," Michael Ward listed the SNA as the most significant achievement, followed by the MPS (2004, 50). That is, the core organization behind the SNA, the UNSO, was also partly responsible for the formal development of the MPS.

In addition, the USSR did not simply formulate the MPS and impose it on other CMEA states. Despite the obvious power differential between the USSR and other CMEA states, those other states made critical contributions to the development of the MPS. The CMEA as a whole and its individual states also interacted with the UN, in some cases bypassing, if not opposing, the CMEA (and USSR) to some degree.

A prominent Hungarian statistician, László Drechsler, said that "the difference between the SNA and MPS is analogous to the difference between the smallest common denominator and the lowest common multiple in mathematics" (Árvay 1994, 224).[26] He meant that the CMEA countries collected and analyzed much more data than the MPS officially requested but submitted only the required information. In contrast, the 1968 SNA was so extensive that almost no state implemented it fully, but whatever they did do corresponded to the document.

In this way contestation within the CMEA was managed by permitting flexibility beyond the formal requirements of the MPS. Such divergent national practices affected institutions at the international level. Hungary provides one case of pragmatic innovation in this regard. János Árvay explains:

> Hungary has always played an active role in broadening the scope and deepening the observation of economic activity, standard of living, external relations within the CMEA Statistical Commission. Wherever it was not possible to reach agreement with the other member-countries, the Hungarian Central Statistical Office followed its own way in developing its own statistical system, while also adhering consistently to the standards approved jointly. (1994, 231)

26. Drechsler worked in Hungarian statistics and at the UN. He had been chairman of the IARIW. His 1961 PhD thesis addressed the issue of international comparisons between the MPS and SNA, and he was widely considered an expert in this field.

It is interesting in this passage that Árvay points out that Hungarians followed the rules and helped the CMEA, but when that didn't work out, Hungary "followed its own way."

Indeed, Hungary introduced its own hybrid national accounts system in 1970.[27] This system was consistent with the MPS, allowing Hungary to submit required data to the CMEA, but it also allowed for the compilation of all the macro-statistical aggregates of the SNA (Árvay 1994, 231). Where there were points of conflict in the two systems, Árvay explains that Hungary went with the system recommendations that fit its economic circumstances.

Although Hungary strayed the furthest from the MPS, variation in national accounting practice also occurred elsewhere in the CMEA. In Poland at the beginning of the 1980s the work of the national statistical office was subject to review by an independent government organization. The four CMEA countries that belonged to the World Bank and the IMF (Yugoslavia, Romania, Poland, and Hungary) submitted data based on the SNA. Poland, Romania, and Yugoslavia used only the MPS in their own official statistical publications, however (Árvay 1994, 264).

SNA Revision from 1968 to 1993

The 1968 SNA was initially published in English. By 1970 it had appeared in the other official UN languages. Soon afterward, important economic events led to thoughts of possible changes (Harrison 1994, 169). The 1973 oil crisis and resulting inflation spurred interest in rethinking the way that national accounts handle inflation; the use of input-output tables that were sometimes a couple of years old became problematic. In addition, the rise of monetarism sparked interest in improved financial statistics and cooperation between central banks and NSOs.

In 1975 an "inter-regional seminar" in Caracas focused on implementation of the 1968 SNA. Regional meetings followed in Africa in 1975 and 1979, in western Asia in 1978, and in Europe in 1978 and 1980 (Harrison 1994, 170). For the UN Statistical Commission's twentieth session in 1979, a report on these meetings was prepared. It argued for the formation of an expert group to consider implementation and future work on the SNA. An expert group with representatives from ten countries and some international organizations met in the spring of 1980 in New York. The group decided not to overhaul the SNA but unanimously agreed that some "clarifications" were necessary.

---

27. For a detailed description of the system, see Árvay 1973.

The twenty-first session of the Statistical Commission in 1981 called for a second expert group. Its eleven national and international representatives met in 1982. This group agreed with its predecessor: the SNA needed "clarifications and updating" but not a major revision. However, it took an important step toward further international collaboration in its report:

> It is apparent that those international organizations, regional commissions, and specialized agencies that are directly involved in the development of the systems and standards need to be brought together on a cooperative basis. The burden of work can then be shared and conflicting or duplicative efforts can be avoided. In terms of implementing a common set of standards, furthermore, representation of those directly involved is essential. (UNECE 1982, cited in Harrison 1994, 171)

The 1982 expert group also recommended the formation of a permanent working group, which became the Inter-Secretariat Working Group on National Accounts (ISWGNA or Inter-Secretariat Group). ISWGNA initially included the UNSO, the OECD, and Eurostat; later the IMF and World Bank also joined. Further Statistical Commission meetings in 1983 and 1985 returned to the issue of reviewing the SNA and called for "clarification and simplification and harmonization among different international statistical systems" (Harrison 1994, 172). At this point several systems were in use: NIPA in the United States, the ESA in Europe, and the MPS.

The Inter-Secretariat Group decided to hold eight meetings, with approximately two per year starting in 1986. The first was to review the structure of the 1968 SNA. Six others would address more specialized topics (price and volumes, the external sector, the household sector, the public sector, production accounts and input-output tables, and financial accounts and balance sheets). A final meeting in 1989 would summarize progress in order to prepare a revised SNA for the 1991 Statistical Commission meeting. The expert group comprised six "core experts," three from developed countries and three from developing countries, and six subject specialists from around the world (Harrison 1994, 172).

The first meeting in 1986 was scheduled ahead of an "inter-regional" meeting of developing country representatives. The meeting addressed the applicability of the SNA to developing countries, but those countries did not argue that economic differences necessitated different statistical systems. Anne Harrison, a core member of the expert group, writes:

> There was unanimous agreement that the concerns of developing countries needed to be reflected in the SNA, and there was a very clear message that all developing countries were not alike; there were greater

> differences between developing countries than between some developing countries and some developed countries. With this in mind, therefore, it was felt very strongly that there should not be two versions of the SNA, a "full" version for developed countries and a cut-down version for less developed countries, but that a single version should be expounded, capable of meeting the requirements of the conditions in countries at all stages of development. It would be for individual countries to decide how much of the System they could and would implement, given resource constraints and policy considerations. (Harrison 1994, 173)

The Inter-Secretariat's goals of clarification, simplification, and harmonization led to substantial changes in the SNA, even though that was not its intent (Harrison 1994, 173). The line between "clarification" and "change" turned out to be fuzzy. For example, on the issue of the production boundary, "clarifying" what kind of household or artistic production should be included actually changed the production boundary slightly.

Nor was "simplification" easily defined. Different users and compilers had different ideas of what would be simpler. In addition, simplification of the theoretical structure conflicted with the desire to integrate new and different kinds of data into the system and ultimately proved impossible. In the end, the concept of simplification was applied primarily to publications on the SNA; people agreed that they should be more user-friendly.

The expert group meeting on the external section with the IMF did make significant progress toward the goal of greater harmonization in the SNA (Harrison 1994, 176–78). Both sides agreed to adjust balance of payments statistics. The joint session also approved additional steps toward harmonizing government accounts and financial statistics. ESA and the SNA reached an important agreement where the ESA would be rewritten by 1994 in order to be consistent with the revised SNA (these documents were published as the 1993 SNA and the 1995 ESA).

Some other harmonization efforts, however, did not succeed (Harrison 1994, 177–78). Despite many meetings and a general agreement on substance, the expert group could not come to agreement with the drafters of the UN's International Standard Industrial Classification of All Economic Activities (ISIC) to use the same language as the SNA. Similarly the expert group could not reach a final agreement with the ILO or COFOG (Classification of Functions of Government).

By the sixth expert group meeting in March 1988, it became obvious that the group was in the midst of a major revision to the 1968 SNA. Harrison describes the intentions and efforts of the participants:

> Here was a group of people determined to achieve an overhaul of a major statistical system with the intention that this system should serve the statistical community well for the next twenty years. Indeed it was at this meeting that the need to be forward-looking and to think about likely innovations in accounting practice and policy concerns was first articulated. (Harrison 1994, 179–80)

The final meeting to summarize the expert group's progress was supposed to take place in late 1988. Peter Hill of the OECD was tasked with writing up the final report, but there were still many unresolved issues. To settle these questions, three meetings were scheduled for 1989. As it turned out, the group actually met six times from January 1989 to October 1992. For these later meetings, the group structure changed to include the core members plus one specialist from each specific area. The group assigned André Vanoli[28] to work with Peter Hill in drafting the final report (the so-called "Blue Book").[29] By September 1989 it was acknowledged that the need to circulate documents at regional meetings would prevent any new SNA from being ready by the Statistical Commission's 1991 meeting, as originally planned; the target date was postponed until 1993. Altogether, from 1986 to 1992 the expert group met fourteen times, with five sessions in Europe, six in the United States, one in Moscow, one in Zimbabwe, and one in Mexico.[30]

The expert group meeting December 3–7, 1989, in Moscow, had particular relevance for the future of the SNA as a single system, although the results of the meeting reflected the real ambiguity at the time in the relationship between the SNA and MPS. The meeting had been intended to explore further linkages between the SNA and MPS, and at the meeting the group concluded a number of harmonization agreements that entailed changes to both systems. Harrison writes, "The boundary between intermediate consumption and compensation in kind received considerable attention, for example, and it was noted that the MPS had an explicit treatment of losses which was missing in the SNA but should usefully be included" (1994, 182). This work on *both* systems suggests that the idea of integrating the two systems was still in play, despite such major political events as the fall of the Berlin Wall less than a month before meeting.[31]

---

28. André Vanoli, a former director of the French Central Statistical Office and chairman of the Council of the IARIW, has been president of the French National Accounting Association since its founding in 1983.

29. Carol Carson of the US also helped in managing the revision.

30. For a list of all meetings, dates, locations, and participants at each meeting, see Harrison 1994, 191–93, annexes I–II.

31. Some accounts suggested that the wider political events had rendered the idea of integration obsolete, but there was nevertheless debate over of what integration might entail in theory and practice (Árvay 1994, 234–35).

A more radical change in the meeting's agenda, however, was the recognition that the revised 1993 SNA would need to be able to accommodate all types of economies. According to Harrison, "suddenly and unexpectedly there was a requirement that the Blue Book should adequately cover the conditions in centrally planned economies" (1994, 182). Such an expansion of the SNA was a very significant departure from the initial plans for the SNA revision, but it was also compatible with the use of both systems by CMEA countries. So while an important change for the SNA, it was not yet the end of the MPS.

From 1990 to 1992 a great deal of work went into drafting the Blue Book, revising the draft, and getting comments from other ad hoc groups, including a series of regional commission meetings throughout 1990. A complete draft was presented in September 1992 at an interregional meeting in Mexico, where more than sixty countries commented on the draft (Harrison 1994). The Statistical Commission approved the revised draft in February 1993 and it was published in December 1993, first in English, then in other languages.

Mutual Constitution and Contestation in the Development of the 1993 SNA

The 1993 SNA Blue Book reflected the institution's role as a universal system. The 1968 SNA had a separate chapter for developing countries, but the 1993 SNA integrated such concerns into the core document. It also emphasized flexibility: although the framework is supposed to be applicable everywhere, it recognized that the specific conditions of a country might necessitate extensions and the use of so-called satellite accounts (Bos 1994, 202).

In describing the development of the SNA, Michael Ward wrote that the UNSO responded to the economic ideas of the time and "adopted a genuinely international policy perspective" (2004, 43). Unlike the 1953 and the 1968 versions, which were mainly written under the direction of Richard Stone and primarily reflected the experiences of developed countries, the 1993 SNA incorporated the views of experts from all types of economies during the revision process over the course of the fourteen expert-group meetings and regional conferences.[32] Like the MPS, the 1993 SNA resulted from contestation, debate, and mutual learning among those who crafted the revised draft and participated in the process.

---

32. On the bilateral and multilateral cooperation that led to the improvement of national statistics, see Apelt and Kahnert 1992. On the diversity of people who contributed to the 1993 SNA, see Ward 2004, 85.

The revised draft had "approximately 100 significant changes from the 1968 version" (Harrison 1994, 183).[33] When it was presented to the scores of country representatives at the interregional meeting in Mexico it was, by and large, well received. According to Harrison, however, there were eight areas of resistance. In two cases (gold as a financial asset and mineral exploitation) the recommended changes were upheld. In two other cases (imputed rent on government and nonprofit buildings serving households and whether to handle own-account—marketable, but not marketed—consumption as market or nonmarket) the 1968 treatment was retained. In one case (free bank services) a compromise was reached. Finally, representatives objected to the omission of three topics in the revised version—the environment, consumer subsidies, and the formal/informal sector distinction. The only resolution of these issues was a promise to make the topics a priority at future meetings.

The 1993 SNA did not alter the production boundary to include housework or environmental costs. Bos argued that the production boundary had "hardly been changed since the 1947 report" (1994, 198). Changes to the production boundary may be the most controversial but are also potentially the most consequential. Harrison notes that those working on revisions to the SNA have spent a lot of time debating things that are unlikely to affect GDP, public policies, or welfare, such as whether and how to impute rent for government and nonprofit buildings, while the SNA has been criticized by economists for ignoring areas that would have significant effects such as unpaid housework, environmental costs, human capital, and research and development (1994, 189).

Competition among International Organizations on National Accounts

In the course of revisions in the decades leading up to the development of the 1993 SNA, the UNSO lost its role as the leading force in national accounts. This shift had taken place by the 1970s. The complex structure of the SNA took time to implement and update and some other international organizations such as the World Bank were frustrated at how long it took to get current estimates of GNP, especially for developing countries (Ward 2004, 96–98). Because the World Bank wanted information quickly to assess its loans and other development programs,

33. For a complete list of changes from the 1968 to the 1993 SNA, see Harrison 1994, annex III. For further discussion of the content of the 1993 SNA, see Kendrick 1996, an edited volume written by participants in the process of the SNA revision. It contains chapters devoted to various aspects of the 1993 SNA, with separate comments following each chapter by participant authors.

it began doing its own calculations of per capita GNP (annual income) in U.S. dollars (using the Atlas method for dollar conversion, with the goal of improving cross-national comparability owing to exchange rate fluctuations, although comparability was not actually improved). Even UN agencies adopted the World Bank's GNP calculations, despite discrepancies between the UNSO and World Bank figures. As a result, the UNSO lost its leadership role.

The World Bank, however, had a different mission than the UNSO. Michael Ward, who worked in the data development group of the World Bank for fifteen years, was very critical of the World Bank GNP figures. In discussing the Bank's efforts to help countries construct GNP, Ward noted that the "so-called field missions...were far more in the nature of quick fixes to improve GNP and growth-rate numbers that were clearly out of line than substantive exercises in data evaluation" (2004, 98). He made an exception for the World Bank's work on national accounts in Russia and the FSU as well as in China.

Ward explained that the World Bank was not implementing the SNA in various countries; rather it had developed a quicker method of calculating GNP using a "Revised Minimum Standard Model" (RMSM), a set of estimates produced by statistical models. Ward wrote:

> To many statisticians working "at the coal face," this development of data artifacts, which replaced more robust but time-consuming procedures in some countries, seemed dangerous because it rolled assumptions and hypotheses into official numbers. Genuine measurement took a back seat. In reality there were no recent official GNP estimates based on actual detailed source data in many countries, especially the poorest. The Bank's procedures demonstrated that key numbers could be generated by institutional pressures and constraints and equally could be arrived at using models influenced by particular policy objectives, assumptions, and institutional imperatives. (2004, 100)

Ward argued that with a few exceptions, including the World Bank's management of the International Comparison Program, the bank "did little or nothing to provide technical assistance or offer training to developing countries to help improve the quality of their national income statistics or to make them more current" (2004, 101). He continued: "The Bank's overriding operational concern with current GNP rather than with the overall structure of the accounts has had important negative implications. The widespread desire of politicians to have 'a number,' whatever its credentials, has undermined more substantive statistical inquiry in general" (2004, 102).

In contrast to this negative assessment of the World Bank, Ward suggested that the IMF was now at the forefront of improving national accounts statistics through its data dissemination standards (SDDS and GDDS) and other technical assistance programs. He cited several examples of IMF success in improving national accounts data.

This discussion of differences in goals and practices of the UNSO, World Bank, and IMF regarding national accounts highlights the point that contestation over national accounts occurred not just between adherents of the MPS versus the SNA, or between national and international levels, but also among organizations at the international level. It also suggests an important issue in implementation of the SNA, namely that the data demands from international organizations are not homogenous and that international organizations had different, sometimes contradictory, influences on the work of NSOs.

The formation of the Inter-Secretariat Group and the formal collaboration of all the key international organizations in the revision of the SNA has reduced these organizational conflicts. According to Ward, since the mid-1990s there has been more interest in coordination across international organizations on statistics (2004, 47–48).[34] This collaboration continued with the 2008 update.

The End of the MPS

It may seem as though the end of the MPS was a foregone conclusion, the result of the revolutions of 1989 and the collapse of the USSR in 1991. Although those political events did have an enormous influence on a range of CMEA institutions—including the existence of the CMEA itself—the historical record on the MPS is more complicated.

Árvay notes that when he began his paper for an IARIW conference in 1992 on the evolution of national accounts, no one foresaw the end of the CMEA and the USSR or the political, economic, and social transformation of Eastern Europe. He writes, "For the last three decades, up to 1989 the parallel existence and full autonomy of the two systems seemed to be destined to last for ever" (1994, 233). Anne Harrison also notes that although the revision of the 1968 SNA had from the start planned to address needs of developing countries, the integration of the MPS and SNA came "quite late in the process in 1989." Yet even that late plan for "integration" of the two systems would not last. Harrison continues, "By the time the *1993 SNA* went to print, the pace of reform in most previously planned economies was such that it was clear the SNA would supplant the MPS in a very short space of time" (1996, 339). Outside analysts, too,

34. For example, among the IMF, the World Bank, Eurostat, the OECD, the WTO, and within UN agencies ECE and Conference of European Statisticians, ILO, and UNCTAD.

failed to anticipate either the end of the MPS or the quick implementation of the SNA. Writing for a CIA conference on Soviet GNP in May 1989, Kostinsky and Belkindas analyzed events at Goskomstat USSR. Beyond the calculations of GNP based on MPS data, they write, "we know of no plans to release more complete GNP accounts" (1990, 192). They do not mention the possibility of introducing the SNA in the USSR.

The MPS came to an end because of combined action in the CMEA states and also at the international level in the UN and other international organizations such as the OECD. Just as the MPS had not simply been imposed on the states that used it, its end was a result of decisions at both the international and the domestic levels. A confluence of actions by CMEA NSOs, interactions between state and international representatives, and steps taken by international organizations led to the end of the MPS. It is in this sense that the eventual hegemony of the 1993 SNA was "accidental."

Changes to National Accounts in CMEA States

While the MPS and the SNA were undergoing revision, the USSR was entering a period of institutional changes that would eventually transform the entire political and economic landscape. Mikhail Gorbachev took office in 1985, and his perestroika and glasnost' programs were well underway by 1987. Also in 1987, TsSU USSR was renamed Goskomstat USSR, and a revolution in statistics would soon begin.

After decades of opposition, the USSR published GNP figures for the first time in its main statistical yearbook for 1987 (Goskomstat SSSR 1987, 15, as cited in Kostinsky and Belkindas 1990, 183). However, GNP was not reported in terms of any recognized method with the standard components but as three figures: 825 billion rubles total, which was then separated into material production of 668 billion rubles and 157 billion rubles for nonmaterial production.

In mid-1988, Goskomstat put out its first official publication on the concept of GNP. The brief document included definitions and put forward five methods for compiling GNP. It was published as a booklet (Goskomstat SSSR 1988, cited in Kostinsky and Belkindas 1990); then in June 1988 it appeared in *Vestnik statistiki* (VS 1988), Goskomstat's own journal, which was widely distributed domestically and abroad. The five methods included three based on compilation of primary statistics: the production method (*proizvodstvennyi metod*), the distribution method (*raspredelitel'nyi metod*), and the end-use method (*metod konechnogo ispol'zovaniia*). These bear some resemblance to the three Western GDP methods (production, income, and expenditure) for calculating GDP. More important, however, Goskomstat also specified two "conversion" methods (which they called "keys," *kliuchi*). In these two methods GNP is calculated as an aggregate, but its components are not calculated independently, so these keys are essentially methods for adding services to the existing MPS-based "national income" figures (Kostinsky and Belkindas 1990, 184).[35] In a July *Vestnik statistiki* article, senior Goskomstat officials wrote that the last two conversion methods were the way that GNP was going to be calculated at Goskomstat for the next few years; hence as of mid-1988, it seemed that the SNA was not actually going to be implemented, at least according to Goskomstat USSR (Ivanov et al. 1988).[36]

The effects of Goskomstat's actions were not confined to the USSR. Once Goskomstat began publishing GNP figures, the other countries of the CMEA followed suit, and some went further. Hungary stopped submitting MPS data internationally and instead submitted only SNA-based data (Blades and Harrison 1992, 101).

Another important factor was what was happening within the Soviet republics. Perestroika and glasnost' had opened the door to officially sanctioned experimentation and discussion of alternatives in a range of institutional areas. There was an explosion of nationalist mobilization in some Soviet republics in the late 1980s. These republics challenged central authority in many areas, including statistics. Some republics, such as the Baltics (Estonia, Latvia and Lithuania) published their own statistics, including alternative economic data, sometimes in local languages (Heleniak and Motivans 1991, 479–80).[37] These new publications included estimates of national wealth at the republican level for 1987 and 1988 (Nesterov 1997, 1472–75). This decision exposed the huge economic differences among the republics of the USSR.

More important for the present discussion is that these republican-level national wealth estimates were not based on a standard Soviet methodology. Nesterov has argued, "as a result, the TsSU was forced to elaborate specific detailed methodological guidelines for the Union Republics for their experimental calculations of national wealth for 1987 and 1988" (1997, 1472). Those guidelines were published in 1989.[38] It is clear that the alternative republican statistics and implied criticisms of the central statistical authorities compelled, or at a minimum

35. See the appendix in Kostinsky and Belkindas 1990 for details on all five methods.

36. One of the authors of this article, Youri Ivanov, was also one of the participants in the expert group meetings in 1990 and 1991.

37. See Heleniak and Motivans 1991, 480–88, for an extensive discussion of the content of new publications and changes to existing ones up to 1991. On the availability of various statistics for the pre-1991, 1991, and 1992 periods in the CIS see Noren 1994. On availability of GNP data, see Kostinsky and Belkindas 1990, 190.

38. National wealth figures for all union republics appeared in the 1989 yearbook (Goskomstat SSSR 1989) and in the union-level yearbooks for 1989 (Nesterov 1997, 1475).

helped motivate, Goskomstat to reconsider its own practices and methodology for both the MPS and estimates of GNP.[39]

The mixed recommendations and practices among CMEA states continued through 1989. In July 1989 in an interview with *Izvestiia* (a major national newspaper), the newly appointed head of Goskomstat USSR Vadim Kirichenko openly called for a move to international standards (Berger 1989). As of 1989 Gosplan started to use GNP growth rates, instead of the MPS-based NMP, in its plan targets: for 1989 the target growth rate was 6.6 percent (Goskomstat SSSR 1987, 184).

The introduction of GNP in the USSR, while an important shift from past practice, should not be confused with the introduction of the SNA, nor did that introduction mark the end of the MPS or of many other Soviet-era practices in statistics. Kostinsky and Belkindas write, "Although Goskomstat's new interest in GNP accounts might be a sign of reform, evidence suggests otherwise. As indicated above, Goskomstat's first efforts at estimating GNP are simply values derived by adjusting the existing national-income-produced [MPS-based] accounts" (1990, 191).[40] Despite Goskomstat's plans to improve the compilation of price indices, that had not happened by 1989. Kostinsky and Belkindas write, "the GNP instructions on converting to constant prices show no recognition of the criticism of Goskomstat's measures of growth. All the flaws of the official economic growth statistics carry over to GNP. Furthermore, they may be exacerbated by inflated measures of growth in the service sphere" (1990, 185). To illustrate this point, Kostinsky and Belkindas did some simple calculations with the GNP figures published by Goskomstat in 1987–89 and demonstrated obvious discrepancies in current and constant prices (1990, 186).

The use of the MPS in CMEA states ended, for the most part, in 1990. East European NSOs significantly changed their statistical systems in 1990–91, making the transition from the MPS to the SNA (Blades and Harrison 1992, 102). Hungary went through a different process because of its hybrid system. While implementing the SNA came a bit later in the USSR/Russia, as of 1990 most MPS-based publications, including the flagship periodical, the statistical yearbook *Narodnoe khoziaistvo SSSR*, came to a halt. The yearbook did not resume wide external distribution again until 1994, under a different name. By then, it had vastly different content, by and large in line with the categories of international statistics and the 1993 SNA.

---

39. For further discussion of this point, see Heleniak and Motivans 1991, 479–80.

40. Criticism of the quality of Goskomstat USSR's early GNP estimates was extensive, within and outside the USSR. For example, the CIA analyst James Noren called these perestroika-era attempts at GDP "half-hearted" and "feeble at best" (1994, 14); see also Pitzer 1990; Tabata 1996. From within the USSR, see Kudrov 1993; Nesterov 1997.

The End of the MPS as an Internationally Recognized System

The actions of the USSR, the republics within the USSR, and other CMEA states were critical to the end of the MPS in practice, but international organizations also played a key role. The UN and the OECD in 1989–90 both reacted to events and influenced the course of action taken by countries.

The issue of integration of the SNA and MPS or further linkages between the two systems came up at the February 1989 yearly meeting of the UN Statistical Commission (its twenty-fifth session). According to Árvay,

> during the discussion of these items unexpectedly a sensitive question was raised which had been politely and carefully avoided for thirty years. The representative of Hungary proposed that instead of explaining the differences and creating shorter or longer bridges between the two systems the Statistical Commission should take definite measures for the *integration* of the two systems. This idea received general appreciation from all participants of the Commission. (1994, 234, emphasis in original).[41]

The UN report from the meeting states, "The work on SNA/MPS links... had entered a new phase. The main objective was now the achievement of substantial progress in convergence of the SNA and MPS, with the ultimate goal of integrating the two systems" (UN Statistical Commission 1989, 25, par. 61). Also in 1989 there was a UN Economic Commission for Europe meeting in Geneva in which some CMEA participants suggested an integrated system, rather than two separate systems. The move toward the integration of the two systems was a significant departure from the recognition of two distinct systems, which had been in place since 1971.

As discussed above, the December 1989 expert group meeting in Moscow followed up on these plans for integration but did not resolve the question of integration versus replacement of the MPS with the SNA, because participants agreed on both measures for harmonization of the two systems and the expansion of the SNA to be able to accommodate all types of economies. In the ensuing weeks and months, however, historic changes in political and economic regimes across Eastern Europe overtook the plans for integration.

By 1990 most of the CMEA countries were in negotiations regarding transition to the SNA, not integration of the MPS and SNA. To assist in this transition, the Conference of European Statisticians met in the summer of 1990 in Geneva. In September 1990, the OECD's Centre for Co-operation with the European

41. Other accounts also point to Hungarians as being a driving force behind the move to integrate rather than to compare or link the two systems (Vanoli 2005).

Economies in Transition (created that March)[42] and the UN Economic Commission for Europe sponsored a meeting in Paris on "Statistics for a Market Economy" (Blades and Harrison 1992). All Central and East European NSO directors attended both meetings, and at the Paris meeting the directors unanimously pledged to implement the SNA or the European Community version (the 1993 SNA was still being drafted) within two to three years (Árvay 1994, 235). This Paris meeting seems to mark the end of the MPS as an internationally recommended system. The steps toward "integration" taken during the meetings of 1989 were important, but after September 1990 there was no further discussion of integration of the two systems. Now the discussion involved the timetable for implementation of the soon-to-be-completed 1993 SNA.

SNA 2008

In early 2009 the UN Statistical Commission formally approved an official update to the 1993 SNA: the "2008 SNA."[43] This revision is not a conceptual departure from the 1993 version: it was meant to strengthen the 1993 SNA rather than displace it. Moreover, the changes are primarily clarifications and additions that do not conflict with the ongoing implementation of the 1993 SNA.[44] The preface to the 2008 SNA states that it builds on the "solid existing framework" of the 1993 SNA, and that implementation of the 2008 version is "consistent with continuing efforts to implement the 1993 SNA in all countries" (ISWGNA 2009, xlv).

In brief, five areas of change differentiate the 2008 SNA from the 1993 SNA:[45] methods of accounting for certain assets;[46] recommendations for accounting for financial services;[47] the treatment of globalized production;[48] accounting for government and public sector activity;[49] and a new chapter on the informal

---

42. This is now the Centre for Co-operation with Non-Members.

43. The 2008 SNA, like the 1993 SNA, is formally a product of ISWGNA.

44. Reflecting its relationship to the 1993 version, it was initially called "1993 SNA Revision 1," but the name was later simplified to "2008 SNA" to reflect the year it was completed.

45. For a discussion of changes, see ISWGNA 2009, xliii–xlv.

46. Intellectual property products and "nonproduced nonfinancial assets" such as natural resources, weapons systems, and capital services.

47. Financial derivatives, measurement of nonlife insurance services, nonperforming loans, "financial intermediation services indirectly measured, known as FISIM," and pension entitlements.

48. Remittances, "merchanting" of goods and services that move between countries, and "shell companies."

49. Means of delineating government and the public sector from other parts of the economy, including the treatment of "super dividends," public-private partnerships, restructuring agencies, securitization vehicles, loan guarantees, holding companies, and employee stock options.

economy, including both household activity and the "non-observed" sector. Although extensive, these changes complement and reinforce the 1993 SNA.

The SNA required adjustment for two reasons. First, changes in global and national economies since 1993 necessitated consideration of new types of economic activity, primarily related to the globalization of production and the proliferation of new financial services and products. Second, since its inception the SNA, like all national accounting systems, has continually grappled with how best to account for existing economic activity; as this shared understanding shifts, so too does the SNA. Different national statistical offices and organizations are constantly working on new measurement techniques and accounting rules aimed at removing inconsistencies in the SNA or harmonizing the SNA with other macroeconomic statistics and international standards. When these efforts lead to new collective approaches to economic activity, they necessitate updates to SNA methodology. Thus the 2008 SNA revision indicates new collective decisions about how to account for economic activity, not merely changes in economic structure.

This collective, problem-solving approach to updating the System of National Accounts was reflected in the process, which formally began in 2003 when the UN Statistical Commission asked the ISWGNA to form an Advisory Expert Group (AEG) of twenty country experts to begin work on a revision.[50] After gathering input from a variety of sources, the group agreed on a consolidated list of forty-four changes and thirty-nine clarifications by 2007 (ISWGNA 2007). It then held a series of meetings to discuss and debate the details. Flexibility remains an integral part of the 2008 SNA and is reinforced by the use by individual countries of "satellite" accounts—experimental accounts for new areas such as environmental activity. There are also "supplementary" tables and items for use by certain countries. These satellite and supplementary tables are ways for countries to work through specific issues while maintaining collective dialogue and commensurability of the primary accounts.

The revision process that resulted in the 2008 SNA was the most transparent in its history. The UN has posted a full record of the Advisory Expert Group's meetings—including agendas, minutes, reports, and PowerPoint presentations—on its website.[51] This revision process reveals that mutual constitution between national statistical offices and international rules remains firmly established.

---

50. Three of the twenty country representatives were from the postcommunist region: the Czech Republic, Lithuania, and Russia. The Russian representative was Andrei Kosarev, who, as head of national accounts at Goskomstat from 1995 to 1997, was charged with implementing the 1993 SNA. For the full list of AEG members, see ISWGNA 2009, xlvi–xlvii.

51. See http://unstats.un.org/unsd/sna1993/snarev1.asp, accessed 22 October 2009.

In this round of revisions there was no discussion of alternative systems. The debate over the 2008 SNA occurred in a context in which it was not only the single international standard for national accounts but an increasingly all-encompassing system of economic statistics harmonized with ever more international standards, including those related to balance of payments, environmental accounting, and industrial classification.[52] The hegemony of the SNA, established in the 1990s after its adoption by the postcommunist states, seems not only secure but likely to expand its reach in coming years.

The SNA's hegemony is also indicated by a recent and prominent critique of GDP. French President Nicolas Sarkozy set up a commission of renowned economists and social scientists, headed by Joseph Stiglitz and Amartya Sen, two outspoken Nobel laureates in economics, to reconsider measurement of "economic performance and social progress." In the fall of 2009 they produced a 292-page report strongly critical of GDP and advocating alternative measures (Stiglitz et al. 2009). Yet the commission did not directly criticize the SNA, which seemed surprising given the close timing of the report and the release of the 2008 SNA. The commission seemed to take the SNA for granted and advocated using it to produce different aggregates beyond GDP which would move toward broader understandings of well-being by focusing on the relationships among income, consumption, and wealth, including distributive issues and expanded treatment of household and nonmarket activity. This critique and set of suggestions for future statistical work shares the fundamental assumption of the SNA, that strengthening the work of NSOs in basic data collection and processing according to SNA principles is the basis for any future improvements in the quality of economic statistics across the board. Implementation of the 1993 and 2008 SNA remains as critical as ever, regardless of conflicting perspectives on the value of GDP versus other macro-aggregates.

Looking back at the development of the SNA through various iterations and the rise and fall of the MPS, one sees that at each point there were multiple actors on different levels (international, national, and sometimes subnational) and that the institutionalized systems influenced actions even as they were affected by various actors. There were not only competing ideas and interests but a diversity of practices in national accounts. The development of the SNA as a norm is therefore a good example of mutual constitution and contestation in institutional development.

---

52. These are *The Balance of Payments Manual, The Handbook of National Accounting: Integrated Environmental-Economic Accounting, The International Standard Industrial Classification of All Economic Activities, Rev. 4,* and *The Central Product Classification, Version 2.* See also ISWGNA 2009, xlv, for further discussion of these international standards.

This story exemplifies what a constructivist approach to norms, institutions, and institutional change can contribute. Through process tracing we see that it was not simply efficiency or material interests that drove the development and increasing dominance of the SNA—even though efficiency and material interests are undoubtedly enhanced by its development. This narrative also shows that although power differences and larger geopolitical conflicts such as the Cold War permeated the institutional environment of the time, the SNA's development was by no means simply a reflection of the interests of the most powerful states. Some of the leading postwar powers only belatedly joined the emerging international consensus on the SNA.

Another contribution of this chapter is to illustrate the real possibilities for variance in participation or implementation of the SNA and the context for the choices that were made. What might we have expected after 1990? Was the only choice for postcommunist countries, and Russia in particular, to move full steam ahead with the SNA? The history of the development of the 1993 SNA suggests not. Several alternatives to implementing the SNA existed: the Hungarian model (a hybrid system), the Polish model (submission of certain SNA data to international organizations like the IMF and World Bank combined with use of the MPS at home), and the U.S. model (a national accounting system that is fully compatible with the SNA but responsive to domestic political interests). The MPS could have been revised to be more compatible with the SNA while retaining its name and features specific to the postcommunist context. Indeed, it is remarkable that such a face-saving maneuver was not chosen.

Even if we ignore the variation in Eastern Europe's experience with the MPS and the participation of East European NSOs in the emergence of the MPS as an international system, and argue that the move to the SNA needs no further explanation after 1989 because the CMEA states had accepted the MPS only because of Soviet domination, we would still have to explain why the USSR/ Russia also abandoned the MPS.

Although this chapter outlines the rise and fall of the MPS, the end of the MPS does not in itself explain the vigorous move to implement the SNA by postcommunist states. By understanding the debates and ways in which agreement over the principles of the SNA was reached, however, we gain a better grasp of how NSOs and governments in postcommunist states understood their options regarding national accounts in the early 1990s. From this standpoint we can move to a more thorough examination of the explanations for Russia's decision to implement the 1993 SNA.

4

EFFICIENCY, RESOURCES, AND CAPACITY IN THE IMPLEMENTATION OF THE SNA

Structural explanations suggest ways in which macro-level variables influence institutional change. In these theories, individual choice is constrained by factors that affect the larger entity in which the individual is situated, such as a bureaucratic organization, the state, or the international system—so much so that in explaining outcomes we need not focus on individual choices but on those larger structural entities.

In this chapter, I discuss how theories of efficiency and structural changes in the economy may have influenced the move to the SNA and how they played out in Russia and at Goskomstat. Next I examine state-level variables including per capita GDP, state capacity, and human capital cross-nationally to explain how these factors relate to postcommunist countries' level of implementation. Finally I consider resources, including human capital, at the organization level, within Goskomstat. All these factors suggest constraints or enabling conditions that may have influenced postcommunist countries' implementation of the SNA.

Efficiency

Because some institutions have efficiency advantages, some scholars argue that those institutions will win out over less efficient alternatives (Ouchi 1980; Williamson 1981). Efficiency-based theories suggest convergence across states based on efficient outcomes and explain institutional change by considering the efficiency gained from a particular institution. An efficiency argument would predict that if the SNA was more efficient than the MPS or other systems, then the SNA would (eventually) win out over all alternatives. Such an argument would also account for the development of the SNA itself as a process in which decisions on what to include or exclude and how to process data were based on increasing efficiency.

There are several problems with this argument as applied to the SNA. To begin with, efficiency gains do not explain the timing of the development or implementation of the 1993 SNA. The need for comparable national accounts data had existed since the development of the modern state, but the first SNA was formalized only in 1953. From the late 1960s until the early 1990s, when the MPS rapidly disappeared, the world had a rather stable system of two national accounts systems. Thus efficiency gains alone cannot explain either the initial appearance of the SNA or the persistence of an alternative system. They also do not do a good job of explaining the timing of the MPS's demise.

The historical record on the SNA's development also does not support the idea that efficiency was its driving force (or that of the MPS). Many unresolved competing interests survived the formalization of the SNA in 1953, 1968, and 1993. The debates included myriad conceptual issues which cannot be characterized as concerns over "increasing efficiency."

An efficiency argument also cannot account for the enduring cross-national variation in the implementation of the 1993 SNA. If the SNA beat out all competitors because of its demonstrably greater efficiency, why do all countries not adopt it fully and with haste?

Moreover, national accounts reside side-by-side in many national statistical agencies around the world with census data and population statistics. Despite the view of politicians and the general public, there is scientific consensus that sample surveys produce population estimates that are more accurate and less costly than full enumerations of the population. Indeed, censuses may be among the most inefficient practices of national statistical agencies. But there is also consensus that censuses are politically important events and may have political or social benefits despite their economic inefficiencies. Thus, if efficiency gains explain the victory of the SNA, it remains puzzling why efficiency does not determine outcomes in other areas of national statistics.

Another problem with an efficiency argument is that postcommunist countries chose not to implement many types of institutional reforms, including those related to the rule of law or the eradication of corruption, which would have enhanced efficiency. It is not clear why the efficiency argument would apply only to reform of national accounts.

Finally, efficient outcomes can be misleading in that the outcome does not in itself explain the sources of change. Even if we agree that the SNA is more efficient than other alternative statistical systems, it was not necessarily chosen solely on efficiency grounds. As critics of functionalism have long argued, efficient outcomes do not happen by themselves. If we consider areas such as trade liberalization, we see that although free trade might be more efficient, few would reduce the process by which trade regimes emerge to efficiency gains alone.

Market Transition: Structural Changes in the Economy

Another macro approach to institutional change highlights structural changes in the global or domestic economy. At its core this is a Marxist argument in that the underlying structure of the economy determines the shape and content of political and economic institutions. An example is a market-transition theory in which structural shifts in the economy from a centrally planned economy to capitalism should result in institutional changes when the new institutions meet the demands of the new market structure. With regard to national accounts, there is a key assumption here: that the system of national accounts as an institution reflects or is closely tied to a particular type of economic structure. This theory would not predict variation in national accounting systems among similar types of economies.

If we assume that the SNA is compatible with capitalist economic structures, then all market economies should have the same system of national accounts, and any changes in economic structure toward a market economy should result in a move to the SNA. In this case, efficiency is not the driving factor behind convergence of national accounting systems within types of economies; instead the structural demands of capitalism (or another economic system) determine the system of national accounts. Interests are assumed to be congruent with the economic system.

As perestroika and glasnost' progressed in the late 1980s and economies in Eastern Europe and the USSR moved from central planning to market-based systems, the changing structure of the economies did necessitate some kind of change in statistics. The emergence of private enterprises and market prices for most goods and services, the explosive growth of the shadow economy, and the new demands for banking and financial statistics emphasized the need for national statistical offices (NSOs) in these states to adapt to new economic conditions. In addition, certain functions such as monitoring plan fulfillment, which had been a core activity of Goskomstat, were no longer needed given the demise of central plans. Thus it would seem that the transition to market economies is very relevant in explaining the shift to the 1993 SNA by postcommunist states, and that this explanation should speak to the timing and direction of the institutional change.

The transition to market-based structures, however, is an incomplete explanation because in practice economic structure has not determined national accounting systems, either in the West or in the East. And if we look at the real choices facing Eastern Europe and the Soviet Union in the early 1990s, we see that rapid and comprehensive implementation of the 1993 SNA was by no means the only choice for postcommunist countries in the face of structural economic change.

Economic Structure and Statistical Practices

What is the relationship between economic structure and national accounts? If we go back to the fundamental question of any national accounting system, the production boundary, or what kind of economic activity should be counted in a system of national accounts, we see that this is not merely a function of economic structure. Although the goal may be to mirror the economy, in fact the determination of the production boundary is a theoretical, ideological, and political decision, and one that generates contentious debate among structurally similar countries.

Moreover, the 1993 SNA was specifically revised to be more inclusive of different economic conditions across countries, and it does do a better job than its predecessors of handling the specific needs of developing countries. More countries have signed onto it; hence we might conclude that the fit between the SNA and a country's economy is the key to its implementation. However, the variation among capitalist countries reveals that a market economy is not sufficient for implementation of the SNA. Hence even for the most inclusive SNA to date, the theoretical fit between a national accounting system and a country's economic structure does not explain patterns of implementation.

In planned economies, too, the national accounting system did not always fit the economy. The MPS focused only on material production in its production boundary—but socialist economies nonetheless had services and other economic activity excluded from the MPS. That production boundary—which was a critical distinction between the MPS and SNA—was a theoretical construct informed by ideology and politics, especially Marxism, not a reflection of the real economic structure. If structural economic conditions are determinative, it is hard to explain why the MPS ever had such a limited production boundary.

Goskomstat, moreover, did not respond to market conditions by blindly allowing structural conditions to determine organizational practices. Goskomstat largely ignored certain areas of new economic activity—for example, the black market. Hence structural changes did not result in identical changes in data collection. Some new data series were added to correspond to new economic activity, but other areas continued to be ignored.

If we examine practices within the organization, we see that Goskomstat looked for ways to get around market mechanisms when those market constraints stood in the way of other goals. A vivid example of this concerns the "hiring" of enumerators to work on the 2002 census, for which Goskomstat was responsible. Enumerators were paid, on average, $35–$50 for nineteen full days of work.[1] In the past, the rate of pay had not been an issue because enterprises were required by the central government to supply a certain number of enumerators. In some places, such as Moscow and St. Petersburg, Goskomstat was forced to hire whomever would agree to work for the low wages it offered and even had to rely on universities and institutes to pressure students into working on the census. In many cases, students were forced to work or face expulsion; this type of corvée labor is similar to the practice of students being forced to participate in potato harvests in the old Soviet days. In hiring workers, one official noted that they were helped by the legacy of "executive discipline" in some small towns and villages, in that the administrations in those areas simply did what Goskomstat asked them to do. This example suggests that the emergence of markets alone is not enough to explain the decision to comprehensively move to the 1993 SNA; instead, structural changes in the economy led to a mix of market problems and Soviet-type solutions.

Alternatives to the 1993 SNA

The preceding discussion raised doubts about the relationship between economic structure and particular national accounting systems. Given that, what were the institutional possibilities for NSOs in postcommunist countries at the time of the market transition? To evaluate the role of structural change on the implementation of the 1993 SNA, we have to consider how those alternatives might have dealt with new market-based conditions. In the late 1980s, postcommunist

1. A description of the enumerator's job puts the wage problem in perspective. The census was conducted in October, when even in relatively temperate Moscow the temperature was in the low thirties, with freezing rain on most days. Enumerators went door-to-door to register the population from approximately 10 am to 10 pm, spending most of that time standing in unheated concrete corridors or walking from building to building. Occasionally, friendly citizens invited enumerators inside their apartments or offered them tea, but for the most part enumerators spent their time standing in the cold. It is little wonder, then, that Goskomstat had great difficulty hiring enumerators, especially in the larger cities where both the cost of living and average wages made the census wages unattractive; moreover, the work was temporary.

countries had several realistic possibilities besides moving full steam ahead with implementation of the 1993 SNA.

First, they might have calculated macroeconomic aggregates such as GNP without implementing the SNA. Some East European countries submitted certain SNA-type aggregate figures to international organizations in the late 1980s while retaining the MPS for domestic publications of national accounts.[2] The USSR began calculating GNP in 1988, using a set of conversion "keys" by which MPS data were converted to reach a GNP figure (VS 1988; Kostinsky and Belkindas 1990). The postcommunist states might also have used the World Bank's methodology for estimating GDP in the absence of underlying SNA-type data, as was done in many other countries. All these methods would have given Russia a GNP/GDP figure and other macro-aggregates required by international organizations and would not have entailed a full shift to the 1993 SNA or abandonment of the MPS.

A second possibility for postcommunist states would have been to adopt the Hungarian hybrid system of national accounts, pioneered in 1970. In this case data were collected and processed according to both the MPS and the SNA. Because Hungary had paved the way, many of the issues of compatibility between the systems had been resolved. Hence this option would not have been uncharted territory and could have provided a compromise for those still committed to the MPS and those in favor of the SNA. The use of two systems simultaneously, although not specifically modeled on the Hungarian experience, was discussed and advocated in the USSR in 1989–91. The idea was to "integrate" the two systems, while maintaining the use of both. The historical record suggests that as late as mid-1991 in the USSR there was no intention to drop the MPS.

A third and perhaps more conservative approach, fitting the commonly held image of Goskomstat, is that postcommunist countries might have opted to make more gradual, incremental adjustments to their statistical systems. A piecemeal approach to institutional change would have eliminated outdated Soviet practices (like monitoring plan fulfillment) and gradually introduced data previously excluded from Soviet statistics, such as services and the informal economy. Goskomstat could have started by filling in the data gaps in its previous system: for example, Kostinsky and Belkindas reported that new input-output tables were published in 1987 but were still lacking critical data, which Goskomstat promised to provide eventually.[3] Goskomstat might have also slowly introduced sampling

2. Poland, for example, submitted such data to the IMF, which it joined in 1986 (IMF 2009a).

3. In particular, they noted, "the first set of input-output data to appear in over 10 years was a selection of results from the 1987 table recently compiled by Goskomstat. However, even at the six-sector level, only an incomplete table is provided, without even total final-demand and value-added vectors or total outputs" (Kostinsky and Belkindas 1990, 191).

to replace the full enumeration data collection methods of the past. This might have been done in cooperation with international organizations or even with increased coordination and would have been a continuation of some of the experimental approaches begun in the late 1980s. The result would have been steadily increasing compliance with international standards that eventually resulted in something like the U.S. model: a distinctive national accounting system fully compatible with the SNA. In other words, a limited, structure-influenced change in data content and methodology resulting in gradual evolution of the system over time might have been chosen. According to the leadership of Goskomstat, this option of gradual change was discussed but ultimately rejected in favor of full implementation of the 1993 SNA (Sokolin 2004).

Finally, Goskomstat and other NSOs in Eastern Europe and the former Soviet Union might have agreed to the 1993 SNA in the early 1990s but then waited to implement it. A reasonable argument could be made that a period of political and economic turmoil, including extremely high inflation, as was the case in most postcommunist countries in the early years of transition, was not the time to switch to a whole new system of price-based accounting of national economic activity and that reform of the statistical systems should have occurred after stabilization. An alternative as suggested by Noren (1993, 1994) would have been to collect volume rather than price-based data, which would be more reliable given the instability of prices.

Indeed the most likely scenario for Goskomstat, especially given its history and the general experience of Russia's lackluster progress on other institutional reforms, would have been to pursue symbolic acceptance of the SNA and a gradual shift toward its implementation, resulting in limited progress in the first five to ten years. This approach would have been consistent with the experience of most other countries, especially those facing similar economic and political conditions.

In sum, although some type of change to the Soviet statistical system was likely, given the structural changes in the East European and former Soviet economies, the decision to fully implement the SNA was not the only choice, nor was it the most obvious or likely path for postcommunist NSOs based on structural changes alone. That is, structural changes in the economy are an important part of the explanation as a key condition increasing the likelihood of some kind of institutional change, but they are not determinative of the choice for the 1993 SNA in particular or the level of implementation of the SNA. An explanation based on structural economic conditions would predict that countries with similar economic structure should have the same institutional arrangements, an argument not borne out by the path of SNA development and the variation in SNA implementation among capitalist economies. Why postcommunist NSOs decided to stop what they had been doing in the 1980s, reject the MPS or any version of it, and move resolutely toward implementing the 1993 SNA remains a puzzle.

State-Level Variables: Income, State Capacity, and Human Capital

We can also ask whether state-level structural variables—the resources, both material and human capital, available for institutional change—influenced the implementation of the 1993 SNA. Material resources are needed to pay for equipment as well as to hire and retrain staff, while human capital, including skills and experience, is necessary to undertake new or difficult tasks. We can measure this resource availability across countries with variables such as per capita GDP, state capacity,[4] and education, and we would expect a positive relationship with implementation of international institutions. Indeed, a quick glance back at the regional distribution on the first SNA milestone assessment as shown in figure 1.1 suggests that income at least matters. The two regions that do best overall are also the wealthiest regions of the world, and the worst region is the poorest.

However, there is an important exception to this general finding; as a group, aside from North America and Western Europe, postcommunist countries have gone further in implementing the SNA than any other geographic region or group of states, and it is not clear that this is due to greater income or state capacity in the region. In addition, if we look at the CMEA,[5] the average SNA milestone assessment was 2.0, slightly above the FSU/East Europe regional average of 1.89 (the mean score for all countries was 1.60).[6] CMEA is a theoretically interesting regional grouping because it includes those countries most closely allied economically with the USSR, or states that were most under the influence of the Soviet statistical and economic system.[7]

To probe these relationships further, I used ordered logit to examine the relationship among structural factors, postcommunist status, and SNA milestone achievement level (the only quantitative assessment for which systematic country level data was available). Even controlling for income, state capacity, human

4. Income or other measures of economic development are highly correlated with state capacity (Fearon and Laitin 2003, 80).

5. Including the twenty-four that were members as of 1987, excluding East Germany

6. If we exclude Cuba and Vietnam, which are still "communist," the CMEA postcommunist average is 2.09.

7. Other CMEA states also influenced Soviet views on statistics and the development of the MPS.

Table 4.1 The effect of income, state capacity, and human capital on SNA milestone level (ordered logit)

	MODEL 1	MODEL 2	MODEL 3	MODEL 4	MODEL 5	MODEL 6
GDP per capita[a]	.126***	.132***	.090***	.096***	.101***	.106***
	(.025)	(.026)	(.030)	(.030)	(.027)	(.028)
Adult literacy[b]	.016**	.014*	.005	.003	.010	.008
	(.008)	(.008)	(.009)	(.009)	(.009)	(.009)
State capacity[c]			.030***	.030***		
			(.007)	(.007)		
Democracy[d]					.014**	.015***
					(.006)	(.006)
Eastern Europe and FSU states	.687*		.971**		.763*	
	(.416)		(.430)		(.417)	
CMEA states		.937**		1.221***		1.057***
		(.428)		(.441)		(.430)
Log likelihood	−268.08	−267.04	−248.62	−247.32	−265.31	−263.95
Pseudo R2	.09	.09	.14	.15	.10	.10
Observations	185	185	182	182	185	185

Notes: Standard errors are in parentheses; *** significant at the .01 level, ** significant at the .05 level, * significant at the .10 level

[a] GDP at constant 1990 prices in thousands of U.S. Dollars, average 1992–97 (UN Statistical Division 2008).

[b] Adult literacy 2000 (UNESCO 2003). Missing country data have been replaced with regional averages from the same table.

[c] WGI, "Government Effectiveness" (World Bank 2008). I use the data from 1998 because that is the closest to the 1992–97 period for the SNA data, for which there was data for most countries available (182 out of 185).

[d] WGI, "Voice and Accountability" (World Bank 2008). The primary reason that I use the WGI measure for democracy over Polity or ICRG is because WGI had fewer missing countries.

capital (literacy), and democracy, status as a CMEA member (or FSU/East European state) has a positive and significant effect on SNA achievement. Table 4.1 shows the results of six models predicting SNA milestone achievement.

In the table, models 1 and 2 consider the effect on SNA achievement of being in the FSU or Eastern Europe (model 1) or CMEA (model 2), controlling for income and literacy. For income, I included average GDP per capita in thousands of U.S. dollars for the period of the SNA milestone assessment, 1992–97. Literacy should be related to human capital, a necessary resource for the SNA reform. For literacy I used UNESCO's "Adult literacy" indicator.[8] In these two models, income, literacy, and status as a postcommunist or CMEA member are all significant.

8. It measures the percent of people aged fifteen and above who are literate (UNESCO 2003). Many other education measures could not be used because of missing data on countries and regions of interest in this study.

Models 3 and 4 add a control for state capacity. State capacity is difficult to measure, and the measures we have are not without their problems (e.g., many measures lack coverage for all countries, and they tend to be highly correlated with other measures, such as income and democracy). Nevertheless, under the rubric of state capacity, I use the World Bank's Worldwide Governance Indicator (WGI), "Government Effectiveness."[9] When state capacity is included, literacy drops out, but income, state capacity, and status as a postcommunist or CMEA member are all significant.[10]

Models 5 and 6 add a control for democracy.[11] Because the SNA institutionalizes transparency in economic data, it might be more likely to be implemented by democracies that are generally more committed to transparency in governance than dictatorships. For democracy I used the World Bank's WGI, "Voice and Accountability."[12] Because this democracy measure was highly correlated with state capacity (0.81), I treated it separately. Here again, literacy drops out as significant, but income, democracy, and status as a postcommunist or CMEA state are significant.

In all the models, income measured by GDP per capita is significant, as are the other controls, state capacity and democracy. Literacy was not significant when either state capacity or democracy was included in the models. Regional status in East Europe or the FSU or CMEA, however, was also significant in all models, and the effect was slightly stronger and more statistically significant for CMEA states. Taken together, these structural factors do not explain much of the overall level of variance, which suggests that there is more going on in implementation of the SNA than is captured in these variables. Moreover, especially for the measures of democracy and state capacity, there is a great deal of variance among postcommunist countries, which is somewhat at odds with the relatively uniform high level of achievement in implementation of the SNA by these countries.

In sum, these results indicate that state-level structural variables do matter to some degree for implementation of the 1993 SNA. Indeed, they may be necessary

9. It measures "perceptions of the quality of public services, the quality of the civil service and the degree of its independence from political pressures, the quality of policy formulation and implementation, and the credibility of the government's commitment to such policies" (World Bank 2008).

10. Arguably state capacity in postcommunist states was lower in the years immediately following the transition than in the communist era, yet that was when the move to the SNA began. I use the WGI data from 1998, which is the earliest available with coverage of postcommunist states, so in this quantitative analysis the capacity measure for postcommunist states is probably somewhat higher than it would have been during the initial years of SNA implementation.

11. There are a number of democracy measures, but WGI is the most comprehensive for this time period.

12. It measures "perceptions of the extent to which a country's citizens are able to participate in selecting their government, as well as freedom of expression, freedom of association, and a free media" (World Bank 2008).

but not sufficient conditions for SNA success. But rather than explaining away postcommunist success on the SNA, this quantitative analysis only heightens the question of why some states—the newly capitalist and not especially rich or capable postcommunist ones—seem to be so much more able or willing to measure their economies according to capitalist principles.

Organization-Level Resources

Because bureaucratic organizations are the places where many international institutions are implemented, it also makes sense to consider resources at the organizational level. The resources available to an organization charged with implementing an institutional change are likely to be correlated with the wealth or capacity of the state, but there may be variation in resource allocation across bureaucratic organizations. Although resources come mainly from domestic sources, foreign assistance can also play a critical role in funding institutional reform (World Bank 1998; Goldsmith 2001). In this case, organizations with greater levels of material wealth and human capital should be more likely to implement the SNA. Indeed, structural approaches at the state and organization levels were the primary focus of implementation efforts by the Inter-Secretariat Working Group on National Accounts for the 1993 SNA (UN Statistical Commission 2008, 10).

An examination of resources within Goskomstat yields insights that complement quantitative analysis at the state level. For Goskomstat as an organization, the immediate transition period was a time of material poverty not unlike that faced by other postcommunist bureaucratic agencies, societies, and states. In contrast, human capital at Goskomstat was relatively high—a legacy of the communist educational system—as it was at other postcommunist NSOs. This contradictory combination of low material resources and high human capital complicates the role of "resources" in explaining implementation of the SNA.

Material Resources at Goskomstat

As a state organization, Goskomstat depends almost entirely on the Russian state budget for funding. During the most intensive period of statistical reform at Goskomstat, 1992–96, the Russian economy registered substantially negative growth rates. This decline followed several years of negative growth in the late Soviet period, and the situation would not turn around until after 1999. In addition, the government faced record-breaking inflation and its own inability to collect taxes. This severely limited the financial resources available for Goskomstat's move to the SNA in the early 1990s. Meanwhile, the transition to a market economy meant that whereas during the Soviet period resources had been allocated to Goskomstat regardless of overall economic conditions, in the early years of the post-Soviet period the organization lacked even basic supplies (like paper) and computer equipment—despite the pressing need for technological improvements and staff retraining that a move to the SNA required.

In one of the earliest articles discussing Russia's commitment to the SNA, Pavel Guzhvin, the acting head of Goskomstat, noted that that although it was regrettable that Russia found itself in need of foreign assistance, Goskomstat might need foreign aid to implement the SNA (Guzhvin 1992a). Even so, a commitment by Goskomstat to the SNA had been made. Later *Vestnik statistiki* articles noted the lack of financing as a severe constraint on meeting the target dates for implementation (Zharova 1993a, 1993b).

The most significant source of extrabudgetary funds at Goskomstat was a loan from the World Bank for $30 million in 1999 (World Bank 1999).[13] From this loan, $20 million was to be spent on equipment (Belkindas 2001). The Russian government contributed an additional $20 million to the project in 2004. The World Bank loan went along with technical assistance from a host of international organizations, and international expertise did filter through the organization via nationwide conferences dedicated to retraining as well as educational materials that were distributed to regional offices. These resources, broadly understood, no doubt greatly aided implementation of the SNA. In general, postcommunist countries have received a great deal more technical assistance for implementation of the SNA from international organizations than have other middle income or developing countries. However, the infusion of funds and expertise followed Goskomstat's commitment to implement the SNA by several years.

Another, smaller source of extrabudgetary income for Goskomstat that has existed since perestroika is sales from publications. In Moscow purchases are made directly at the Goskomstat store. In the regional offices payments have to be made at state banks (which are not necessarily located nearby), then receipts are presented at the regional offices for the publications. Funds from these sales are supposedly deposited directly into the federal budget, but regional offices report that they are allowed to draw on some percentage of revenue from their local publications for office expenses such as equipment or renovations. There are no reliable quantitative sources available on the size of revenue from publication sales, but in interviews local officials said that these sales did not constitute a significant portion of the organization's budget.

13. There was an additional emergency $1 million loan for updating mainframes for Y2K (Belkindas 2001). This initial $30 million loan was repaid in December 2006, and was followed by another $53.5 million loan in 2007.

In the 1990s Goskomstat employees with academic degrees earned approximately $50 per month. In 2004, after several efforts under President Vladimir Putin to increase the wages of state civil servants, wages at Goskomstat for university graduates rose to around $100 per month for employees in the regions and about $200 per month for those in Moscow. To put this in perspective, at the time workers at McDonald's in Moscow earned about $200 per month. The salaries at Goskomstat were low even by Russian standards. Relative to other state institutions that required technical and statistical skills, such as the Ministry of Finance or the Central Bank, Goskomstat offered much lower prestige as well as pay and therefore had greater difficulty in attracting and keeping skilled workers. The private sector paid several times the salaries of state institutions.

Several indicators point to the limited resources available to Goskomstat. The first post-Soviet Russian census was supposed to have taken place ten years after the last Soviet census of 1989. This critical event for both Goskomstat and the Russian state was delayed twice due to lack of funding and faced severe budget constraints even when it did finally take place in 2002. If we count Goskomstat publications, we find far fewer of them in 1991–93 (both in the number of publications and the size of the print runs). The quality of the paper in those that did appear in print is terrible: the 1992 issues of *Vestnik statistiki,* the organization's flagship journal, are a case in point.

In the late 1990s and the 2000s, Goskomstat was better off, but at the time of the decision to implement the SNA and in the first phase of that implementation, its material resources were very limited.

Human Capital at Goskomstat

Assessment of human capital at Goskomstat is more complex. The communist commitment to education, both ideological and material, left the postcommunist states with highly educated populations and hence a large pool of well-trained potential statisticians (as well as mathematicians and economists). But relative to the private sector and other organizations Goskomstat was poorly situated to attract the most talented employees. It remains to be seen whether the current educational system in the postcommunist countries, hampered by massive resource constraints, will continue to produce high-quality statisticians, especially ones willing to work for the state's low wages.

A challenge for human capital at NSOs concerns organizational prestige. National accounts in Russia, as elsewhere, is a low-status and low-paying job relative to other professions that demand mathematical and statistical skills. One World Bank official said in an interview that national accounts is the "least prestigious profession on earth." In just about every country there is a common hierarchy of state economic and statistical work where the high-prestige organization is the central bank, followed by the ministry of finance, then by the NSO. Outside economists in the private sector and academia also do not necessarily think highly of those who work in NSOs. For developing or transition countries, international institutions that worked with NSOs were another source of the "brain drain" that affected Goskomstat's most talented staff.

The breakup of Goskomstat USSR into independent republican state statistical committees and the formation of Statkom CIS led to several shifts of skilled personnel among these different organizations.[14] Vladimir Treml has observed that during the Soviet period, Goskomstat USSR in Moscow monopolized the supply of statisticians with the best training in methodological and theoretical work. After the USSR collapsed, Goskomstat Russia inherited the most skilled employees of Goskomstat USSR. However, some analysts feared that the breakup of Goskomstat USSR into constituent units and Statkom CIS would drain Goskomstat Russia of skilled workers and resources.[15]

Some of the most qualified Moscow-based statisticians were lured to newly independent republican committees that offered higher salaries and benefits. Statkom CIS initially attracted methodologically sophisticated employees, but over time it became a place for senior officials who retired from Goskomstat Russia, including M. Korolev, Y. Ivanov, N. Belov, and V. Shevchenko (Treml 2004).[16] The most recent chairman, Vladimir Sokolin, also took a post at Statkom CIS after retiring from Goskomstat Russia in 2009.

Another indicator of the level of prestige and employee compensation at Goskomstat is apparent in the gender breakdown: Goskomstat is overwhelmingly—approximately 90 percent—staffed by women. In some regional offices this number approaches 100 percent, as most of the men are located in the Moscow office and in relatively high management positions (the top four positions are held by men). Nevertheless, some important management positions are staffed by women, including the head of the department of National Accounts and the head of the Census. Of the seventeen department heads at the organization, ten are women. If one considers gender biases in the labor market, suggesting that qualified women get lower-paying and lower-status jobs, the rate of female

14. Statkom CIS was set up in 1992 to coordinate the move to the 1993 SNA for the Commonwealth of Independent States (CIS), which is a subset of the former Soviet states.

15. See Demchenko 1992 on fears of resource losses. For counter arguments see Guzhvin 1992a; Noren 1994, 23.

16. During my interviews in 2004, the apparent differences in resources between Statkom CIS and Goskomstat Russia were very stark. Though they share the same building, the offices I saw in Goskomstat Russia were renovated and modern, whereas the Statkom CIS offices seemed to have changed little from the Soviet period—some offices still even had busts of Lenin.

employment at Goskomstat is a striking indication of the status of national statistics.

I asked many Goskomstat officials about this gender distribution. Most of the time, they insisted that the work was very "routinized" and therefore suited to women. For example, one regional official said:

> Women comprise 93% here. Men find this type of work unattractive—it is monotonous and demands perseverance and attention to detail. Those who work here get professionally deformed, so to say—the person gets used to analysis of numbers and stays concentrated on that when it comes to other things, even when watching TV. For example, my brother who is a policeman—he is so used to scanning traffic flows that he immediately sees drunk drivers; similarly, statisticians immediately see if something is wrong with indicators. Statisticians are naïve idealists. They think that the regular patterns that they discover really describe reality and when they are confronted with reality, they do not believe it and eagerly return to their observations. (GKS29 2003)

A second reason cited by officials for the high numbers of women was the pay.

There are at least two ways to understand this issue of organizational prestige and female employment at Goskomstat. One could argue, as some economists in Russia do, that Goskomstat does not employ the "best and the brightest." But one could also argue that Goskomstat benefits from gender biases, getting well-qualified employees at lower cost. In this case, the percentage of women is not a sign of lower human capital but a sign of labor-market biases.

A final point in analyzing human capital in postcommunist NSOs concerns the issue of "familiarity" with national accounts. Long-time employees at postcommunist NSOs had familiarity with the concept of both their own MPS and, to some degree, the SNA (in all its versions). This familiarity gave postcommunist states an additional advantage, not captured by general measures of education, in moving to the SNA. But familiarity can work both ways. Although it might have made it easier to learn and implement the 1993 SNA, it could also have led to stronger opposition to institutional change than in states without any attachment to an alternative system.

The debate over the draft 1993 SNA shows the "familiarity promotes opposition" argument in action. In discussing eight areas of contention in the draft, Anne Harrison noted that OECD members raised most of the objections. She wondered whether those with experience with national accounts had greater foresight in anticipating problems or whether "those who have implemented a system are more reluctant to consider change than those who have yet to extend their accounts in new directions" (1994, 188). It seems likely that familiarity with the 1993 SNA functions in the same way as other structural factors: it is enormously helpful in implementation, provided actors have decided what they want to do. But it does not necessarily explain the decision to move to, or the development of internal interest in, the SNA.

In sum, organizational resources are a mixed bag. Whereas limited material resources in the crucial early phases of transition negatively affected resources available for implementation of the SNA and Goskomstat's ability to attract and retain talented staff, the human capital legacy from the communist period and the infusion of resources in the later 1990s from international organizations gave postcommunist countries an advantage in implementing the SNA, once they had decided to do so.

Analysis of structural explanations for the implementation of the 1993 SNA yields several helpful conclusions. Implementation of the SNA by postcommunist countries did not go against the general direction of structural forces: the SNA is more efficient than the MPS; structural changes in the economy did influence statistical systems; and state and organizational resources are positively correlated with implementation of the SNA. The general support offered by these structural factors, however, fails to explain variation across similar types of countries.

Structural variables are not irrelevant but they do not tell the whole story. Statisticians need not only the skills and resources to carry out institutional change but the motivation to do so. Although structural factors establish necessary conditions, they do not address either motivation or the mechanisms by which structural factors are translated into bureaucratic action.

5

CUI BONO?

Politicians, Statisticians, and International Organizations in Russian Implementation of the SNA

In contrast to structural approaches, rationalist theories that focus on the role of specific actors direct us to consider the material interests of the bureaucrats on the ground, or those charged with implementing international institutions, and their relations with other political actors. In this chapter I consider these actor-centered theories by analyzing Goskomstat in light of the sources of institutional change implied by these theories.

First, we have to consider changes in relations among actors—most notably, a change in the relationship between Goskomstat and politicians, societal actors, or international actors who seek to impose their interests on Goskomstat statisticians. We also have to examine interests within Goskomstat, including those of the leadership and staff, as well as employee turnover, which might entail the arrival of new actors with different institutional interests—that is, the replacement of conservatives with those interested in institutional change. According to these theories, aside from putting in place "reformers," altering the material incentives available to Goskomstat statisticians for institutional change, including the collective threat of job loss, would be the primary means of compelling compliance from bureaucrats.

Goskomstat and Politicians

The relationship between bureaucrats and elected politicians is now recognized as a crucial variable in understanding organizational outcomes, including institutional change. Whether scholars apply formal principal-agent models or approach the problem through qualitative case studies, they agree on the need to understand the effects of politicians and organized interests on bureaucrats' behavior (Aberbach et al. 1981; Moe 1987; Peters and Pierre 2001; Huber and McCarty 2004).

Bureaucrats, however, are not just pawns of politicians. Heclo (1977) showed that bureaucrats can employ "weapons of the weak" and resist organizational imperatives of politically appointed managers through withholding of services rather than outright noncompliance. Moreover, bureaucrats can take the initiative in relations with politicians (Kingdon 1995). These studies speak to the question of conflict and contestation among the interests of bureaucrats and politicians in determining institutional outcomes.

Theories that focus on the relationship between actors and domestic politicians would suggest that politicians pressured NSOs to implement the SNA. The assumption is that the NSOs opposed the move to the SNA but politicians withheld resources or threatened job loss to ensure cooperation. To explain the level of SNA implementation in postcommunist countries, politicians would have needed either considerable power or material resources to compel compliance, or NSOs would have had to have been agreeable in the first place. The second option, however, leaves us wondering why postcommunist NSOs supported the move to the SNA. To investigate this theory, we turn to the relationship between Goskomstat and politicians in the Soviet and post-Soviet eras. Or, as Paul Samuelson's Soviet translator put it:

> The time has come Walras has said
> To speak of many things[1]

Goskomstat and Politicians in the Soviet Period

The Central Statistical Administration of the USSR (TsSU) was initially formed on the basis of a respectable legacy of relatively independent prerevolutionary Russian statistics that dates to the beginning of the nineteenth century (Goskomstat Russia 1996b). TsSU USSR existed from 1918 until 1930, when its personnel

---

1. Samuelson (Soviet edition) 1964, 219, quoted in Gerschenkron 1978, 563. In translating a chapter heading from Paul Samuelson's *Economics: An Introductory Analysis* into Russian in 1964, the Soviet censors mistook Lewis Carroll's "walrus" for the famous economist, Léon Walras. Gerschenkron conjectured that when they came upon "the walrus," Soviet translators were perplexed: "The Walrus! Why Walrus? The translators must have pondered over the strange word for a long time. Finally, a brain wave made them see the light. Why, it must have been a misprint for Walras, another vulgar-bourgeois economist. Of course, Samuelson-Walras, birds of the same feather!"

and work were transferred to the Department of Economic Accounting (*Sektor narodnokhoziaistvennogo ucheta*) under the State Planning Commission (Gosplan). In 1931 this department became the Central Administration of Economic Accounting of the State Planning Commission of the USSR (*Tsentral'noe upravlenie narodnokhoziaistvennogo ucheta, TsUNKhU Gosplana SSSR*). The changes in 1930–31 were very significant because they were the culmination of Lenin and Stalin's attempts to destroy the institutional and methodological independence of the state statistical institutions (Seneta 1985; Kotz and Seneta 1990).

By renaming TsSU and subordinating it to Gosplan, Stalin made it clear that statistics would work for socialism and the state, in particular plan fulfillment and monitoring, rather than serve abstract scientific or objective goals (Guzhvin 1992a). Moreover, being under Gosplan entailed certain methodological choices for the organization. Noren writes, "the direction and methodology of statistical reporting were established in Gosplan.... To a large extent, the emphasis on gross rather than net output indicators and the reliance on complete enumeration rather than sampling reflected the requirements for monitoring plan fulfillment" (1994, 14).

There are many anecdotal examples of Soviet statisticians being punished for neglecting to present the Soviet Union in a positive light, especially in comparison with the West. Much of the debate in the perestroika period exposed this system of control during Soviet times. For example, Valentin Kudrov, an economist at Gosplan and later critic of Goskomstat, recounts an episode in which an economist, M. V. Kubanin, having just returned from a trip to the United States, published an article in the journal *Problemy ekonomiki* in 1941 (Kudrov 1994, 4). The article claimed that labor productivity in the USSR lagged behind the United States by four to five times. Unfortunately for the author, the article happened to catch the attention of Stalin himself. It was then reviewed in the leading Communist Party journal, *Bol'shevik*, and labeled "slanderous," after which the author disappeared.

In 1948, TsUNKhU was removed from Gosplan, given independent status under the Council of Ministers of the USSR, and renamed TsSU. Although its level of autonomy increased, significant political control over the organization remained. Yet the control of publications and discussion did not eliminate private critical interpretation. Valentin Kudrov (2004) said in an interview:

> When I worked at Gosplan's scientific-research center (in the late 1950s–60s), we were already beginning to wonder how our growth rate could be 10 percent if the U.S. growth rate was 2.5 percent—we were starting to realize that things could not be that simple. The USSR had a goal back then to catch up with the United States in terms of production per capita by 1980. We started writing secret notes to the Central Committee

> because we doubted all these numbers. Here is another example: we asked ourselves, why did we need to produce 250 million tons of steel, if the United States was producing 120 million tons?

Kudrov was in a position to send questioning notes to the Central Committee, whereas many other economists kept their critical interpretations to themselves.

In a 2004 interview, the former chairman of Goskomstat Vladimir Sokolin recounted his own experience with questioning the Soviet system:

> We always doubt when we are young—confidence comes with age. I had an interesting experience. I remember the time when the Soviet Union published a small number of copies (approximately a thousand) of Samuelson's economics textbook. These copies were distributed among the state's top leaders so that they would familiarize themselves with "the enemy's ideology," as they say. Eidel'man let me borrow his copy for one night.[2] Although that was not enough time to read the whole book, I looked through the textbook and realized that a planned economy cannot be responsive to human needs. The individual was the last thing this economy cared about.
>
> This also makes me remember a "Fitil'" [satirical variety show] episode about a shoe shop that sold both Soviet *skorokhody* [type of shoes] and Italian shoes. One night, a pair of Soviet shoes is stolen from the shop. Although there were a number of suspects, investigators immediately decided that the thief was the one with a lazy eye because only he could steal a pair of Soviet shoes when Italian shoes were sitting right next to them. This episode shows that even back then people were starting to doubt the qualitative advantages of Soviet products. This is also how I began to doubt the quality of Soviet statistics, albeit not the quality of statisticians' work.

It is interesting here that Sokolin makes a distinction between the quality of the work of statisticians at TsSU and the quality of statistics produced by the organization.

Goskomstat and Politicians during Perestroika

The first sign of significant institutional change for TsSU came in 1987 in the midst of perestroika. On July 17, 1987, the Central Committee of the Communist

2. See Samuelson (Soviet edition) 1964. M. P. Eidel'man was the head of national accounts at TsSU.

Party passed Resolution No. 822, "On Measures for Fundamental Improvement of Statistical Work in the Country" (TsK KPSS and Sovet ministrov SSSR 1987). The resolution grew out of debates at the Seventeenth Party Congress and plenums in December 1986 and June 1987, and it specified thirty points aimed at reforming the state statistical administration to promote social and economic development.[3] Also in July 1987, the organization was promoted to the level of "State Committee" status, and TsSU was renamed Goskomstat USSR. The Council of Ministers passed another resolution on October 9, 1987, "Acceleration of the Restructuring of the Work and Organizational Structures of State Organs." It underscored the plans in the party resolution and outlined designs for organizational restructuring within Goskomstat (VS 1987).[4] These resolutions were part of the top-down pressure to "reform" and support perestroika. Initially, however, many of the reform proposals consisted of vague prescriptions for improving work and reducing bureaucracy.

From approximately 1987–88 on, Mikhail Gorbachev's policy of glasnost' was in full swing. The policy, which can be summarized as "openness," gave citizens increased access to non-state-controlled sources of information. It encouraged discussion of what was really going on in the Soviet Union and abroad and dealt an enormous blow to the system of control in the USSR. Glasnost' provided the state with more information while allowing society to learn about the state and about itself. For example, it supplied more information about historical events, the economy, the environment, and conditions abroad.

The wide-ranging demands under glasnost' for more openness regarding politics, economics, and society extended to public discussion of national statistics. There was an explosion of new information.[5] Critiques that were initially framed as a means of revitalizing Soviet power evolved into critiques of the system itself and moved from internal debates to published external critiques. Although most published criticism of Goskomstat came from external sources, even officials such as Vadim Kirichenko, the head of Goskomstat in 1989–92, criticized the politicization of statistics during the Soviet period (Berger 1989; Kirichenko 1990).[6] In newspaper interviews and a journal article Kirichenko called for an expansion of glasnost' and greater scientific cooperation to bring trust back to statistics. He also admitted some problems with Soviet statistics. One analyst

---

3. For additional discussion of this Central Committee resolution, see Heleniak and Motivans 1991, 474, 476–77.

4. For additional discussion, see Heleniak and Motivans 1991, 474, 477.

5. Among other publications, Goskomstat established a new journal, *Istoriia statistiki,* in 1990.

6. For external criticism, see Seliunin and Khanin 1987; Orlov 1988; Nazarov 1991.

called the early perestroika period one of "fundamental breakdown in the Soviet statistical system" (Vanous 1987, 1).

In terms of internal organizational structure, Goskomstat has for most of its history been a centralized organization. TsSU controlled budgets, hiring, and decisions related to the content and accessibility of publications for its regional offices. This organizational control, especially at the republic level, broke down during perestroika.[7] Dissident republics, such as the Baltic states, took the initiative to publish their own data, sometimes in local languages.[8]

Moreover, another significant aspect of the power struggle that led to the end of the Soviet Union was the battle between the Russian Republic (RSFSR), led by Boris Yeltsin, and the USSR, headed by Mikhail Gorbachev. Conservatives launched a coup attempt against Gorbachev on August 19, 1991. The next day, with Gorbachev still held captive, then President of the RSFSR Yeltsin issued a decree on measures to ensure the economic sovereignty of the Russian Republic. His recommendations included the transition to accounting based on international standards. Although the SNA per se was not mentioned, neither was it excluded. On December 25, 1991, the Soviet Union was dissolved and the Russian Federation was born.

Goskomstat and Politicians in Russia

Concomitant with the fracturing of the Soviet Union into independent states in 1991, Goskomstat USSR was broken up. During the Soviet period the Russian Republic's statistical organization had been subsumed by the union-level organization. But with the end of the Soviet Union, Goskomstat Russia inherited the core of the USSR organization, including its entire methodological apparatus. Goskomstat USSR became Goskomstat Russia, and other republican-level Goskomstat organizations became the NSOs of the newly independent states.

On December 30, 1991, the heads of the Commonwealth of Independent States (CIS), a subset of the fifteen republics of the USSR, agreed to form a statistical committee. This committee, known as Statkom CIS, officially came into being on February 6, 1992, with former Goskomstat chairman Mikhail Korolev as its head.[9] Statkom CIS was created mainly to work on SNA development and the implementation of international methodology for all CIS countries. Statkom

7. The USSR was a union of fifteen republics. These "union republics" became independent states in 1991.

8. For further discussion of this point, see Heleniak and Motivans 1991, 479–80.

9. For discussion of Statkom CIS's early activities, see Noren 1994, 31–32. The original documents are published in Statkomitet SNG 1992, 13–20, 1993, 5.

CIS was (and still is) located in the same building as Goskomstat Russia, which is the former TsSU/Goskomstat USSR building.

The period from 1991 to 1993 in Russia was one of general institutional instability, much of it caused by the lack of a constitution (which did not appear until December 1993) and the intense power struggle between the executive, President Boris Yeltsin, and the communist-dominated legislature, the Supreme Soviet. Society and the economic system were in flux, and the executive and legislative branches of government were weak; yet they used what power they did have to battle each other for control of the state. In addition, this was the period of sovereignty claims by regions within the Russian Federation. It is fair to say that governance in Russia in the early 1990s was chaotic at best.

President Yeltsin's administration generally, and Prime Minister Egor Gaidar's government in particular, was committed to moving Russia toward a market economy. The Supreme Soviet opposed the neoliberal policies of liberalization, stabilization, and privatization, and it opposed Gaidar. President Yeltsin was never able to get Gaidar formally confirmed as prime minister (he was appointed acting prime minister from June 15 to December 14, 1992). The lack of a constitution or governing institutional framework for the state and the standoff between the president and the legislature stalled or subverted many institutional reforms. The state could liberalize—freeing prices at the beginning of 1992, opening trade to some extent, and giving away property in mass privatization. But most economic reforms of the early 1990s that required any institution building or institutional oversight capacity failed to get off the ground, resulting in massive corruption, among other problems.[10]

National statistics occupied a rare zone of ideological agreement between the presidential administration and the Supreme Soviet. Goskomstat Russia at its inception was formally under the control of the Supreme Soviet, but from the start President Boris Yeltsin's government showed interest in it, evidenced by Yeltsin's early proposal to adopt international statistical standards.[11]

The Supreme Soviet also moved quickly on changes at Goskomstat and in regard to economic statistics for the country. At the beginning of price liberalization on January 14, 1992, the Supreme Soviet ordered Goskomstat, the Ministry of the Economy and Finances, the Russian Academy of Sciences, and other research institutes to develop a state program of transition to an international system of

10. On the poor state of reform of the Russian state bureaucracy in general, see Brym and Gimpelson 2004. On the need to rebuild postcommunist state institutions see Grzymala-Busse and Jones Luong 2002. On the failure of Russian economic reforms generally, see Goldman 1994; Herrera 2001.

11. This support by Yeltsin was also mentioned in an interview with Vladimir Sokolin (2004).

statistics suitable for market economy, and a large working group in the Supreme Soviet was assembled for this task (Guzhvin 1992a, 16; Khasbulatov 1992).

By April a first draft of this state program was presented to the government. The Yeltsin government agreed in principle but sent it back for review, asking for a reduction in costs and a quicker time table for implementation. The working group in the Supreme Soviet approved a revised draft at the end of June 1992. According to Pavel Guzhvin, the program was translated into English and sent to foreign experts, who in principle endorsed the plan but in some cases cautioned against the overly optimistic allotted time for implementation, which was only four years (1992a, 16–17). In July 1992 the amended program was signed by the minister of the economy, the minister of finance, Goskomstat, and the head of the Central Bank.

On October 23, 1992, the Supreme Soviet approved "The State Program of the Transition of the Russian Federation to the System of Accounting and Statistics Accepted in International Practice, in Correspondence with the Requirements of a Market Economy" (Verkhovnyi sovet Rossiiskoi Federatsii 1992).[12] The resolution signified the endorsement of the transition to the 1993 SNA by the legislature and the agreement of the legislative and executive branches of the federal government on the necessity of reforming statistics. It also set a timetable for SNA implementation for 1992–95.

This October resolution asked the government to ensure the implementation of the state program by agencies of the federal executive branch and the regional governments. It designated Goskomstat as the organization to receive budget allocations to implement the program. It specified a budget for Goskomstat, stipulated that wages should be raised in 1993, proscribed privatization, and recommended that all regional and local authorities give statistical bodies discounts on utilities.

Beyond these laws, neither the Yeltsin government nor the Supreme Soviet directly intervened in the implementation of the SNA at Goskomstat. The government was supportive, however, and the type of information that Prime Minister Egor Gaidar's government asked of Goskomstat was in accordance with the move to the SNA. For example, in 1992, the new Russian government asked Goskomstat for a variety of new indicators, such as on inflation. These kinds of informational demands from the government, which were consistent with the SNA but not the Soviet system of statistics, continued even after Gaidar was out of power.

---

12. For details on the contents of the program, see Guzhvin 1993, 7–8; Noren 1994, 32–35; and *Vestnik statistiki* issues from the fall of 1992 and the winter of 1993.

On February 12, 1993, the Yeltsin government issued a resolution "On Measures for Realizing the State Program." It ordered all federal and regional agencies to implement the program, listed specific steps for them to take, and stipulated higher wages for employees of statistical agencies.[13] Furthermore, on April 30, the government granted a statute (i.e., gave official status) to an interagency commission to coordinate the state program.[14]

In July the Supreme Soviet reasserted its control over Goskomstat. On July 23, 1993, the Presidium of the Supreme Soviet approved the "Statute of the State Committee on Statistics." This statute declared that Goskomstat would be under the supervision of the Supreme Soviet and its Presidium and would be independent from the executive branch (chapter 1 article 4). It also charged Goskomstat with the adoption of internationally accepted standards (chapter 2 article 1). Chapter 3, article 8, stipulates that it is the function of Goskomstat, together with the Ministry of Finance and other ministries, to implement the SNA. Finally, it decreed that the chairman of Goskomstat should be confirmed and dismissed by the Presidium of the Supreme Soviet. The chairman could sit on the Council of Ministers (part of the government or executive branch) as long as he was subordinated to the Supreme Soviet (chapter 5 article 1).

At this time the country faced enormous difficulties, and power and authority were deeply fractured. The oligarchs were taking control of the economy, regions were ignoring federal authority and threatening separatist movements, and the parliament was openly defying the president. Things came to a head with the constitutional crisis of September 21–October 4, 1993.

After an ill-fated attempt by the legislature to remove Boris Yeltsin from power and provoke an armed struggle in Moscow, President Yeltsin took the decision to bomb the parliament (with the parliamentarians still inside). He disbanded all regional legislatures, created new federally appointed regional executives, and put an end to constitutional debates by establishing a draft constitution and pushing through a constitutional referendum in December 1993.

Formal authority over Goskomstat shifted to the executive branch. On September 22 President Yeltsin issued a resolution transferring authority over several government agencies, including Goskomstat, to the Council of Ministers. Goskomstat was not placed under the control of any ministry, nor was it made a ministry-level state organization. Instead, it became one of a small number of "state committees" in the executive branch.

As the executive-legislative conflict described above suggests, the Supreme Soviet and the President argued over who had jurisdiction to name the head of

13. This resolution was updated on June 20.

14. A resolution of August 30 updated the list of the interagency commissions.

Goskomstat. Pavel Guzhvin had been head of Goskomstat RSFSR since 1985, and, although not formally confirmed, he replaced Kirichenko as head of Goskomstat Russia in 1992. Kirichenko, like Gorbachev, had headed a union-level body, Goskomstat USSR, that ceased to exist.

On September 26, 1993, Yeltsin appointed Pavel Guzhvin as chairman of Goskomstat Russia, although various sources make it clear that he was already acting chairman since 1992.[15] Guzhvin's official appointment was not a change of leadership, but it did reflect the growing power of the executive branch. A month later, on October 28, 1993, Yeltsin dismissed Guzhvin and appointed Iurii A. Iurkov in his place.[16] The appointment of Iurkov so quickly after Yeltsin had established control over appointments at Goskomstat does not suggest a high degree of control by the government over the Goskomstat leadership in 1992–93, or presumably they would have replaced Guzhvin earlier.

Despite these events, the Russian state remained weak, and much of the institutional work of economic reforms went by the wayside. Hence the implementation of the 1993 SNA in the early 1990s really stands out among attempts at institutional reform in Russia.

Overall, Goskomstat gained a great deal of autonomy from political actors after the end of the USSR, when the decision to move to the SNA was taken. In an interview, former Chairman of Goskomstat Vladimir Sokolin (2004) noted Yeltsin's early support but said that "once Russian statistics became independent, changes picked up speed."

Vladimir Putin, who succeeded Yeltsin as president in 1999, supported strengthening of the state (or "vertical power"). By every measure, the state—vis-à-vis the regions, the oligarchs, society, and so on—is far stronger than in the Yeltsin period. There is scholarly consensus that Russia is no longer a democracy. National television media are controlled, and human rights organizations or opposition political parties (to the extent any still exist) face constant harassment.

Yet until very recently there has been little political infringement on Goskomstat's work. The reform of the statistical system—begun in the heyday of late perestroika democratic experimentation—continued through the authoritarian era of Putin (and his hand-picked successor, Dmitry Medvedev). Goskomstat has full control over its economic publications. A presidential commission oversees

---

15. For examples, articles by Guzhvin in *Vestnik statistiki* in September and October 1992 list him as "chairman of Goskomstat Russia." His short official tenure, from September to October 1993, may be why Guzhvin is not listed in the official history of Goskomstat (Goskomstat Russia 1996b).

16. On November 19, 1993, Prime Minister Chernomyrdin replaced V. M. Kozlov and Iu. A. Polenov with Valerii V. Dalin and Vladimir L. Sokolin as vice-chairmen of Goskomstat. Sokolin became chairman of Goskomstat in 1998, after Iurkov and Dalin were arrested.

census publications, but a comparison of accessibility of the 2002 and earlier censuses shows a stark increase in quantity and accessibility of data (Herrera 2004).

Moreover, Goskomstat largely benefited from the general reform of the state bureaucracy under President Putin. The parliament finally passed a basic law on statistics in July 2004 (Pravitel'stvo Rossiiskoi Federatsii 2004), followed by a series of updates (Pravitel'stvo Rossiiskoi Federatsii 2008). Before that, there was no overall law on statistics that regulated the sharing of data between government organizations, the collection of data from the public, and the protection of privacy and confidentiality. The laws have made it much easier for Goskomstat to get cooperation from other actors, furthering implementation of the SNA. Also in 2004, Goskomstat was renamed the Federal Service for Statistics (*Federal'naia sluzhba gosudarstvennoi statistiki*, nicknamed "Rosstat"), although it remained "at large" in the executive branch, independent of any ministry. It was moved to the purview of the Ministry for Economic Development in 2008.

Today, Goskomstat remains a centralized organization. All regional offices still report directly to Moscow and all authority relating to the work of the organization stems from the center. Regional offices do have authority over supplemental local publications, but all methodological decisions, including anything related to the SNA, are determined in Moscow. In addition, employees in regional offices are federal employees. In one interview, when asked, given all the organizational upheaval since perestroika, is there anything that had not changed at the organization, a top Goskomstat official said, "The structure did not change: hierarchical bottom-up reporting and most of the staff have remained in place" (GKS4 2003).

The Relationship between Goskomstat and Politicians for SNA Implementation

The last two decades brought a radical change in the political context for Goskomstat as the USSR broke up and Russia became an independent state. The relationship between Goskomstat and the politicians has gone from subservience to one primarily regulated by laws wherein Goskomstat has a great deal of autonomy. During Soviet times, Goskomstat actors were beleaguered by, and at times literally controlled by, Communist Party politicians and doctrine. But this extreme political pressure ended with perestroika and the collapse of the Soviet Union. It was in this period of greater institutional autonomy that Goskomstat decided to embrace the SNA.

Nevertheless, some key politicians and societal actors, such as President Yeltsin and acting Prime Minister Egor Gaidar, enthusiastically supported the move to the SNA. Despite this congruence of interests between politicians and

Goskomstat bureaucrats, the record of governance in the early Yeltsin era does not suggest that politicians in either the executive or legislative branch had the power to force change within Goskomstat. In addition, there is much evidence of internal interest within Goskomstat for the move to the SNA.

Goskomstat developed a somewhat contradictory relationship to the general political context in the sense that it gained autonomy in the period of hopeful democracy in the early 1990s, but retained that autonomy and professional commitment to the SNA even as the state retreated from democracy and international engagement under President Putin. In addition, while the government introduced many institutional reforms meant to bring transparency and efficiency to Russia in the early 1990s, the success of the SNA is unusual.

Thus a simple legislative politics model does not really fit this case of institutional change, because the executive branch and the legislature were much more concerned with battling each other than with overseeing the implementation of the SNA. A principal-agent model is probably not appropriate either, because the interests of principals (politicians, international actors, etc.) and agents (those within Goskomstat) were largely aligned. Overall, the evidence does not point to pressure from politicians in either the executive or legislative branches as the primary cause of implementation of the SNA in Russia.

Goskomstat and Society

Beyond politicians and bureaucrats, especially in democracies, the interests of various societal actors, or actors outside the state, are also important to institutional outcomes. This influence can work either through support for specific institutional changes (Skocpol 1992; Jenkins-Smith and Sabatier 1993) or lack of opposition (Heclo 1974). Many case studies on institutional reform in postcommunist countries (Hausner 2001; Nelson 2001; Tanzi 2001; Johnson 2003) or developing countries (Geddes 1994, 41) focus on politics and interests both within state organizations and in society.

Indeed, in the postcommunist state-building and reform literature, actor-centered analyses that focus on the interests of political and economic elites dominate (Grzymala-Busse and Jones Luong 2002). This competition or even conflict among elites can lead to failures in building state capacity (Roberts and Sherlock 1999), or even disintegration of the state (Ganev 2007), but a confluence of interests among elite and societal actors can also serve as a basis for state building (Volkov 2000).

In explaining the SNA by citing the interests of societal actors, we would expect to find evidence of interest and sufficient power or resources of societal actors to get NSOs to implement the SNA. To test this theory, we have to analyze the relationship between Goskomstat and societal actors.

During the Soviet period, TsSU had minimal contact with the Soviet public. To the extent that communication between TsSU and society did take place, it was a one-way relationship in which Goskomstat published statistical material, some fraction of which was available to the general public, but did not debate, discuss, or get feedback from the public.

That changed with perestroika and glasnost'. Early on, access to Goskomstat publications was greatly expanded. In 1987 an information-publication center (*informatsionno-izdatel'skii tsentr*) was created, which functioned as a retail store for publications (TsK KPSS and Sovet Ministrov SSSR 1987). This center was one of the first open points of access for foreigners as well as ordinary citizens to Goskomstat data.[17]

Meanwhile, newspapers and journals subjected Goskomstat to scathing criticism. In widely cited articles, the unorthodox economist Grigorii Khanin called attention to the need for change at Goskomstat and in Soviet statistics more generally. Khanin's articles in *Novyi mir* in 1987 and *Kommunist* in 1988 represented a watershed in the debate over Soviet statistics.[18] One analyst called the 1987 article a "bombshell" (Schroeder 2001).

Goskomstat was forced to respond to public disapproval in the press and in academic journals, because it was no longer possible after 1987 to censor or disregard criticism. When I asked Chairman Sokolin if Goskomstat had been influenced by any of the criticism of the organization in academic journals or the popular press in the late 1980s and early 1990s, he said that he disagreed with a lot of the criticism but that it had some impact. He remarked, "If someone is constantly telling you that your makeup makes you look ten years older, whether you agree or not with that person, eventually you're going to go look in the mirror" (Sokolin 2004).

Changes in the economic and political structure during perestroika required Goskomstat to address the problem of horizontal relations with other state organizations and how to get data from those organizations. In meetings between the U.S. Bureau of Economic Analysis (BEA) and Goskomstat in 1989, Goskomstat

17. To date, the center retains the same name and function as a retail store for Goskomstat publications, and it is the only part of the Goskomstat building open to the public without a special permit (*propusk*).

18. See Seliunin and Khanin 1987; Khanin 1988. While Khanin's work is well known, few economists today agree with him. Kudrov (2004), a strong critic of Goskomstat who was also once a coauthor with Khanin, said: "[Today] I personally trust Goskomstat more than I trust Khanin. He has now become a Communist and speaks about the contributions of Stalin and other villains, so why should I trust him?" Nearly everyone, however, agrees that his articles in the late 1980s were extremely influential. For further analysis of the impact of the Khanin and Seliunin articles, see Ericson 1990.

officials discussed their lack of access to some kinds of data, like military budgets, but also interagency tension within the Russian bureaucracy about reporting requirements (Kostinsky and Belkindas 1990, 185). In addition, while responsibility for trade statistics was shifted from the Ministry of Foreign Trade to Goskomstat in 1988, Goskomstat did not have a framework for getting data from firms or a way to handle prices on exports and imports (Kostinsky and Belkindas 1990, 185). Goskomstat also had problems with a lack of financial data. Gosbank and the Ministry of Finance kept most data on currency emission and bank balance sheets as well as government budgets and spending and other financial data (Noren 1994, 14–15). Before the laws of 2004–8, in general, Goskomstat had to get special permission every time it needed data from other state organizations. Given the weak central authority in the early 1990s, Goskomstat could not rely on the government or other political actors to enforce cooperation.

The onset of privatization imposed a new responsibility on Goskomstat: to report on the activities of private enterprises. Goskomstat had at best mixed success in this area. In examining the early 1990s, Noren noted considerable under-reporting in nonstate activity such as new private business or private agricultural activity, as well as in traditionally ignored areas such as prison and military production (1994, 14). Overall, speaking of the situation as of 1993, Noren concluded that Goskomstat "is ill-equipped to handle the problems inherent in dealing with reporting units no longer operating under central planning while at the same time trying to introduce new methodologies more in line with international practice" (1994, 23).

In the post-Soviet environment Goskomstat also faced, and to some extent continues to face, resistance from ordinary citizens. Since the perestroika period, public trust in Goskomstat has been extremely low. Distrust was exacerbated by a scandal in 1998 (see below) and the absence of legal protections for privacy and confidentiality of data until the 2004 law. Individuals and firms are reluctant to cooperate with Goskomstat, and both the media and the public remain critical of the organization. Nevertheless, because the public must now *voluntarily* provide data to Goskomstat, the organization must increasingly build relations and trust with societal actors.

On one hand, since the end of the USSR, Goskomstat has faced an uphill battle in obtaining cooperation from other state organizations, as well as firms and citizens; this lack of trust and cooperation has impeded full implementation of the SNA. On the other hand, societal interests had minimal influence on the direction of institutional change at Goskomstat. In the critical period of the early 1990s, there was no organized group of societal interests capable of, or interested in, controlling the methodological and organizational course of Goskomstat. This, along with the absence of political interference, gave the leadership of Goskomstat unprecedented latitude for reorganization and institutional change.

Goskomstat and International Actors

International organizations and developments in the global economy can also pressure institutions to change. The relationship among international economic conditions, domestic economic policy, and institutional change has been studied extensively and with increasing nuance.[19] Although these arguments include an element of structuralism, they focus on how evolving international economic conditions affect the preferences or interests of domestic actors.[20] The crux of these arguments is that shifting economic conditions, at home and abroad, alter material incentives, which in turn leads to institutional change. To apply such an argument here, we need to find evidence that actors in NSOs, or even NSOs themselves, materially benefited from the move to the SNA.

During the Soviet period, TsSU statisticians had arms-length ties with the international statistical community. They participated in the development of the SNA and the MPS as well as in the International Comparison Program in the 1970s, but this was in many ways an "imagined community" of national statisticians because many East European and Soviet statisticians working on national accounts never actually met statisticians in the West. They also maintained a stable division of the world into communist and capitalist economies and their respective statistical systems. While there was professional engagement at the international level on the SNA and MPS as systems, it primarily took the form of comparisons of work done by individual countries, or by the West versus the East, rather than collaborative engagement in the process of constructing national accounts. Statisticians from the West did not work with their TsSU counterparts on Soviet statistics. Foreigners from the West were generally denied access to even the TsSU building in Moscow.

This situation changed dramatically during perestroika. In 1987 the U.S. Census Bureau and Goskomstat began a program of cooperation that included exchanges of official delegations, methodological information, and publications (Heleniak and Motivans 1991). According to Kostinsky and Belkindas (who were both at the Center for International Research at the U.S. Census at the time)

19. For overviews, see Gourevitch 1978; Murphy 1994; Keohane and Milner 1996.

20. This could work, for example, through coalition politics (Rogowski 1989), sectoral reactions (Frieden 1991), firm reactions (Milner 1988), and asset portfolios (Frieden and Rogowski 1996).

national accounts, and in particular the connection between the old NMP and newer GNP estimates, were a primary topic of discussion (1990, 183).

At the same time debate was taking place within Goskomstat, and Westerners were invited there. The demographer Murray Feshbach was the first Westerner to enter Goskomstat's building by official invitation, and he was followed in February 1988 by Vladimir Treml, an American economist who delivered a lecture to Goskomstat officials on the problems with Soviet statistics from the point of view of a Western analyst.[21]

Former Chairman Sokolin said in an interview that there was a great deal of debate about national accounts and the SNA during perestroika within Goskomstat and among Russian economists and statisticians. In his words, "this discussion lasted two to three years, starting in 1986–87, and the Academy of Sciences, as well as various economic institutes, took part in these deliberations" (Sokolin 2004). Sokolin noted that officials at Goskomstat were reading Western publications, such as those by Peter Hill, the OECD statistician credited with cowriting the 1993 SNA Blue Book.

Foreign interaction grew in terms of frequency and scope throughout the late 1980s. In May 1989 Goskomstat set up a telecommunications link with the UN Economic Commission for Europe's network (ECESTATNET) (Heleniak and Motivans 1991, 479). In June 1989 Goskomstat sent a delegation to the U.S. Bureau of Economic Analysis in Washington, D.C., for a four-day seminar on U.S. and UN accounting. According to Kostinsky and Belkindas, Goskomstat "raised questions on numerous details of these accounting definitions and methods" (1990, 183).

By 1990 international institutions—including the IMF, the World Bank, the OECD, and the European Bank for Reconstruction and Development (EBRD)—were participating to a limited extent in the methodological debates in Goskomstat (Belkin 1992). Pavel Guzhvin reported that Goskomstat had already conducted an employment survey of households and individuals in accordance with ILO standards and a public health survey in cooperation with the World Bank (1993, 8–9).

Another international organization that worked with Goskomstat Russia and other FSU states on the SNA was Statkom CIS.[22] This organization was set up in 1992 primarily to aid former Soviet states in implementing the SNA, and many

---

21. See Treml 1988 for a detailed analysis of changes at Goskomstat from 1985 to 1988 and an overview of problems with Soviet statistics.

22. For discussion of Statkom CIS's early activities, see Noren 1994, 31–32. The original documents are published in "Informatsionnii biulleten'," *Statkomitet SNG* 1, 1 (1992): 13–20; and "Informatsionnii biulleten'," *Statkomitet SNG* 1, 4 (1993): 5.

Statkom CIS officials came from Goskomstat. For example, Mikhail Korolev, the former head of Goskomstat USSR, became head of Statkom CIS, and Youri Ivanov, who was one of the people most involved at the UN in the development of the SNA and MPS during the Soviet era, was a deputy director. More recently Vladimir Sokolin moved to Statkom CIS after retiring from Goskomstat in 2009.

As of 1993 Goskomstat had joined the UN Statistical Commission and the Conference of European Statisticians (CES) (Guzhvin 1993, 12). At the same time it was submitting data regularly to the IMF, EBRD, and other international organizations. Guzhvin also noted that in cooperation with the UN Statistical Commission and the OECD, Goskomstat planned to develop purchasing power parity (PPP) data for 1993 that would be in accordance with the International Comparison Program (1993, 11). Data provided by Goskomstat to international organizations were not unproblematic, unbiased, or complete, but the type and volume of shared data had significantly increased.

By 1994 Goskomstat was very different from what it had been in 1991. One analyst, Vincent Koen, notes that, as the 1990s progressed, Goskomstat became much more open to discussion with foreigners (1996, 321). He writes that when he visited Goskomstat in 1991 and met with both the Russian and USSR statistical committees, he was only allowed to talk to high-level managers. Even then, a deputy director who was an open critic of Khanin (the well-known perestroika-era critic of TsSU), remained in the room at all times. Much of the information he received was already available, and even that was conveyed as if it were secret.[23] By 1994 Koen reported that his meetings "could hardly have been more different" (1996, 321). He writes:

> Although access had by no means become straightforward, it was possible to talk with competent specialists, to informally request data, and to exchange critical views on the credibility of the numbers. Indeed, during those years, spectacular improvements took place, helped by a changing of the guard at the top, and reflected *inter alia* in an explosion of the volume of information released by the statistical authorities. (1996, 321).

In the early to mid-1990s Goskomstat had welcomed and at times initiated contact with foreign organizations. The same types of positive assessments were

23. This practice has not gone away entirely. In 2001 I tried to purchase old statistical yearbooks from Goskomstat's store but was told I could not because the books contained "secret material." However, these books had previously been on sale, were on the open shelves of the store, and were available in public libraries.

confirmed by other scholars in the mid- to late 1990s,[24] including those from the World Bank who at times were in weekly or even daily contact with their Goskomstat counterparts.[25] In addition, one of the key authors of the 1993 SNA, Peter Hill, visited Goskomstat in the early 1990s (Sokolin 2004).

Another aspect of Goskomstat's relationship with international organizations in the 1990s was that Goskomstat collected and processed data *together* according to international standards, rather than presenting data as finished products to international organizations. Collaborators included the UN, the World Bank, the IMF, the EBRD, Eurostat, and state statistical agencies of the United States, Germany, France, Italy, and the Netherlands (Treml 2001, 21; Vlasov 2001; VS 2001).

In the past there had been a clear line between Soviet publications and Western ones. Initially, alternative data and alternative models for the construction of national statistics—presented by foreign or nonstate actors under glasnost' and available in scholarly journals or books as well as newspapers—functioned as a substitute or supplement to official statistics. However, in the post-Soviet period these alternative statistics and the methodologies used to construct the data became models for official Russian state statistical work. As the 1990s progressed, joint projects increasingly blurred the line between the work of Russian and foreign organizations.

The most significant example of collaborative effort was the "Russian Federation: Report on The National Accounts," published jointly by Goskomstat and the World Bank (Goskomstat Russia and World Bank 1995). This is an insightful and comprehensive treatment of national accounts in Russia for 1991–94, which provided not only estimates of GDP but also penetrating analysis of the sources and methods used in its compilation. It detailed the progress on SNA implementation as well as the difficulties faced by Goskomstat at the time. The report combines an insider's view with a frank external perspective and in that sense is truly a joint effort by Goskomstat and the World Bank. It would be hard to overstate what a sea change in publications this report represents in terms of the relationship between Goskomstat and international organizations.

Despite their valuable efforts in deciphering Soviet statistics, established Sovietology-oriented organizations such as the U.S. Central Intelligence Agency (CIA) played little role in the implementation of the SNA by Goskomstat in the 1990s (beyond the data and analysis they had provided prior to the end of the Soviet Union). CIA work on Soviet statistics stopped completely in 1991, and in

---

24. See Treml 2001, 21, for a similar assessment.

25. For example, Misha Belkindas of the World Bank worked especially closely with the top leadership of Goskomstat in compiling the first SNA publication in 1995 (Goskomstat Russia and World Bank 1995).

any case their methods were no longer suited to the new environment at Goskomstat. Whereas CIA analysts had pored over published material from afar with almost no direct contact with Goskomstat officials, and the CIA had attempted to translate Soviet data into more comprehensible Western categories, in the post-Soviet period Soviet categories gradually ceased to exist. Analysts from other international organizations worked inside Goskomstat with the direct cooperation of Goskomstat's top leadership as well as lower-level employees to implement international standards.

Can we say, though, that increased contact with foreigners and international organizations explains Goskomstat's decision to adopt and quickly implement the 1993 SNA? The timing of events suggests the answer is mixed. The most intense period of contact with the international community *followed*, rather than preceded, Goskomstat's decision to move to the SNA. There is no question that support from international organizations improved the quality of postcommunist countries' statistics and their ability to implement the SNA, but that close interaction does not explain the initial decision by Goskomstat to drop the MPS and move to the SNA. Thus, we can say international organizations played an essential role in implementation of the SNA, *after* postcommunist NSOs had enthusiastically embraced the shift.

Another way to think about the role of international actors in institutional change at Goskomstat is in terms of pressure. Did international organizations force Goskomstat to adopt the 1993 SNA by threatening to withhold resources or impose other sanctions? There are several reasons to doubt this. First, the SNA is not a formal treaty and international organizations have a limited ability to compel SNA implementation in any country. Otherwise, we would not see so much variance among countries. Conditionality restrictions on loans from international financial institutions cannot "cause" a complicated institutional change that requires large-scale reform within a bureaucracy. Nor is there evidence of such conditionality restrictions in postcommunist countries in the period under discussion. Moreover, much of the data that might be demanded by international organizations is in the form of macro-aggregates that these organizations can themselves estimate, which could substitute for, rather than incentivize, deeper institutional reform.

Even if we posit a diffuse sense of international pressure stemming from structural changes in the economy and the use of the SNA by Western countries, such pressure could explain only the decision to symbolically commit to the SNA, not the level of achievement in implementation. Russia could have remained at the level of minimal compliance occupied by most countries. Instead, the postcommunist countries surpassed the median level of implementation in every international assessment.

Finally, we simply cannot ignore the evidence of widespread support for the SNA inside Goskomstat. As with politicians, international organizations supported the move to the SNA, but contacts with or pressure from abroad cannot in themselves account for the internal change in interest at Goskomstat.

Actors within Goskomstat

In mapping attitudes within Goskomstat, we have to consider the interests of both the leadership and the lower-level staff. The key issue is why interests shifted in the early 1990s. We should consider turnover in the organization, because new "reform-minded" actors may have brought new interest in the SNA.[26] We should also consider incentives that may have been used to change the interests of existing actors. I take up both these questions in the sections that follow.

Leadership of Goskomstat

Table 5.1 outlines the leadership at Goskomstat and its predecessors. Before perestroika, the leadership at TsSU was very stable: two directors in forty-five years. Vladimir N. Starovskii served from 1940 to 1975 as head of TsUNKhU in 1940–48 and of TsSU in 1948–75. Lev M. Volodarskii took over as head of TsSU from 1975 to 1985. In the perestroika era, there were two directors: Mikhail A. Korolev was appointed in 1985 and oversaw the transition from TsSU to Goskomstat USSR. Korolev was removed on July 12, 1989 (Pravda 1989), but went on to become the first head of the newly created Statkom CIS in 1992 (and later a member of the Bureau of the Conference of European Statisticians). Korolev's replacement was Vadim N. Kirichenko. In describing Kirichenko at a CIA conference in 1990, Kostinsky and Belkindas called him "a highly respected economist" and said his appointment "may indicate renewed impetus toward reforms in the statistical system" (1990, 190).[27] While Kirichenko was not from Goskomstat, his previous post was chief of the economic section of the USSR Council of Ministers administrative department, and hence he was not an outsider to the system.

Pavel Guzhvin inherited the leadership of Goskomstat Russia after the end of the USSR, replacing Kirichenko, and serving as acting chair until his brief formal appointment in September 1993. Guzhvin was both an insider and a proponent of the move to the SNA. He had headed Goskomstat RSFSR since 1985 and led

---

26. For example, in East Germany after unification most of the bureaucracy was replaced with new employees, and especially people from western Germany (Derlien 1993).

27. Kirichenko was fifty-eight at the time of his appointment.

Table 5.1 Leadership of TsSU USSR and Goskomstat Russia

	YEARS	TITLE, ORGANIZATION
Vladimir Nikonovich Starovskii	1940–48	Head, TsUNKhU, Gosplan USSR
	1948–75	Head, TsSU USSR
Lev Markovich Volodarskii	1975–85	Head, TsSU USSR
Mikhail Antonovich Korolev	1985–1987	Head, TsSU USSR
	1987–1989	Chair, Goskomstat USSR
Vadim Nikitovich Kirichenko	1989–92	Chair, Goskomstat USSR
Pavel Fedorovich Guzhvin	1985–91	Chair, Goskomstat RSFSR
	1992–93	Acting Chair, Goskomstat Russia
Iurii Alexeevich Iurkov	1993–98	Chair, Goskomstat Russia
Vladimir Leonidovich Sokolin	1998–2000	Acting Chair, Goskomstat Russia
	2000–04	Chair, Goskomstat Russia
	2004–09	Director, Federal Service for Statistics
Aleksandr Evgen'evich Surinov	2009–present	Director, Federal Service for Statistics

the Leningrad oblast statistical committee before that (GKS29 2003). He wrote several critical articles in *Vestnik statistiki* in 1992 supporting the move to the SNA while criticizing Goskomstat USSR (but not statistics at Goskomstat RSFSR).

In October 1993, amid the shakeup following the constitutional crisis and President Yeltsin's bombing of parliament, there were leadership changes at Goskomstat: Iurii A. Iurkov was appointed chairman, and Vladimir L. Sokolin became vice-chairman. Iurkov was generally well respected, and both he and Sokolin supported the SNA. However, these two were not radicals or new to the organization. Both had been mid-level managers in Goskomstat USSR (Treml 2001, 4). Sokolin worked at Goskomstat/TsSU since 1971 and was a methodologist during the Soviet period. In describing the personnel at Goskomstat as of 1993, Noren writes, "the truth is that most of the old apparatus is still in place" (1994, 23).

The shift in leadership at Goskomstat in 1998 from Iurkov to Sokolin, however, demands further attention. In June 1998 Iurkov, Vice-Chairman Valerii Dalin, the head of the data processing center, Boris Saakian, and more than twenty other officials were arrested and charged with "systematic distortion of statistical data" for the purposes of helping certain large enterprises avoid taxes. It was reported that Iurkov pleaded guilty. More specific charges followed: that Goskomstat officials understated production in exchange for bribes and sold confidential business information to competitor firms (Gordon 1998).[28] The details of this case and its conclusion remained unclear for more than five years, until the case

28. See Treml 2001, 6, on the details of Iurkov's arrest.

was finally decided in court in February 2004. In the end, Iurkov, Saakian, and another department head, Viacheslav Baranovskii, were found guilty of forming "a criminal group that in 1995–98 sold information both to private firms and to government departments, including the Labor Ministry and the former Federal Agency of Governmental Communications and Information (FAPSI)" (RFE/RL 2004). Iurkov and Saakian were sentenced to four and a half years and four years, respectively, in a strict-regime labor camp; Baranovskii was given a four-year suspended sentence. The five other defendants received amnesty. Iurkov and the others were not convicted of the "systematic distortion" charge or of falsifying any data. Following Iurkov's arrest and his immediate dismissal in 1998, Vladimir Sokolin became chairman, a post he retained until 2009, when he retired and became head of Statkom CIS.

The reasons for the arrests remain somewhat puzzling. They may have been legitimate prosecutions of corruption. But some people have speculated that Iurkov was close to former Prime Minister Victor Chernomyrdin and that his arrest was linked to Chernomyrdin's fall from grace. Selective enforcement of laws, including politically motivated arrests, is not unheard of in Russia, especially under Vladimir Putin. Since the details of the case have not been made public, it is hard to know exactly why Iurkov and the others were arrested.

From the standpoint of what the arrests tell us about SNA implementation, at a minimum they suggest, if we can believe the charges, that Iurkov was not an enlightened, Westernizer who cared deeply about bringing transparency and the rule of law to statistics, which is largely the point of the SNA. Yet Western scholars and Goskomstat employees alike give Iurkov credit for his positive leadership on SNA implementation. In terms of the effect on Goskomstat, Sokolin (2004) told me in our interview that the arrests reduced the agency's prestige and trust among the public but had little effect inside the organization. Lower-level employees confirmed this view.

From 1985 to the present Goskomstat's leaders have displayed a remarkable consistency: despite being "insiders," they all supported the move to the SNA. In the early years of the transition Korolev, Kirichenko, and Guzhvin published articles calling for the restructuring of statistics and the move to international standards (Korolev 1987; Kirichenko 1990; Kirichenko and Pogosov 1991; Guzhvin 1992a, 1993).[29] Iurkov oversaw the transition.

Interviews and content analysis of *Vestnik statistiki* also support the argument that there was internal Goskomstat support for the move to the SNA. They show that the decision to move to the SNA happened very rapidly between 1988 and

29. See also the interview with Kirichenko in July 1989 (Berger 1989).

1992. Even up to 1991 there was still talk of integrating the SNA and MPS and using two systems, but in published articles by mid-1992 there was total commitment to the SNA, including detailed plans on the conversion to the SNA written by senior Goskomstat officials.

If Goskomstat officials did not support the move to the SNA, *Vestnik statistiki* would not have published articles in support of it. This was a time when Soviet censorship was over and the strategic value of the journal to outsiders was minimal. Also, the key author in *Vestnik statistiki* for the early statements of support for the SNA conversion by Goskomstat was Youri Ivanov, who has published dozens of very consistent articles on the SNA in the Soviet and post-Soviet period. All of his work presents the argument that the statistical system should follow the structure of the economy, and his articles also document the assertion that there was a change in support for the SNA in approximately 1992, a claim he repeated in an interview in 2004 (Ivanov 2004b). It is hard to see how or why these statements of support for the SNA in *Vestnik statistiki* might be coerced or inauthentic; rather it is far more likely that they reveal the timing in the change in support for the SNA within Goskomstat.

Overall, in examining the views of the leadership of Goskomstat, it was a case of the conversion of insiders to reform, not the arrival of "reformers," that explains the interest in institutional change.

Goskomstat Staff

Although a large organization, Goskomstat consists of a relatively small number of employees in Moscow (less than 3 percent of the total), and numerous employees located in regional offices. The agency has a central hierarchy, and regional employees report to the Moscow office. There are regional differences, but the center determines the organization of work.

The workforce seems to have been cut by more than half since the Soviet period, but the published figures are inconsistent. Goskomstat USSR employed about fifty thousand people, a figure also reported in the history published in 1996 (Goskomstat Russia 1996b). However, a 1997 report on the size of federal agencies listed Goskomstat's total staff as 31,484 employees (Goskomstat Russia 1997, 44). That number has since declined further, according to the agency website. On April 18, 2001, it listed thirty thousand; by December 10, 2005, that number had fallen to twenty thousand. During regional interviews in 2003, many regional office directors said that their staff was approximately half the size it had been in 1991. Currently, the 2008 law on statistics specifies that the organization should have no more than 652 employees in the Moscow office, and 22,800 in regional offices (not counting security and cleaning staff), bringing the total to

23,452 (Pravitel'stvo Rossiiskoi Federatsii 2008). The number of staff reported on the website in Russian in 2009 is 23,000 (Rosstat 2009a), although the English version reports 30,000 (Rosstat 2009b).

A critical question for the analysis of institutional change at Goskomstat is what accounts for this reduction in staff. Were employees who disagreed with the move to the SNA fired? The timing of the staff reductions suggests not. The major staffing cuts came when Goskomstat USSR was split into its constituent republican units. Before the move to the SNA, Goskomstat had the task of plan monitoring and opposed sample surveys, instead collecting data though full enumeration of all firms; it also had antiquated data-processing technology and needed a large staff. The move to sampling and the end of central planning probably accounted for much of the reduction in staff.[30] According to my interviews with both central and regional officials, the staff reductions were accomplished not through mass layoffs but by a combination of attrition and closing of irrelevant departments. Hiring of new people took place at the end of the 1990s. The increase, too, was not sudden or massive but the gradual hiring of skilled younger employees.

It is significant that the vast majority of people working on the SNA in the early 1990s had previously worked on the Soviet MPS. They were not outsiders or new employees. Irina Masakova, who headed the Department of National Accounts since 1997, began working at Goskomstat in 1972. Similarly, many other senior Goskomstat officials have worked at the organization for decades.

In interviews several officials noted the consistency of the agency's staff. Sokolin (2004) said: "Statistics is inherently very conservative. The Ministry of the Economy can change but not statistics. We have a long-term agenda and it is clear to us. Although the content of our work has changed significantly, our goals, staff, and so on have remained the same." One official who had worked at Goskomstat for over three decades said that the one thing that had not changed was the "high level of our specialists' qualifications" (GKS44 2004). Another official said, "We continue to hire people who love numbers, who have worked for us for many years, and who are disciplined" (GKS43 2003). Acknowledging the contradiction between extensive staff reductions and vacancies and the idea of staff continuity, one official explained: "The average age of our employees and our staff turnover are both high—those who stay do so because of their devotion to statistics" (GKS29 2003).

In explaining the move to the SNA, the retention of older employees is critical. Even if those who disagreed with the move to the SNA were let go, that

30. For more on this point in CMEA states, see Blades and Harrison 1992, 102.

would not explain the strong support for the SNA among employees who worked at the organization for decades. These people had been devoted to the Soviet statistical system and continue to praise it, yet decided to abandon it in favor of the SNA.

Material Incentives for SNA Implementation

Niskanen (1971) argued that bureaucracies are organizations of self-maximizing individuals.[31] Following his logic, institutional change should occur when bureaucrats stand to gain materially from reform. For example, trips abroad or other perks, in addition to increased wages, might serve as positive incentives for a particular institutional change. In addition to carrots, sticks may work. Bureaucrats could be threatened with job loss or lower pay if they fail to support a particular institutional change. At the organizational level, material incentives might be used selectively to support "reformers" and weed-out "conservatives," thereby changing the composition of an organization in terms of its overall orientation toward a particular institutional change.

Given the sweeping changes in the political and economic environment, both domestically and internationally, might the material incentives for bureaucrats within Goskomstat have changed dramatically, hence sparking new interest in the SNA? Did bureaucrats get bonuses for completing reforms or fear a loss of resources from the state if they did not? To answer these questions, we need to consider the material incentives available to employees of Goskomstat during the shift to the SNA.

The tight resource environment at Goskomstat and in Russia as a whole limited the possibilities for positive incentives. There were no real raises (given inflation) or bonuses for increased productivity or progress on SNA implementation. The average wage for an employee at Goskomstat in the early 1990s was approximately $50 per month, and without positive incentives to compel a change, one would have expected workers to do the minimum necessary, rather than to work harder or learn something new.[32]

The loan from the World Bank in 1999 did not result in additional salary or bonuses for Goskomstat employees. Instead it went primarily to the central

31. For an update on the influence of this work, see the edited volume that revisits and expands Niskanen's insights (Blais and Dion 1991).

32. Although it was all they received, the staff did consistently receive salaries during the 1990s. Unlike some other Russia state organizations and private enterprises at the time, Goskomstat did not have a wage arrears problem.

Goskomstat office in Moscow to pay for equipment and technical assistance from Western consultants (World Bank 1999). Related to international cooperation, a limited number of top employees at Goskomstat did obtain some perks in the form of trips to conferences and the like, but these rewards largely followed, sometimes by years, the commitment to implement the 1993 SNA.

One area where material incentives may have operated, at least in a limited way, was publications. According to one analyst, "in a way, openness was also forced upon Goskomstat by hardened budget constraints, as selling statistical publications became a way to raise revenue" (Koen 1996, 321).[33] That is, revenue prospects have increased the incentives for Goskomstat to meet the needs of businesses and consumers in its publications and to interact more with consumers. In a 2001 survey of print and Internet publications of the regional branches of Goskomstat there did not appear to be a central template for the presentation of data. Websites varied in style and features, and there was little consistency in the type of information available at the regional level, except in one area—every regional website advertised the sale of local economic information.[34] As of 2005 the websites have been standardized, but they still contain a page listing publications and another page listing various services and contact information for the "marketing" departments. In interviews in 2004, some regional offices were very proud of the scope of their publications and their level of responsiveness to local businesses. This incentive would not explain the move to the SNA by the organization as a whole, because the level of discretion by regional organizations on what to publish is limited, but it would suggest a possible incentive for better-quality publications and for greater openness with societal actors.

In terms of incentives at the organizational level, the collective threat of job loss or organizational obsolescence may have been a motivating factor, but the evidence of sincere interest in moving to the SNA by Goskomstat employees seems to challenge this argument. In addition, as with other material incentives (and structural approaches), the more likely path, and one well trodden in Russia (and around the world), would have been to pay lip service to politicians and international actors, agree to the transition to retain organizational resources and jobs, but to do the bare minimum. Finally, the move to sampling required by the SNA accounted for many of the job losses, and the consequences of moving to sampling were certainly known to Goskomstat officials. If the agency wanted to preserve jobs, moving to sampling was a big step in the opposite direction.

---

33. See also Heleniak and Motivans 1991, 474.

34. Based on research assistance from Yulia Woodruff, who conducted a survey of regional Goskomstat websites in July–August 2001.

Overall, it seems unlikely that the employees of Goskomstat were motivated to switch to the SNA by personal financial gain. The resources for material incentives just were not there. Moreover, material incentives seem to be a limited option for most bureaucracies in compelling institutional change. Bureaucracies employ relatively high-skilled workers with college or graduate degrees at below-market wages; often the implicit tradeoff for low wages is job security. Thus we would not expect people who work in bureaucracies generally to be primarily motivated by money, and this very much seems to be the case at Goskomstat.

In 1990s Russia, all key actors agreed on the need to shift to the SNA. The state, especially the Gaidar government, clearly supported the move. Societal actors in Russia and international organizations also strongly favored the reform. But the government and international organizations had little ability to force their will on Goskomstat. Although societal actors supported change within the agency, they, too, had limited influence because of Goskomstat's closed organizational structure. Thus state, societal, and international interests favored reform but were not able to mandate it.

If we shift our focus to the employees of Goskomstat, we see that the actors charged with reform had considerable interest in the SNA. But this interest leaves unanswered the question of why Goskomstat employees who had previously supported the MPS became so committed to its Western alternative. Actor-centered theories are a step toward explaining bureaucratic reform, but they present an incomplete story: by focusing on material incentives they cannot tell us what motivated statisticians to embark on such a radical departure from their previous work.

In the early 1990s, many Soviet statisticians still worked at Goskomstat. The leadership changes since perestroika have promoted people from within. And despite significant reductions in staff, most of those who remain have long histories with the organization. There was no wholesale replacement of Soviet-era Goskomstat employees with "reformer" types, in either leadership or rank-and-file positions, and therefore we cannot explain institutional change by citing a change in actors. Nor can we invoke incentives, since the resource constraints on the organization greatly limited the use of material incentives to compel a change in interests in favor of the SNA.

Hence, after examining the roles of politicians, societal actors, and international organizations' relationship with Goskomstat, as well as the interests of Goskomstat employees and material incentives for adoption of the SNA, we are left with the same question we started with. Among those Goskomstat employees who implemented it, where did the interest in moving away from the Soviet system and toward the SNA come from?

6

PROFESSIONALS IN THE SERVICE OF THE STATE

The Organizational Identity of Russian Statisticians

Valentin Kudrov captures the central question of this chapter when he writes, "It seems to me that the present Goskomstat in large measure preserves the frame of mind of the old USSR Central Statistical Administration and, having made some changes, has turned into a kind of mutant that has yet to restructure its work fully" (1993, 130). Social identities affect how actors understand the world, how they view others, what they aspire to do, how they do things, and where their interests lie. To understand why actors at Goskomstat committed so quickly to the SNA after decades of support for the MPS, we thus have to consider the identities at work. Was it socialization into a new identity that led Goskomstat officials to embrace the SNA in the early 1990s?

To answer this question satisfactorily, we have to examine whether any identity change took place. To do that, we must first clarify what we mean by social identity and identity change. The definition and framework for evaluating identities that I use here is based on my previous collaborative work on measuring identities (Abdelal et al. 2006, 2009). There we define a social identity as a social category that varies along two dimensions—content and contestation. Content describes the *meaning* of a collective identity. Contestation refers to the degree of agreement within a group over the content of the shared category. In this chapter I organize my examination of social identities and identity change in the implementation of the SNA according to these types of content and contestation.

Where Identity Is Located

Beyond a general definition and framework for measurement of identity, however, we have to address the question of where identity is located. One issue is of scale: international, national, or organizational. Another is of specificity: Is identity content contained in statements by individuals or groups or must we look for sources of more diffuse social understandings?

Given the implications of a constructivist approach that would suggest interaction between the international and national levels, we have to consider identity at multiple levels to assess its role in implementation of the SNA. In this chapter I explore the content and contestation of identity at the international, national, and organizational levels. Of these, I emphasize the organizational level—identity at Goskomstat—as most important in identifying the interests of actors charged with implementing the SNA.

Regarding specificity, I try to get at shared understandings (agreement and disagreement over content) by considering the statements and actions of individuals. In particular, I am interested in statisticians and economists working on national accounts at Goskomstat, other NSOs, and international organizations. In addition, we have to bring in what we know about social identities more diffusely held in Russia as a whole and at the international level. The idea is that an organizational identity does not exist as an island—it is shaped by the larger identity context that surrounds it—yet organizational identities may not be entirely synonymous with larger national or international identities because contestation is always happening. For this reason, it makes sense to examine the specific content of organizational identities while not forgetting the broader context.

The real, multi-level lives of individuals involved in national accounts illustrate that these levels are not mutually exclusive. Officials at NSOs are also state-level officials and often work on national accounts on behalf of international organizations, complicating a neat delineation of groups. For example, Mikhail Korolev began his career as an academic statistician in the 1960s at the Moscow Institute of Economics and Statistics. From 1972 until 1989 he worked at Goskomstat (and its predecessor organizations), eventually becoming chairman, and following that he headed Statkom CIS. Korolev was as tied into the hierarchy of Soviet statistics as anyone, but at the same time, he was also active in international circles. He was a member of the UN Economic Commission for Europe's Conference of European Statisticians and the UN Statistical Commission beginning in the 1970s and he was elected chairman at UNSC in 1979.

Hence to understand social identities related to the SNA we have to look at many levels. The boundary that separates in-group and out-group members can blur; identities at one level may be in conflict with those of another. As I argue below, this was an important tension for Goskomstat officials, especially in the Soviet period.

Measuring Social Identities and Identity Change

The content of social identities may take the form of four types that do not mutually exclude one another: cognitive models, social purposes, relational comparisons with other social categories, and constitutive norms. In the broadest sense, a cognitive model may be thought of as a *worldview,* or a framework that allows members of a group to make sense of social, political, and economic conditions.[1] The cognitive content of a collective identity describes how group membership is associated with explanations of how the world works and of the group's social reality—its ontology and epistemology. For example, according to Brubaker, Loveman, and Stamatov, "what cognitive perspectives suggest, in short, is that race, ethnicity, and nation are not things in the world but ways of seeing the world. They are ways of understanding and identifying oneself, making sense of one's problems and predicaments, identifying one's interests, and orienting one's action" (2004, 47). Cognitive content, rather than implying an identity-based theory of action (à la norms or Social Identity Theory), implies a theory of identity-based interpretation and development of interests.

The content of a collective identity includes relational comparisons when the identity is defined in terms of references to other collective identities. An identity may be defined by what it is not—that is, by some *other* identities. Relational content of collective identities can include the extent to which one social identity excludes the holding of another (exclusivity); the relative status of an identity compared to others; and the existence or level of hostility presented by other identities. Gender and class identities present obvious illustrations of relational content; even the category of "transgendered" references sex-based differences between men and women, and it is hard to imagine any definition of class that did not include a comparison with other economic groups. However, gender and class identities are not the only types that have relational content: many ethnic and religious identities also include relational comparisons. Such comparisons are usually targeted: Chinese may compare themselves to Japanese or Koreans in terms of defining who they are, but not to Mexicans or Algerians.

1. Some scholars use other terms besides "worldviews." Denzau and North (1994), for example, use "shared mental models."

The content of a collective identity may also be purposive, in the sense that the group attaches specific goals to its identity. This purposive content is analytically similar to the commonsense notion that what groups want depends on who they think they are. Thus identities can lead actors to work toward particular group purposes or goals. For example, most national identity groups share the goal of supporting their nation-state or, in the case of nationalist movements, establishing a nation-state. Similarly, a religious identity might include shared purposes, such as working to increase converts, reduce poverty, or end the death penalty.

Finally, the normative content of a collective identity specifies its constitutive norms—the practices that define that identity and lead other actors to recognize it. For example, for an ethnic group this kind of content could include "rules" on language use, religion, and dress codes. Note that types of identities can be embedded in norms: Armenians are also Christians, and to convert to Islam would make others in the group seriously question one's "Armenian-ness." Also different types of identities may have different norms, but with some overlap: religious identities may have norms that include dietary restrictions and birth or marriage ceremonies but may also include dress codes or language use similar to ethnic group norms. All the rules that determine group membership and putative attributes of the group can be thought of in terms of constitutive norms, which can be informal or formal so long as they set collective behavioral expectations for members of the group. Moreover, these constitutive identity group norms usually derive from a broader set of social norms that emanate from multiple centers of authority. Hence constitutive norms also link particular identity groups to larger historical and social contexts.

The content or collective meaning of identities is neither fixed nor predetermined. Rather, content is the outcome of a process of social contestation within the group. Indeed, much of identity discourse is the working out of the meaning of a particular collective identity through the contestation among its members. Individuals are continuously proposing and shaping the meanings of the groups to which they belong, so content is always contested and contestation is the key to understanding how the meaning or content of identities change over time. Specific interpretations of the meaning of an identity are sometimes widely shared among members of a group and sometimes less widely shared. At a minimum, contestation can be thought of as a matter of degree—the content of collective identities can be more or less contested. Indeed, the further apart the contending interpretations of a collective identity prove to be, the more that identity will be fragmented into conflicting and potentially inconsistent understandings of what the group's purposes or relations should be.

Because the content of an identity is the product of contestation, the very data that a scholar extracts from a group elucidate, in manner and degree, the members' consensus and disagreement over content. By treating contestation as an empirical question, one can take snapshots of the degree of stability or flux in identities as they evolve, as they are challenged, and as they are constructed and reconstructed, hence addressing the theoretical tension between measurement and the fluidity of social identities. To address the question of a change in social identities then, we can examine the changes (or the lack thereof) in the four types of identity content over time.

Cognitive Content: Marxism and Evaluations of Soviet Statistics

People who share an identity also share specific interpretations or understandings of the world, while people outside the identity group probably do not share those interpretations—this is what is meant by the cognitive content of identity. In the case of Goskomstat, two aspects of cognitive content are especially noteworthy. First, Goskomstat statisticians shared a Marxist understanding of the relationship between the structure of the economy and other political institutions, including statistical systems. Second, Goskomstat statisticians shared a generally positive view of Soviet statistics. If we look outside of Goskomstat, we see that Western economists shared neither a Marxist understanding of the role of the economy in determining statistical institutions nor a positive assessment of Soviet statistics; on the contrary, the Western perspective is decidedly negative. At the international level, among the community of national statisticians, Marxism is not a shared part of the identity content, but the view of Soviet statistics is neutral, suggesting some solidarity with Soviet statisticians. An examination of views of Marxism at Goskomstat and views of Soviet statistics over time reveals relatively little change in this type of identity content.

Marxism

Marxism influenced the worldviews or cognitive schema of Soviet citizens as well as national statisticians at Goskomstat. Marxist discourse and categories of analysis are evident throughout Goskomstat publications and discussions of Soviet and CMEA statistics. A review of *Vestnik statistiki* shows that Marxist discourse permeated the journal during the Soviet period.

A visible change in Goskomstat publications after the end of the USSR was the lack of explicit Marxist-Leninist and communist discourse. An examination of statistical yearbooks as well as *Vestnik statistiki* from the 1960s to the present demonstrates a fundamental change in categorization as well as content from the discourse of Marxism-Leninism to one of international statistical methodological norms. For example, up until 1988 there were sections of *Vestnik statistiki* devoted to the party conferences and congresses and subsections such as, "In Aid to the Agitator and Propagandist," which after 1994 was retitled, "Statistics: Facts, Estimates, Forecasts." Less dramatic was the shift from categories like "Social-Economic Analysis" to "Macroeconomic Analysis," a more common term in international circles.

This discursive change is also evident in the laws governing statistics. The language of the 1987 Central Committee resolution is quite different from the 1992 Program for Statistical Reform and the 1993 Program on the Shift to a System of National Accounts. These changes have made Goskomstat publications much more similar in form, as well as content, to their Western counterparts.

While some of this attention to Marxism was certainly externally imposed, its pervasiveness at Goskomstat and throughout Soviet society is still remarkable and suggests at least some level of authenticity. Moreover, as the link between the economy and statistics at Goskomstat suggests—e.g., the common recitation that statistics is a mirror of the economy—the move away from explicit Marxist terminology does not necessarily suggest a move away from Marxist understandings of statistics. I consider evidence on this point in more detail in the next chapter, but it is worth highlighting here the more generalized influence of Marxism on Goskomstat identity.

A final example of the legacy of Marxism at the organization comes from an article by Pavel Guzhvin (1992a), which was meant to explain the new direction of Russian statistics toward the SNA. Guzhvin wrote that Goskomstat had to move closer to international standards, but he noted that the shift would not be as easy as it sounded, thanks to the rigid habits among the staff at Goskomstat (1992a, 3). He stated that although Marx's original model of calculating national income had been useful to central planning, it no longer fit the current market economy (1992a, 4). For this reason, he declared that it was time to adopt a new theoretical model, the SNA, and to bid adieu to the MPS. Guzhvin wrote that Goskomstat statistics were still "very much within the Marxist scheme" (1992a, 4), and that Goskomstat specialists would have to give up the Marxist tradition in which they had been trained, which would be psychologically difficult. As he put it, "the task of our employees in the reorientation of their brains truly is not easy" and "we have a difficult task of retraining our statisticians to stop thinking in terms of Marx and start thinking in terms of the SNA" (1992a, 5). As it turned out, the move to the SNA at Goskomstat, although a break with the past, was not so psychologically difficult because it did not entail a renunciation of the past.

Goskomstat's Evaluations of the MPS and Soviet Statistics

Another way in which identity seems to have affected the understandings of Russian/Soviet statisticians is in their positive evaluations of the quality and contributions of Soviet statistics.[2] In this section, I provide evidence for continuity in the view of Soviet statisticians toward the MPS over time. To the extent that the interpretation of Soviet statistics is a part of cognitive content of Goskomstat identity, this suggests a continuity in Goskomstat identity as well.

The few early Soviet works that mention national accounts at all—Moskvin's articles in *Vestnik statistiki* (1949, 1950) offer one example—discuss the concepts of "social product" or "national income" and their foundations in Marxism. They take a critical stance toward capitalist methodology but emphasize the spectacular growth of the USSR compared to Western countries. Moskvin boasts that industrial production in the USSR since 1930 had multiplied by nine times, whereas the rate in "capitalist Europe" was flat (1949, 17).[3] Other Soviet sources cited the figure of 650 percent growth in industrial output from 1928 to 1940, but these figures were not accepted in the West.[4] Discussion of these very high growth rates, in conjunction with the emergence of the SNA after WWII, was the catalyst for debates regarding the Soviet statistical system itself. It also signaled a growing divide between Western and Soviet economists and statisticians in their interpretations of the economy and the best way to evaluate it.

An article by A. Yugow, which grew out of a 1947 symposium on the Soviet economy organized by Seymour Harris, sums up many of the advantages of the Soviet statistical system:

> Accounting of all economic phenomena on a national scale and the possibility of statistically following all economic phenomena in their complete economic cycle give Soviet statistics such great advantages in comparison with the statistics of other countries that the forms, methods, and results of the work of the statistical organs of the U.S.S.R. are highly instructive to all who work in the field of the theory and practice of economic statistics, even in cases when these data are not entirely exact and commensurable in particulars. The gathering of primary

2. I use "Russian" here in the sense of "citizen of Russia" (*rossiiskii*) rather than ethnic Russian (*russkii*).

3. The citations in the article are limited to Marx, Lenin, Stalin, and Sobol, whose work was used in the development of the MPS.

4. For an early assessment of national income in Russia and the USSR from 1913 to 1934, see Clark 1939.

> materials, the formulation of problems, and the effect of the plan upon economic factors in the U.S.S.R. provide an almost "laboratory" picture; in any case, they reflect the existing facts far more clearly and fully than in other countries, where the statistical study of national problems and those of individual branches is not only greatly complicated, in view of the technical incompleteness of the data, but is also deliberately distorted because of private interests, trade secrets, competition, etc. (Yugow 1947)

Yugow's characterization of Soviet statistics lays out several claims about the superiority of Soviet statistics that would be echoed repeatedly by others: that Soviet statistics present a more comprehensive, methodologically more precise, and less biased representation of the economy than those of Western countries. Although one might think that Yugow's view is a relic of the communist past, he raises points not very different from later articles. The celebratory tone remains even in current analyses of Soviet statistics at Goskomstat.

A review of *Vestnik statistiki* from the 1960s to the present shows that nearly every article is positive on Soviet and CMEA statistics.[5] In articles that discuss the UN, authors go out of their way to note that other countries similarly recognize the value of Soviet statistics (VS 1968, 1971, 1979). In comparisons of the MPS and SNA, some authors suggest not only the great achievements and superiority of Soviet and CMEA statistics (Tsyrlin 1970; Driuchin 1977; Leshchev and Antsiferova 1978; Volodarskii 1978; Tsyrlin 1981; Leshchev 1985), but the improvement of the SNA thanks to Soviet statistics (Simchera 1976). Similarly, some articles highlight the way that Soviet and CMEA statisticians have aided the development of statistics in other countries (Lukach and Nesterov 1969; Kudinov 1979; Konevskii 1981, 1987).

Contestation

Despite examples of strong views, within the Western and Soviet discourse there was also some contestation. Soviet statisticians from the 1960s on experienced a growing sense of doubt about the Soviet economic system. For some this translated into a criticism of the statistical system. Valentin Kudrov (2004) described in an interview that he first questioned Soviet statistics in the late 1950–60s because the overall growth and industrial production figures were so many times higher than for the United States. It took him some time, however, to conclude

5. There are too many to cite here, but on the CMEA there were approximately forty-nine articles in 1968–91.

that Soviet statistics were seriously flawed. He read some of Abram Bergson's work in 1961 and that was a start, but he said, "In the end, I fully realized that we were lying when I worked in Geneva [1986–90]. They even asked me there directly: 'Why are you lying?' So I did not realize it until rather late."

Similarly, Vladimir Sokolin (2004) recounted his experience with reading foreign publications, such as the famous Samuelson economic textbook (Samuelson 1947) and beginning to doubt the superiority of the Soviet economic system. He quickly added that even though he had doubts about the Soviet economic system, he did not doubt the quality of statisticians' work.

There is some evidence of contestation in *Vestnik statistiki* as well. For example, in the 1980s the view was still that Soviet statistics were superior, but there was also recognition of some achievements in statistics in other countries (Kudinov 1982; Konevskii 1983). Kudinov wrote that some things could even be borrowed from capitalist statistics, but only after "critical evaluation" (1982, 49).

Nevertheless, in the Soviet period there is little doubt that on the whole, Westerners and Soviets disagreed about the quality of Soviet statistics. A critical question is whether this difference in interpretations of the value and contributions of Soviet statistics was based on identity differences. Did the Soviets really believe in the quality of the MPS and Soviet statistics? Given what we know about political control in the USSR, it is reasonable to question whether these positive statements reflect that control rather than indicate the cognitive content of a shared identity among Soviet statisticians.

We can evaluate the authenticity of these views, however, by looking at another type of evidence: how officials at Goskomstat evaluated Soviet statistics in the absence of political control, during perestroika and later. If the writings of Goskomstat officials and Soviet analysts were insincere due to political control, one would expect the analysis of the Soviet system to change following political liberalization in the late 1980s. By and large, that did not happen. To this day Goskomstat officials retain a positive evaluation of the MPS and Soviet statistics.

Post-1991 Views of the MPS and Soviet Statistics

A key indicator of Goskomstat's view of its own past and the quality of the MPS and Soviet statistics is its publication in 1996 of an organizational history, titled *Russian State Statistics, 1802–1996* (Goskomstat Russia 1996b).[6] This book, which is jointly written in Russian and English, was published in the midst of completing the first phase of transition to the SNA—a seeming renunciation

6. This book was prominently displayed on Goskomstat's website until 2009.

of the Soviet statistical system. Yet it is essentially a list of Russian and Soviet achievements in statistics, with hardly a critical word for the Soviet past.

The agency praised the first national accounts work done in the USSR for 1923–24, published by P. I. Popov (1926). They also reprinted part of the preface where Popov noted the unique achievements of the USSR in national accounts: "neither in the statistical nor the economic literature, be it Russian or West European, were there any examples of such work. In doing this work we had to solve independently not only some technical problems of conducting research but also the methodological premises" (Goskomstat Russia 1996b, 63).[7] In reviewing the achievements of Russian and Soviet statistics, the editors bypassed any criticism of the Stalin period and noted, "Statistical science in the 1920s–30s inherited the traditions of Russian statistics and essentially enriched the theory of statistics" (Goskomstat Russia 1996b, 69).

Had the 1996 book been published before perestroika, it might have been an unremarkable addition to the hundreds of self-congratulatory articles in the Goskomstat publication record. But it appeared right at the time that Goskomstat was finishing the first stage of implementation of the SNA, and hence provides important window into the way that Goskomstat statisticians managed their understanding of the relationship between the SNA and the MPS. It suggests that they are able to both embrace the implementation of the SNA and celebrate the Soviet statistical system. In addition, the 1996 book and the record in *Vestnik statistiki,* especially post-perestroika, provide evidence that Goskomstat employees were not secretly anti-Soviet all along. If that had been the case, the kind of vehement burst of anti-Soviet criticism that arose in newspapers and journals during perestroika should have been more prevalent in post-Soviet Goskomstat publications. If the pro-Soviet sentiment had been just a function of political control, there should have been more criticism of the Soviet period after Goskomstat was freed from Soviet political influence, especially in 1991–98, the years with the greatest level of political freedom.

Another example of the positive view of the Soviet past is a recent analytical book about Goskomstat edited by Vladimir Sokolin and five vice-chairmen (Goskomstat Russia 2004). This book celebrates the contributions of Soviet statistics with only limited references to past problems. They write: "Statistics as a science and as a practical activity received a big boost in the USSR. . . . Despite certain ideological dogmas and restrictions, many positive results were achieved: for example, for the first time in human civilization a unified system of economic

7. The book does not mention that Popov's work was subsequently ignored for decades at TsSU.

accounting was constructed" (Goskomstat Russia 2004, 16). The last sentence refers to Popov's 1926 work on national accounts.

Goskomstat officials also have much praise for the MPS. They frequently equate the MPS with the SNA as an equivalent system in terms of status, technical achievement, and quality of data produced. This view of the two systems drew support from the International Comparison Program in the 1970s and 1980s, which essentially gave parallel treatment to the SNA and the MPS (UN Statistical Office 1977; Ivanov and Ryzhov 1978; Ivanov 1987). Many Soviet statisticians believed that their system was simply an alternative to the SNA and, although based on differences in "fundamental concepts and definitions," it nevertheless shared with the SNA many commonalities. Ivanov wrote in 1987 that the "SNA and MPS belong to the same family of systems of macro economic aggregates designed to ensure a coherent description of the economic process, of the interrelationships among various economic magnitudes" (1987, 2). Similarly, Leonid Nesterov has argued that some aspects of the SNA were based on MPS principles and that national wealth estimates were made throughout the Soviet period (1997, 1472).[8]

Interviews conducted in 2003–4, well after the move to the SNA, reveal the same approach to the MPS and the SNA. For example, one official noted that the MPS and the SNA are "two different principles for assessing macroeconomic development" (GKS50 2004). Another made it clear that s/he thought that other countries respected the MPS, and that the transition to the SNA did not entail the dismantling of the Soviet statistical system. S/he said: "Nobody looked down on us. We did not have to destroy significant parts of our statistical system" (GKS49 2004). When asked how the two systems compare, several officials declined to judge, for example, one said, "Indicators were good both then and now" (GKS29 2003). Even Valentin Kudrov (2004) said, "In general, the new system is not better or worse—it is just completely different." Irina Masakova (2004), who headed national accounts at Goskomstat since 1997, said, "My whole professional background had to do with macroeconomic statistics; the MPS is similar to the SNA."

Western Evaluations of Soviet Statistics

In contrast to Goskomstat statisticians, Western economists did not hold positive views of Soviet statistics. At the 1947 symposium where Yugow presented his view of Soviet statistics a divergence of views between Western economists

8. In particular, he cites the UN guidelines for tangible assets and balance sheets (UN Statistical Commission 1977, 1979).

and Soviet economists on the quality of Soviet statistics was already developing. The symposium's other authors cast doubt on Soviet claims regarding growth in income and productivity (Clark 1947), industrial output (Gerschenkron 1947), total output (Baran 1947), and wages (Bergson 1947). Abram Bergson clarified the critique of Soviet statistics in a way that would resonate in scholarly work for the next forty-five years: "Not only does the Soviet government make a practice of withholding information about its economy; too often it seems not to be especially concerned with making clear the precise meaning of the information it does release" (1947, 234).

As the Cold War heated up, Westerners increasingly expressed outright distrust of Soviet statistics. In a 1953 symposium on "Reliability and Usability of Soviet Statistics" the criticism of Soviet statistics went far beyond complaints of outdated price indices and data limitations to a more comprehensive critique of the Soviet statistical system itself (Rice 1953).[9] By 1953 the objections to Soviet statistics had shifted to a critique of the system's basic methodological and technological deficiencies. Harry Schwartz (1953) evaluated the statistical system as a whole and concluded:

> The evidence suggests that on the whole Soviet statistical techniques are less advanced than those in the western world and that modern developments in the fields of sampling theory, correlation analysis, and the like are used only slightly or not at all. Certainly little interest in such matters is evidenced in Soviet statistical textbooks and in the journal of the Central Statistical Administration. That this should be so, if it is so, is surprising in view of the great contributions made in the past by Russians in the field of probability and statistical theory. It can only be explained on the basis of the dead hand that totalitarian ideology and Stalin worship impose upon Soviet statisticians as they do upon creative work in many other fields.

As the twentieth century progressed, the view that statistics and national accounts in the Soviet Union had fallen victim to political ideology became more and more widespread, especially among U.S. academics and policy analysts. At the same time, accounts in the USSR continued to view the MPS and Soviet statistics in positive terms, even citing the contribution of Soviet statistics to the field more generally.

---

9. This symposium grew out of a panel at the meeting of the American Statistical Association and was published in *The American Statistician*. Participants included Abram Bergson, Alexander Gerschenkron, Frank Lorimer, Harry Schwartz, and Lazar Volin.

The International View of the MPS and Soviet Statistics

The people working on the development of national accounts in international organizations had an arguably different relationship to Soviet statisticians from other academic analysts in the West. Whereas Abram Bergson and others associated with the Central Intelligence Agency were unquestionably not part of the identity group that Goskomstat officials thought they belonged to, international statisticians from the UN Statistical Office had a different relationship to their Soviet counterparts. If we examine their views on Soviet statistics, we see a middle ground between the sharp criticisms of Western academics, on one hand, and unbridled positive Soviet assessments, on the other. Although UN statisticians do not ignore the problems of Soviet statistics, their criticism is noticeably muted.

Given that the Cold War and considerations of diplomacy might have hindered analysts' ability to speak freely, I consider some accounts of Soviet statistics produced after the end of the Cold War by statisticians writing as private citizens rather than as representatives of their respective international organizations.

In explaining the UNSO's early choice of Richard Stone's version of the SNA rather than the MPS, Michael Ward wrote,

> In the final analysis, despite a respectful acknowledgement in the direction of socialist statistical systems and some limited technical recognition of the formal structure of the system of material balances [MPS] (and the "normal" standardized pricing procedures that went along with it for quantity audit and accounting purposes), UNSO embraced the system of trade and production statistics adopted by the developed Western industrial nations. (2004, 44)

This statement of the UNSO's views on the MPS stands in marked contrast to those of the academic participants in Harris's 1947 symposia.

Another interesting view on the value of the MPS versus the SNA comes from János Árvay. We might expect Árvay, as a Hungarian, to express some negativity toward the MPS given its strong connection to the USSR and the Soviet domination of the CMEA states. In an article on the rise and fall of the MPS, however, Árvay repeatedly cited the merit of comparing it with the SNA, saying, "the building of bridges between the two systems had invaluably great importance!" (1994, 233; see also 218). He noted how at the time the comparison projects were well received and promoted the development of statistics as well as détente. But he also expresses his disappointment that things have changed: "There is a threat of belittling the role of the MPS and the work done to link the SNA and MPS in the previous decades and the exaggeration of the SNA in the present time and in the near future" (1994, 233).

Several important books on the history of national accounts have been written by international participants in the development of the SNA and the MPS. In virtually all of them the discussion of problems with the MPS and CMEA statistics is marked by neutrality, or at most a detached puzzlement as to the reasons for inconsistencies and gaps. One finds only a hint that anything was seriously wrong with Soviet statistics and none of the negative judgment so prevalent in the work of other Western academics (Bergson 1953b; Noren 1994; Schroeder 1995). For example, in describing Soviet statistics in the 1920s–50s, Vanoli called the situation regarding national income statistics "confused" (2005, 20). He praised the good work of Popov (1926) for 1923/24, then said, "from the 1930s on, the resulting official series will linger for at least twenty years within a limited scope and refer to some aggregates of output valued at 1926–27 constant prices." That was it—no further criticism or judgment, despite the fact that the use of outdated 1926–27 price indices was a major criticism of Soviet statistics among Western academics and policy analysts.

Árvay's discussion of the development of national accounts in the USSR takes a similar tone. Árvay is fairly positive toward official Soviet statistics up to the mid-1930s, but he does note that from the mid-1930s to the end of the 1950s, "the scope of macroeconomic data was drastically restricted" (1994, 220). As a criticism, this seems rather mild in comparison to other accounts.

In an article detailing changes in Central and Eastern European national accounts in the early 1990s, Derek Blades and Ann Harrison two core members of the Expert Group who worked on the development of the 1993 SNA, addressed the issue of "charges of deliberate misrepresentation" in CMEA statistics. They write, "While instances of this have been noted, Western suspicion on CEEC's [Central and East European countries'] statistics were largely based on unfamiliarity and incomprehension" (1992, 102). This is a quite different assessment of Soviet and East European statistics from the one found in the West and is somewhat closer to that among Soviet statisticians.

Assessing Change in the Cognitive Content of Goskomstat Identity

The cognitive content of identity affects the way that groups interpret information and posits that a shared identity will result in a shared understanding among group members. Other groups having different identities may interpret information differently. If we review how three groups—Western academics and policy analysts, Soviet or Goskomstat officials, and national accounts statisticians in international organizations—evaluated Soviet statistics, we see that there were differences, with the Western academics being very negative, Goskomstat statisticians being positive, and the people from international organizations neutral or even positive; individuals in this last group to some degree share an identity with Goskomstat officials as part of the community working on national accounts.

There could be a variety of reasons for these different understandings, but in terms of explaining the implementation of the SNA, the critical fact is that despite a change in explicit Marxist rhetoric, these identity-based interpretations—cognitive content—have remained relatively stable, even in the face of Russia's move away from the Soviet system in the early 1990s. The positive assessment of Soviet statistics in the post-Soviet period reflects continuity in identity content over time, suggesting internal dissatisfaction with the past system is not likely to have been a source for the decision to implement the SNA.

Relational Comparisons: Statisticians as an Identity Group

In examining the relational content of identity at Goskomstat, we are interested in how Goskomstat statisticians compared themselves to other statisticians and to what extent these comparisons changed over time. We take the same approach to international actors. In examining these relational comparisons we see that the boundary between Goskomstat and the community of statisticians working on national accounts is quite fluid.

Today there are very close ties between officials at Goskomstat and other international statistical organizations. This is evident even from a cursory glance at Goskomstat's website, which has numerous links to international organizations and other NSOs, but it is also evident in Goskomstat's publications, which extensively cite works by statisticians abroad. Although the level of interaction with international organizations has definitely increased since perestroika, it is worth considering whether or how Goskomstat's identity in relation to other groups has changed and what the continuities are.

If we examine Goskomstat publications going back to the Soviet period, before the 1968 SNA or the formalization of the MPS, we discover serious engagement with the work of foreign statisticians working on national accounts (Kudrov 1960; Rozovskii 1962; Zagladina 1963; Maslov 1965). Despite some predictable Marxist-inspired criticism—in discussing U.S. national accounts, Kudrov reacts to a Department of Commerce definition by saying, "this definition is a vivid manifestation of the vulgar bourgeois concept of national income, resting on three notorious whales: utility theory, the theory of factors of production, and

Smith dogma" (1960, 32)[10]—there is also evidence of internal debate. In the same 1960 Kudrov article the footnotes show contradicting views among the Soviet statisticians on the best methods for recalculating national income, including a note from the editors disagreeing with Kudrov.

Similarly, Zagladina's 1963 article is a detailed discussion of U.S. publications on national income and GNP compared with "aggregate social product." Here again are the obligatory references to the "bourgeois" essence of the American method and the problematic inclusion of services in GNP, but the tone of the article is not as dismissive of American statistical science as it could have been; rather she presents a debate between American statisticians and Soviet colleagues, both of whom were invited to improve on the author's ideas.

In a 1965 article by Maslov the editors of *Vestnik statistiki* wrote a preface explaining the attention given to the SNA in the journal. They first noted that the SNA "represents a significant phenomenon in the development of contemporary statistics of capitalist countries" and that "the statistical bodies of the United Nations have in recent years paid great attention to that system" (Maslov 1965, 44). For these reasons they said that the journal would address the SNA starting with the Maslov article and that in response to readers' interest in the subject, the journal would return to the topic in future, which they did.

If one counts all articles on statistics in foreign countries and international organizations, from 1968 to 1991 there were thirteen articles per year on average, including book reviews, extended methodological discussions, and short articles. In terms of relational comparisons these articles are of three types: comparisons between the East and the West (or socialist versus capitalist statistics), which primarily take the form of comparisons of the SNA and MPS at the UN or other international venues; comparisons among the CMEA states, which primarily emphasize cooperation and mutual success; and analysis of statistics of other regions (namely, Africa, Europe, Latin America, Asia, and the world) and individual countries (for example, Algeria, Austria, China, Cuba, Finland, Japan, Mongolia, Uganda, the United Kingdom, United States, and Vietnam) with the idea that these cases can offer instructive comparisons with the Soviet or CMEA experience.

The dominant type of engagement with the larger international community of national statisticians concerned the comparisons between the East and the West at the UN. The journal reported on the UN Statistical Commission itself (Lukach and Nesterov 1969), its meetings, and especially the discussion of the SNA versus

10. This is a widely used Russian idiom, a reference to the folk belief that the world is floating on the backs of many fish but primarily three whales. Hence three whales are the three main pillars on which something rests.

the MPS at those meetings (VS 1968, 1971, 1979; Konevskii 1981, 1983, 1987; Shevchenko 1989). From the late 1960s on, many articles that described the SNA did so in technical rather than polemical terms, with the aim of explaining it rather than critiquing it (Lukach and Nesterov 1969; Ivanov and Riabushkin 1971).

There was also much attention to the recognition of Soviet statistics and the MPS by the West (VS 1968). One article noted how frequently the USSR appeared in UN yearbooks over time (Lukach and Nesterov 1969), showing it to be increasing, implying that the importance of the Soviet statistics in the world was also increasing. Another article discussed M. A. Korolev's appointment as chair of the UN Statistical Commission in 1979, which the article noted was a sign of the high level of international prestige accorded to Soviet statistics and statisticians (VS 1979).[11] A third article noted that an international seminar on "Statistical Services Ten Years From Now," held in Washington in March 1977, had two keynote lectures, from a Briton (representing the West) and a Russian (representing the East) owing to the equal status of both systems (Driuchin 1977). This idea of equal status for the MPS and the SNA was repeated over and over in *Vestnik statistiki.* Articles claimed that the two systems were equal and that the UN had recognized this fact since 1971 (Lukin 1977, 74; Leshchev and Antsiferova 1978; Konevskii 1981).

In conjunction with the first formal UN comparison project (UN Statistical Office 1977; Ivanov and Ryzhov 1978; Ivanov 1987), there was increasing emphasis on the value of comparisons and what might be learned from that experience (VS 1971; Ivanov 1972). After the UN published its methodology for comparing the SNA and the MPS in 1977, many more articles discussed comparisons between the systems: (Lukin 1977; VS 1979; Ivanov and Ryzhkov 1981; Konevskii 1981; Tsyrlin 1981; Konevskii 1982; Antsiferova 1983; Konevskii 1983; Leshchev 1983; Antsiferova and Zarubin 1984; Konevskii 1987; Zarubin and Sergeev 1990). One article even noted that the 1975 Helsinki Accords had recognized the importance of statistical comparisons (Ivanov and Ryzhkov 1981).

By the 1980s one could find discussions of the SNA that were not ideological at all but focused on the technical details of comparisons between the SNA and the MPS (Ivanov and Ryzhkov 1983). Although there were some canned statements about Marxist-Leninist statistical theory being the only truly scientific one, some authors nevertheless acknowledged respect for the considerable achievements of Western statisticians (Nesterov 1990). A deputy head of Goskomstat wrote of the positive and valuable experience of Western economists and statisticians (Zarubin and Sergeev 1990).

11. Korolev would later head TsSU and Goskomstat in 1985–89.

In addition to the relationship between statisticians from communist and capitalist states, there was also engagement with the CMEA. A series of articles noted the close cooperation and shared achievements of the CMEA (Stanev 1968; Kuzin'skii 1979; Antsiferova 1983; Leshchev 1983). Meetings of the CMEA Standing Commission on Statistics were also detailed (Leshchev 1974, 1977; Lukin 1977; Leshchev and Antsiferova 1978; Kudinov 1979; Leshchev 1985). Moreover, there were extended discussions of statistics in CMEA states: Bulgaria (Stanev 1968), Poland (Kavalets 1969), and East Germany (Donda 1970).

Reviews of Western and UN publications kept *Vestnik statistiki* readers up to date on what was happening internationally in regard to statistics and national accounts (Kudrov 1970; Simchera 1970; Tsyrlin 1970; Lukin 1980; Nesterov 1988). In one book review, Kudrov (1970) began by noting that in recent years several works on the SNA had been translated into or written in Russian, and that Soviet scholars therefore were generally familiar with the system. Ivanov wrote that the differences between the systems were well described in the literature (Ivanov and Ryzhkov 1981).

A fundamental fact that emerges from this analysis is that Goskomstat did not learn about the SNA in the late 1980s. The evidence is overwhelming that the SNA was discussed in the USSR while the 1993 SNA was being developed in the 1960s–80s.

The delineation of the sources of knowledge about the SNA, however, was somewhat vague. Clearly Goskomstat personnel were reading Western and UN sources, but these Soviet publications and their authors were themselves a source for other Russian statisticians' knowledge. For example, Andrei Kosarev (2004), who headed national accounts at Goskomstat in the early 1990s, said in an interview that his knowledge of the SNA came primarily from the Soviet economists Youri Ivanov and Boris Isaev.[12] In evaluating relational comparisons by Goskomstat officials, we see that even during the Soviet period, when actual contact with foreign statisticians was quite limited, Goskomstat personnel knew of their foreign colleagues' work and passed it on to others who enjoyed less access to outside sources.

A more explicit statement of mutual learning between "East" and "West" comes from Blades and Harrison. In their article on national accounts in Central and Eastern Europe, although their overall emphasis was on what Western statisticians could do for "their colleagues" in the East, they argued:

> it is well to remember that the West has lessons to learn from the East. The West accuses the East of deliberate falsification of statistics, but the

12. Ivanov had worked at the UN for eleven years on developing the SNA while simultaneously working in Goskomstat's department of national accounts.

> West has problems that may be equally serious—the errors arising from disinterest on the part of respondents; too often they give only partial replies, inaccurate ones or none at all. The East is very conscious of the errors inherent in sampling and non-response—problems of which their Western counter parts are theoretically aware, but which they often over look in practice because of persistent exposure. (1992, 106)

They also cite examples of statistics on the informal economy and social statistics as areas where the West can learn from the East.

In an interesting take on the conflict between supporting government policy and professional statistical standards, Blades and Harrison write, "staff in some CEEC offices have explained that they sometimes refused to publish data or stopped working in areas where they feared that professional standards were no longer being maintained" (1992, 102). Others might have just said that NSOs in the East lacked a sense of professionalism, but Blades and Harrison suggest the opposite—that they were professionals and occasionally had to refrain from certain kinds of work if they could not uphold their professional standards. In this way Blades and Harrison imply a shared sense of professionalism between statisticians in the East and the West.

National Accounts: The "Least Prestigious Profession on Earth"

One type of relational comparison that is consistent for international organizations and NSOs is the portrayal of statisticians involved with national accounts as hardworking and underappreciated, suggesting a level of solidarity in suffering vis-à-vis other occupations, especially economists who are better paid and doing more prestigious work. Anne Harrison summarizes this point of view: in discussing the importance of the 1993 SNA at the 1991 meeting of the UN Statistical Commission, she said, "the Director of the United Nations Statistical Office said that national accounts was too important to be left to the national accountants" (1994, 188).[13] Even as a joke, that is an extraordinary public statement by the head of the world's leading body on national accounts.

In an article detailing the development of the 1993 SNA, Harrison takes time to explain the personal dedication of statisticians working on national accounts. She notes that some of the expert group meetings lasted ten days, followed or preceded other meetings, and required a lot of preparation time. Everyone working

13. The UN Statistical Office was renamed the UN Statistical Division after 1989.

on the SNA revision had other full time jobs.[14] Nevertheless, Harrison says, "the inputs provided by these people came from voluntary unpaid overtime." For that reason, she asks people who think the revision process took too long to "pause to consider the degree of effort this voluntary contribution represents and note the personal contribution and dedication of most of those individuals involved, which in many cases was carried through changes of positions, and in some cases organizations, during the revision process but with a continued commitment to the completion of the task at hand" (1994, 187).

Harrison goes on to address the difficultly in convincing people to work on national accounts:

> One of the problems of producing good national accounts is that one needs staff to work on the accounts who are meticulous in their attention to detail, who are content to assemble a lot of detail that piece by piece is not particularly interesting, but together gives a comprehensive view of the economy, and generally be content to work in an area where public appreciation and esteem is rather low-profile. (1994, 189)

She argues that a more positive message about the SNA needed to reach the wider statistical community. By convincing people that the SNA had been revised thoroughly and that appropriate measures were being taken to address the remaining pressing demands, work on national accounts might become more attractive. New graduates might become convinced that "working in a statistical office could be as interesting, challenging, and rewarding as the presently more high profile activity of economic forecasting and policy analysis" (Harrison 1994, 190).

This same discourse of national statistics as low prestige and hard work was echoed in my interviews with Goskomstat personnel. In discussing the transformation of Goskomstat's work since perestroika, many officials attributed successful reform to the efforts of Goskomstat employees, and in these remarks they frequently used the terms "enthusiasm," "devotion to work" (*predannost' delu*), and "professionalism." Irina Masakova (2004) explained the agency's success: "The enthusiasm of our specialists working here and their devotion to work—it is on this basis that we have achieved the level we are at today in statistics. Another important factor is the professionalism of our specialists." Andrei Kosarev (2004) said, "From my personal experience in statistics, I can say that my staff worked not because of wages but because they were used to it, interested in it, and enthusiastic about it." Another interviewee attributed the agency's achievements

14. Except Peter Hill, who had two years of leave from the OECD (1988 and 1991/92) to write up the Blue Book.

to "the devotion to work by people working in statistics as well as the general line of Goskomstat" (GKS44 2004). In explaining how the sense of professionalism and international ties were helpful to Goskomstat's work on implementing the SNA, one person noted: "Theoretically, it was easier for us statisticians to enter the international system because we speak the same professional language as statisticians from other countries. This facilitated our transition and spared us the psychological stress of the transition" (GKS50 2004).

Assessing Change in the Relational Content of Identity at Goskomstat

Goskomstat personnel had a long history of engagement with statisticians in other countries, in print if not in person. With the end of the USSR, face-to-face meetings multiplied, but the sense of community among statisticians was not fundamentally transformed. Statisticians in Russia and abroad shared a sense that they worked hard and that their work was underappreciated by others, but the relational content of identity at Goskomstat does not seem to have undergone a major change from the Soviet to the post-Soviet period.

Shared Purposes: The Goals of National Accounting

Another type of identity content is shared purposes—the goals toward which members of an identity group strive. These goals can be multiple and at times conflicting, and members of a group can disagree about them or how to prioritize them. At the international level, however, the goals of national accounting and statistics are now fairly well established. The UNSO for much of its existence worked to make national statistics comparable and to establish international standards based on scientific principles, and it largely achieved these goals.[15] According to Michael Ward, one of the UNSO's most important achievements was "the establishment and universal acceptance of standard international classifications, common statistical definitions, and recognized data frameworks around the world" (2004, 53). One can find similar goals listed as objectives of many international organizations that work with statistics, including the OECD, IMF, Eurostat, and the Conference of European Statisticians (CES).[16]

15. On other issues of interest to the UNSO, see Seltzer 1995, cited in Ward 2004, 46.

16. See www.unece.org/stats/archive/00.e.htm. See also Franchet 1992 for the case for further standardization by the CES.

In line with such goals, the UN Statistical Commission published a report called the "Fundamental Principles of Official Statistics," which lists the "ten commandments" for the work of NSOs (UN Statistical Commission 1994). This document grew out of a 1992 UN Economic Commission for Europe resolution that had been adopted by numerous other organizations. The principles promote:

1. relevance, impartiality, and equal access of data;
2. professional standards based on scientific principles and ethics;
3. accountability and transparency in methodology;
4. prevention of the misuse of data;
5. use of a variety of sources of official statistics;
6. confidentiality;
7. law-based statistical practices;
8. coordination of all national statistics;
9. use of international standards; and
10. international cooperation.

The CMEA states accepted a version of these ten commandments in conjunction with the implementation of the SNA (Blades and Harrison 1992, 105). Numerous other NSOs and international organizations endorse them, and the UN has begun to assess the implementation of these principles for all member states (UN Statistical Commission 2004a).

While these shared goals seem uncontroversial, they presume a level of democratic governance and accountability, as well as organizational autonomy and capacity for NSOs. Not all states or NSOs follow every principle, and most dictatorships would have little interest in them. Even within Europe their application has been uneven. At the fortieth anniversary meeting of the CES in 1992, Blades and Harrison acknowledged that not all states met the shared standards and emphasized that not only countries in Central and Eastern Europe fell short (1992, 105). Nevertheless, these standards are shared more fully than ever before.

Goals of National Statistics in the USSR and Russia: Science and Professionalism versus the State

Russia accepts all ten fundamental principles as shared goals with the international national statistics community, even if it has not fully implemented them. The paragraph on the Goskomstat website that describes the objectives of the organization essentially reproduces the first principle in the UN document.[17] But this was not always the case.

---

17. See www.gks.ru/wps/portal/english and http://unstats.un.org/unsd/methods/statorg/FP-English.htm.

Many of the ten principles are at odds with an authoritarian regime and a politically controlled organization, as was the case with the USSR and Goskomstat. Yet Soviet statistics were not simply fabrications or political propaganda. Goskomstat had conflicting goals: it served the state, most notably in monitoring central plan fulfillment; at the same time, its employees respected statistics as a profession and criticized their Western colleagues for not being "scientific" enough.

The politicization of Goskomstat dates to the beginning of the USSR. Lenin in 1922 said, "The Central Statistical Administration should not be 'academic' or 'independent'...but an organ of socialist construction" (Kotz and Seneta 1990, 87). The Cheka, the internal security force of the new Soviet state, expressed this view even more bluntly: "Our work should concentrate on the information apparatus, for only when the Cheka is sufficiently informed and has precise data elucidating organizations and their individual members will it be able...to take timely and necessary measures for liquidating groups as well as the individual who is harmful and dangerous" (Cheka circulars, 1920–21, as cited in Holquist 1997, 415).[18] A half-century of Soviet rule did not alter such views: in an article commemorating the sixtieth anniversary of Soviet statistics, L. Volodarskii (1978), the head of TsSU, used a quotation from Lenin as his epigraph: "Statisticians should be for us practical assistants, not scholars." With this quotation, he highlighted the ability of statistics to aid in economic development and policy making by providing the data the state and party leaders need at the expense of a focus on academic or theoretical matters. Overall, it is now well established that statistics were politicized in the Soviet period. One official nonchalantly explained, "in Soviet times, statistics fulfilled the goals set by the Party and functioned within strict limits" (GKS50 2004).

Many have argued that the politicization of data and national statistics was not simply a function of political control but something more deeply ingrained in those who worked at Goskomstat. Valentin Kudrov writes, "in this system worked people of a specific type, Soviet people or *Homo sovieticus*, who had a repressed pseudopatriotic calling, a calling based on an all-penetrating ideology and the concept of 'educational work.' It was precisely from their hands that the statistical distortion of reality was managed" (1994, 4–5). Vadim Kirichenko, former head of Goskomstat, also argues that politicization of data geared toward enhancing the image of the USSR was an internal, deeply held practice:

> It is essential to eliminate a directive, which has been shaped over decades, to demonstrate mainly successes and advantages and to keep silent on inadequacies and the critical situation in the social and

18. Also noted in D'iakonov and Bushueva 1992, 40.

> economic growth of the country and its regions. Such an approach, such an orientation, has practically become part of the "genetic code" not just for one, but for many generations of statisticians. (1991, 11–12, cited in Kudrov 1994, 5)

At the same time statisticians at TsSU—like Kudrov himself—were engaged, at least in print, with the wider profession of statistics.

A year before Volodarskii quoted Lenin on the purpose of statistics, *Vestnik statistiki* published an article that discussed the common goals of UNESCO and the CMEA (Lukin 1977); a couple of years later, another article emphasized shared goals with international community of statisticians (VS 1979). In 1982 an international seminar on systems of data gathering and processing took place in Moscow under the aegis of the UN European Economic Commission (Kudinov 1982). This was reported as a collegial event where statisticians from different countries had common goals, shared concerns, and the ability to discuss and solve problems together. The Irish representative even wrote a poem to sum up the seminar:

> What awaits us in five years?
> Maybe the stars will tell
> There should not be a terrible nightmare in the future
> Statistics can bring peace
> Work together and discuss everything
> Reflect on problems and resolve them.
> (Kudinov 1982, 49, published in Russian)

Another article written by a Finnish statistician comparing the CMEA and Finland noted that statistics plays an important role in promoting peace and strengthening friendship between nations by providing valuable information and allowing people to understand one another. The epigraph of this article was "reliable information—guarantee of peace" (Niitamo 1982).

These articles in *Vestnik statistiki* suggest that Goskomstat statisticians were aware that the international community of statisticians was increasingly committed to transparency and coordination, practices that in many ways were antithetical to the goal of serving the Soviet state.

Goskomstat's conflicting goals reflect the surrounding context of Soviet and Russian identities. In one of the most insightful and comprehensive works to date on this topic, Ted Hopf (2002) put forward a topography of social identities in the USSR and Russia for 1955 and 1999. He summarized the primary identities for 1955 along dimensions of modernity, class, and nation, with a composite discourse of "New Soviet Man" as a function of positions on modernity and class (2002, 40–81). In 1999 identities were primarily based on understandings of the relationships between the Russian self and others: historical (sovereignty, great power, nation, orthodoxy); external (West, United States, Europe, East and their positions on class, markets, democracy, and difference); and internal (rural-urban, center-periphery, and Chechnya) in the context of modernity. Four primary discourses come out of these identity positions: New Western Russian, New Soviet Russian, Liberal Essentialist, and Liberal Relativist (Hopf 2002, 154–59).

Although the framework for identity used here differs from Hopf's framework, his identity topographies capture well the contestation that is critical to understanding identity at TsSU/Goskomstat and the context of social identities of the time more generally. In addition, we can think of some of the types of identity content discussed above using Hopf's categories. In particular, the dual social purposes of Goskomstat can be understood through Hopf's class, modernity, and nation dimensions; the goal of being modern, scientific, and professional existed alongside the goal of supporting the revolution in a class position as part of the intelligentsia. However, some international statistical practices, such as the inclusion of nonmaterial production (services) in GNP or use of sampling, were seen as bourgeois and capitalist and hence opposed to the Soviet and revolutionary position.

Another way of getting at the broader context of social identities in the USSR and Russia as they related to Goskomstat is to consider the literature on the history of science and politics in the USSR. There we see that science and politics have been deeply connected since the beginning of the USSR.[19] On one hand, there was reverence for science and engineering. Education in engineering and technical subjects was a gateway to an administrative career (Armstrong 1965, 652), and Soviet bureaucrats valued an "engineering approach" to social problems.[20] Farmer writes, "the Soviet political elite is ridden through and through with the technocratic ethos" (1992, 163). On the other hand, political elites often viewed technocrats and the scientific intelligentsia with suspicion, especially in the early years following the revolution.[21] Bureaucrats sometimes found their commitment to the Soviet system at odds with their commitment to science, because the Soviet system entailed adherence to Marxist-Leninist principles, which sometimes conflicted with scientific approaches.

---

19. For an overview of the complex relationship between science and politics in the Soviet Union, see Bailes 1978; Graham 1993.

20. On the impact of science and technology on politics and society in the USSR, see Graham 1990.

21. On technocrats and technocracy in the Soviet Union, see Armstrong 1965; Bailes 1978; Lampert 1979; Farmer 1992, 162–69; Graham 1993, 160–67. On the intelligentsia more generally, see Bauer et al. 1959, chap. 18.

Soviet statisticians had to balance their professional obligations and their loyalty to the Soviet state. As international support for the SNA grew, they also had to decide how to reconcile Soviet practices with those of the global community of statisticians. As I argue in chapter 7, they mediated this tension in part with a conditional norm that legitimated different types of national accounting systems based on different economic structures.

Change in Goskomstat's shared goals began in the late perestroika era, when international engagement rose and political control declined, leaving the organization with far more autonomy than at any time during the Soviet period. The goal of supporting the state was subordinated, though not completely abandoned, to the goal of international commensurability. But this new purpose was not a completely new shared goal. Instead it built on the agency's earlier support for scientific principles and professionalism.

In a report to a CIA conference on the state of Soviet statistics, Kostinsky and Belkindas made a remarkable claim: "Goskomstat and the CIA are pursuing the same goal: an accurate measure of the size and growth of the Soviet economy" (1990, 183). Given the past differences between Goskomstat and the CIA over approaches to national accounts, that must have seemed like a significant break from the past. However, Kostinsky and Belkindas suggested that Goskomstat was primarily motivated by the need for better information about the economy, not an interest in "reform" per se.

Only a short time later, however, Goskomstat adopted the SNA, and officials explicitly cited the international commensurability of data as an objective. In 1993 Pavel Guzhvin ended an article in *Voprosy ekonomiki,* a leading economic journal in Russia, by saying, "we hope to raise statistics to a level that will satisfy the demands of the market economy and will make it possible to compare indicators of the Russian national economy's development with analogous indicators of other countries" (1993, 13). In another article on Russian statistics in the same issue of *Voprosy ekonomiki,* Igor' Pogosov called for Goskomstat to implement a range of international standards including those of the UN Statistical Commission, the Food and Agriculture Organization, ILO, World Health Organization, IMF, UNESCO, and UNEP (Pogosov 1993). *Vestnik statistiki* also ran several articles dealing with international standards.

When I asked lower-level regional Goskomstat personnel about changes in methodology at Goskomstat, respondents almost universally noted that it was important for Russian statistics to be comparable with other countries and for Russia to be part of the international system. One official noted:

> I was working on branch classifications at TsSU and studying at the Foreign Trade Academy. I was writing my dissertation on the MPS and the SNA and I realized that comparisons were impossible; this was 1987–88.

> This is how I realized the importance of introducing SNA in Russia, that is, to see how we fit into international society. (GKS49 2004)

In this statement the issue of statistical comparisons is linked to the broader issue of Russia's place in the world.

Assessing Change in the Purposive Content of Goskomstat Identity

It is fair to say that Goskomstat today fully embraces the principle of international commensurability of data. Thus we can conclude that, in contrast to the cognitive and relational content of identity at Goskomstat, this is one area that has significantly changed over time.

We might ask whether support for the Soviet state was actually identity content. Since commitment to this goal diminished after the loosening of political control, perhaps it was more the result of outside pressure than an ingrained part of Goskomstat identity. But as noted above, even officials within Goskomstat acknowledged that serving the Soviet state was a deeply held belief among statisticians—part of the "genetic code" according to one former chairman. Moreover, as the discussion of norms and habits below will demonstrate, in its practices, Goskomstat has not fully shed the goal of supporting the state.

Constitutive Norms: Practices at Goskomstat

The final type of identity content that I consider is constitutive norms, the shared practices and habits that constitute group membership. Below I discuss three areas of practice: the use of sampling for surveys; the skillful manipulation of rules to achieve desired results; and the way that data errors or changes are handled. All three practices distinguished Soviet statistics from national statistics in other, non-CMEA states. Marxist discourse and the conditional norm that delineated the use of the SNA and MPS receive detailed examination in the next chapter.

Probability Theory and Random Sampling: Pathetic Trickery or Science?

An important, perhaps crucial, figure in the development of modern probability theory was Andrei Kolmogorov, a Soviet mathematician. He was appointed professor at Moscow State University in 1931, the year that TsSU was placed under the authority of Gosplan, stripping it of some of its institutional autonomy. Kolmogorov wrote *Foundations of the Theory of Probability*, an influential treatise published in German in 1933 (and still in print in English as late as 2000). Probability theory is the basis for statistical sampling, where a selection of observations is chosen for analysis to make statistical inferences about a larger population. Sampling allows one to extrapolate information about a population from a small amount of data. For example, rather than collect data from every member of a population or every firm to learn about unemployment or production, a sampling approach would survey a subset of the population or firms, then apply statistical methods to draw general inferences from these samples. Although the USSR's contributions to probability theory placed it at the forefront of statistical science, it rejected the practice of survey sampling in favor of full enumeration in its national statistics.

At the founding meetings of what would become the UNSO in 1946, the UN Nuclear Commission on Statistics set out national accounts and sampling as its highest priorities and established a subcommittee on sampling. The Soviet representative, Sergei Chernikov, objected to the subcommittee's creation (Ward 2004, 51). Even though the subcommittee reserved an open seat for a Soviet representative and despite the participation of prominent international statisticians such as R. A. Fisher, the Soviets did not nominate anyone for the post (Rice 1952, 85).

In his keynote address to a methodology conference held on February 20–21, 1950 at TsSU, V. N. Starovskii, the head of TsSU, said, "harmful bourgeois influences and anti-Marxist distortion in Soviet statistical science and literature hampers its development" (cited in Rice 1952, 82). Starovskii also "identified the main obstacle to the development of statistical science as the formal mathematics school of thought" (cited in Rice 1952, 82).[22] This approach, he said, "considers statistics [to be] a universal science for the study of nature and society based ultimately on the mathematical law of large numbers and not on a Marxist-Leninist theory" (cited in Rice 1952, 82). In discussing this speech by Starovskii, Stuart Rice argued that the Soviets' negative attitude toward probability theory and sampling was increasingly out of line with the international community and indicated a divergence in Soviet conceptions of statistics from international views (Rice 1952).

22. An interesting parallel in the criticism of sampling and statistical inference in comparison to full enumeration is the strong recent political opposition to its use in correcting the undercount in U.S. census data, including a Supreme Court decision against the use of statistics to correct the 2000 census figures for the purposes of determining congressional seats; see Peterson 1999.

Nevertheless, opposition to sampling in the USSR continued for some time. TsSU was committed to full enumeration methods (for firms) or at best using nonrandom quota samples of households for collecting data. Alexander Driuchin (1977), former head of the RSFSR Goskomstat office, explains why. He argues that Western statisticians work under very unfavorable conditions, dealing with private companies who lie to cover up the exploitation of workers. Due to these conditions, Western statisticians are forced to find ways to compensate for deficiencies in data by applying various mathematical methods, but these methods are self-deception. Mathematical theories, which are neither scientifically objective nor unbiased, cannot compensate for the lack of understanding of the real world and real social processes. In contrast, Soviet statisticians do not need these tricks because they use scientific methods and have access to real data (Driuchin 1977, 50–51).

Despite the negative reaction to random sampling and the use of probability theory or other mathematical statistical methods in *Vestnik statistiki*, the discussion also reveals empathy for Western statisticians among Soviet statisticians. In "The Crisis of Contemporary Bourgeois Econometrics" Maslov explained that Western econometricians, unlike their Soviet counterparts, do not have complete data owing to the use of sampling. Therefore they turn to studying "the random and the probabilistic," thereby ignoring reality (Maslov 1975). The point of this, Maslov notes, is to serve the interests of the capitalist classes. His article evinces a mixture of disdain and pity toward Western econometricians; he clearly does not approve of the methods, but he feels somewhat sorry for these people who have no other choice but to do this sort of analysis. Simchera (1976) expresses the same view toward Western statistics and statisticians, recognizing some Western achievements while sharply criticizing the preference for mathematical models. Simchera laments that statisticians in the West invest enormous time and effort studying things the wrong way. On a more positive note, he notes some "shared successes" and explains that Westerners could and sometimes did learn from Soviet statisticians.

Official views on sampling changed in the late 1980s. In July 1987 in a very critical article about Goskomstat, N. Belov, a vice-chairman, called for the use of surveys (Belov 1987, cited in Kostinsky and Belkindas 1990, 189). Guzhvin also recommended sampling in one of his articles discussing the direction of Russian statistics (1992a). Nevertheless, opposition to sampling continued, even though implementation of the SNA required it. The widespread support for the SNA itself did not extend to statistical sampling.

Although the rejection of sampling had been one of the primary complaints lodged against Soviet statistics, Derek Blades and Anne Harrison of the OECD avoided outright criticism of the East, instead pointing out how the CMEA's experience with full enumeration censuses and administrative returns might be useful in a new hybrid model of data collection. They write, "It is perhaps ironic that as the CEECs are moving away from their auditing role and into the areas of sample surveys, many countries in the West are under pressure to rely more on administrative returns" (1992, 104). In the West, commercial statistics were produced mostly from surveys, and government data from administrative returns. Blades and Harrison, however, note: "The French practice of co-ordinating commercial and national accounting practices through a 'Plan Compatible' is often held up as an ideal to other OECD countries; it is a way of working that is very familiar to the CEECs where statistical returns referred explicitly to items specified in national book-keeping practice" (1992, 104). It may seem like a technical detail, but it offers another example of fellow statisticians downplaying criticism of past practices in CMEA NSOs.

Knowhow: Accentuate the Positive, Eliminate the Negative

Goskomstat did not simply make up numbers. Soviet statistics were not based on "free invention," to use Bergson's term. Instead, Goskomstat manipulated definitions and rules to present data in ways that suited their interests, in this case portraying the Soviet economy, and by extension the Soviet state, in the most positive light.

There is ample evidence of these practices. In a newspaper interview in 1989, Vadim Kirichenko denied "outright deception" but admitted that Goskomstat "had previously succumbed to the desire to always present statistics in the best light, including carefully modifying computations or definitions to improve results" (Berger 1989, 2, cited in Kostinsky and Belkindas 1990, 192). Kostinsky and Belkindas argued that Goskomstat had a "predilection for continuing to paint the best picture possible of Soviet economic performance" and that "the most serious charge against Goskomstat since the era of glasnost arrived was that it continued to tamper with the aggregate economic measures" (1990, 191). Viktor Belkin has argued, "unfortunately the virus of the TsSU-Goskomstat occupational disease—the embellishment of reality—is still alive" (1992, 103).

Some examples from the perestroika era illustrate this practice. In 1985 TsSU decided to remove alcoholic beverage production from industrial output; this move followed a steep drop in alcohol production due to Gorbachev's antialcohol campaign, hence the removal reduced the apparent drop in industrial production. As in the past, the change in methodology was not announced and past data were not updated to reflect the change (Volkov and Samokhvalov 1989, cited in Kostinsky and Belkindas 1990, 191). Because the turnover tax on alcohol was an important source of income for the Soviet state, the forced decrease in supply of alcohol led to lower levels of revenue for the state. TsSU manipulated various formulas (especially the weight of alcohol in total retail sales and past year retail trade figures) to inflate current retail trade figures (Vanous 1987, 2–3). The inflated retail trade figures then affected national income statistics via inflated consumption figures. Another example was the introduction of a new "net output of enterprises" indicator lauded by Korolev, which similarly obfuscated what was actually included in production figures (Korolev 1989, cited in Kostinsky and Belkindas 1990, 191).

If we look at this norm of manipulating rules in the broader context of Soviet and Russian identity, we see that it fits in with general shared practices. There is neither outright opposition or blind following of rules but creative utilization of institutions where actors use rules to get what they want. Alena Ledeneva (2006) documents this kind of innovation, which she calls "knowhow," in formal and informal practices in Russia in the 1990s and demonstrates that it can support as well as subvert institutions.

Silences: No Explanation of Changes or Errors

Related to the manipulation of rules is the refusal to discuss such manipulation. Just as Goskomstat regularly came up with creative, rule-based ways to improve the appearance of the Soviet economy, it also developed a habit of not discussing changes in methodology or puzzling inconsistencies and errors in publications. Despite the implementation of the SNA, this Soviet practice carried over into Russian statistics.

Some of the inconsistencies presented themselves to careful readers of Goskomstat publications in the form of revisions of previously published figures. For example, in January 1992 Goskomstat published a net 2.2 percent decline in industrial production for 1991, but in 1993 they published a net 8 percent decline for 1991—a difference of 5.8 percent—without any commentary on the discrepancy between the 1992 and 1993 publications (Kudrov 1993, 128; Pogosov 1993, 20). Goskomstat published figures for budget deficits, too, without any commentary or explanation on where they came from. Pogosov considers these inconsistencies "instances of deliberate publication of incorrect information" and argues that these examples "attest to the nostalgia for tendentious ways of 'improving' indicators. The elimination of 'errors' of this type depends exclusively on the good will of organizations formulating and publishing the data" (1993, 20).

The move to the SNA did not alter this habit of silence. In a careful and detailed analysis of SNA data for 1989–95, Shinichiro Tabata notes the continued existence of the old problem of frequent changes (without comment) to previously published figures (1996, 130). Interviews conducted with economists and other consumers of Goskomstat data in Russia in 2003–4 mention the lack of *specific* methodological notes (explanation of particular changes and discrepancies) as one of the most frequent problems characterizing Goskomstat data.

There are discrepancies even in the information that Goskomstat publishes about itself as an organization. The 1996 organizational history refers to fifty thousand employees (Goskomstat Russia 1996b), whereas a 1997 report lists 31,484 (Goskomstat Russia 1997, 44). But there is no evidence that the agency lost 37 percent of its employees between 1996 and 1997, so one of the numbers, most likely the 1996 one, is in error. The inconsistencies continue: as of 2009, the Russian version of the Goskomstat website reports twenty-three thousand employees (Rosstat 2009a), and the English version thirty thousand (Rosstat 2009b). Although not especially serious, these inconsistencies do correspond to a pattern.

Occasionally, especially in the late perestroika and early post-Soviet periods, Goskomstat officials did admit errors or distortions. Chairman Kirichenko, in his 1989 interview with *Izvestiia,* acknowledged the case of enhancing the apparent growth rate in the USSR by the removal of alcohol sales in the late 1980s (Berger 1989, 2, cited in Kostinsky and Belkindas 1990, 192). In one of his earliest statements as head of Goskomstat, Pavel Guzhvin admitted some problems with Soviet statistics (Guzhvin 1992a). Some articles in *Vestnik statistiki* also acknowledged errors, as when the journal published a highly critical article on the manipulation of the 1937 census (Volkov 1997).

The joint Goskomstat Russia-World Bank (1995) report on national accounts also devotes a significant amount of space to the issue of revisions. In particular, the report notes the need to explain the revision process to users so they understand both the need by policy makers for estimates based on incomplete data and the need to revise estimates as more or better data become available. The report states that Goskomstat should "design and implement an enlightened and transparent dissemination program to the public media and users which explains properly the revision policy on national accounts estimates" (Goskomstat Russia and World Bank 1995, xi). Goskomstat did later adopt the IMF's most demanding dissemination standard, the SDDS.

Nevertheless, despite improvements in treatment of recent data, there has never been a systematic accounting of problems during the Soviet period (lack of coverage and restricted publication of data, faulty price indices, descriptive distortions, etc.), and even specific admissions remain rare. The 1996 organizational history (Goskomstat Russia 1996b) contains hardly a hint of problems in 194 years of Russian and Soviet statistics, illustrating the paradox of appearing to renounce past practices in favor of international standards while celebrating the past.

In this chapter I have examined the content and contestation of the identity of statisticians at Goskomstat and at the international level. By considering the four types of content and contestation at multiple levels we can reach an understanding of identity and identity change at Goskomstat without reducing identity to a single dimension. In brief, although there have been significant changes in some types of identity content at Goskomstat, there has also been a great deal of continuity.

In examining cognitive content—the ways in which sharing an identity affects interpretation of information—I focus on evaluations of Soviet statistics by those within Goskomstat, by Western academics, and by the international community of national statisticians. Overall, Goskomstat officials retain positive assessments of Soviet statistics. This view of the quality of Soviet statistics differs markedly from those of Western academics, who were quite negative in the Soviet era and after 1991. Those working on national statistics at the international level, who to some extent share a professional identity with Goskomstat statisticians, were more muted in their criticism of Soviet statistics than Western academics and were somewhat more sympathetic to the views expressed by Soviet statisticians. Here too there has not been much change over time, despite the end of the Cold War and the possibility for a more frank assessment of the Soviet period by international actors. Thus there does not seem to have been a significant change in the cognitive content of identity at Goskomstat or by other identity groups.

With respect to relational content, although distinctions were drawn between Soviet or Marxist statistics and statistics in bourgeois capitalist states, there was even in the 1960s engagement between Soviet and Western statisticians in the pages of *Vestnik statistiki*, reflecting a collegial professional relationship. In addition, the discourse of national accountants versus other groups is similar in Russia and at the international level, suggesting again a shared identity in terms of relational content. Although there was an increase in the frequency and level of closeness of ties between Goskomstat and their international colleagues in the post-Soviet era, this was not a relationship that developed post-1991 (or post-1989). Rather, the professional engagement reaches back decades before the move to the SNA. Hence in terms of relational comparisons as identity content, there clearly has been a strengthening of international professional ties, but this change does not signal a fundamental rethinking of the place of Soviet statisticians vis-à-vis the wider community of national statisticians.

The shared goals of Goskomstat have changed over time, but this change indicates a realignment rather than a profound break with past goals. Organizational identity at Goskomstat has long had two primary shared purposes that were somewhat in conflict—a commitment to professionalism and advancing the science of statistics combined with loyalty to the Soviet (now Russian) state and need to present data in a way that would enhance the appearance of the Soviet economy. There has been a shift toward professionalism and international commensurability of data and away from serving the state. Yet the shift is incomplete. Practices and norms at Goskomstat reveal many instances during and after the move to the 1993 SNA when Goskomstat's loyalty to the state was evident.

In examining norms at Goskomstat, in this chapter I focus on three: the position on sampling, the manipulation of rules, and the silence regarding changes to data and other inconsistencies. On sampling there has been a change: where Soviet/Russian statisticians were once strongly opposed, they now have accepted sampling. With manipulation and silence regarding errors, there has been significant continuation of past practices. Hence we cannot say that all Soviet-era organizational norms have been overturned. Nor has there been a wholesale adoption of the professional norms of international statisticians.

In summary, what can we say about identity as a variable in Goskomstat's move to the 1993 SNA in the early 1990s? Overall there was not a significant change in identity or socialization into a new identity that would explain the timing of SNA adoption or the level of implementation. To the extent there were changes in identity content—in relational content toward stronger ties with national statisticians at the international level, in shared goals toward support of international comparisons and standards, and in norms such as sampling—these changes were mainly concomitant with the shift to the SNA or even part of it rather than precipitating factors.

One exception might be the change in shared goals, since support for greater professionalism and international commensurability may date back to the 1970s. However, it is not clear why this shared goal at Goskomstat led to replacing the MPS rather than building bridges between it and the SNA or integrating the two systems. Specific changes in identity content still do not adequately explain why Goskomstat so enthusiastically abandoned the MPS and embraced the SNA in the early 1990s.

Identity does play a role in the move to the SNA—but not via a *change* in identity. What I have left out of this chapter is any discussion of a particular type of identity content, conditional norms. By surveying the terrain of identity at Goskomstat, we see that there was much contestation as well as contradiction. A crucial tension was in the shared goals of Goskomstat, between the support for international standards and support for the Soviet state. I argue that this tension led to some creative solutions in the form of a conditional norm regarding the appropriateness of the SNA, where the SNA was deemed appropriate for capitalist, market-based economies and the MPS was the appropriate system for centrally planned economies. This norm was part of the identity of Goskomstat, a behavioral prescription for the identity group, and it did not change over time. Instead, as the structural economic conditions of the types of states specified in the norm changed dramatically in the late 1980s, the norm linked those structural changes to a different understanding of appropriate action by Goskomstat and other CMEA NSOs.

7

STATISTICS AS A MIRROR OF THE ECONOMY

The SNA as a Conditional Norm

In this chapter I continue the discussion of identity at Goskomstat but take the analysis in a different direction. Here I make a case that a critical variable in Russia's move to the SNA was a conditional norm that specified the type of economy as a condition of the appropriateness of national accounting systems, with the SNA the appropriate national accounting system for market economies and the MPS appropriate for centrally planned economies. This argument builds on the discussion of identity content and contestation outlined in chapter 6: the tension created by conflicting shared goals and fractured relational comparisons contributed to the development of a conditional norm that could preserve Soviet practices and professional legitimacy in the face of growing international support for the SNA. This stable norm, in conjunction with a change in structural economic conditions, then prescribed the appropriateness of an abrupt institutional change toward the SNA and away from the MPS.

National statisticians are the holders of norms about the appropriateness of statistical systems. Although statisticians at Goskomstat were to some extent part of the international community of statisticians, the content of identity at Goskomstat differed in some significant ways from that of other national statisticians. These differences included cognitive content, with Goskomstat statisticians holding Soviet statistics, including the MPS, in much higher regard; relational content, with the distinction between socialist and capitalist or bourgeois statisticians; shared purposes, with Soviet statisticians working for the state as well as subscribing to internationally shared professional goals; and constitutive practices or norms, such as those regarding sampling, the treatment of rules, and errors or changes in data. As a result of these distinctive features of identity, Goskomstat statisticians diverged from the international community of statisticians regarding the appropriateness of the SNA.

Since its formalization in 1953 the number of countries using the SNA had risen steadily, although it was not yet an international norm and there was still significant variation in national practices. The process of revising the SNA in the 1960s–70s and the formalization of the MPS, as well as the recognition of two international systems, necessitated consideration of the appropriate conditions for each system—national statisticians had to ask and answer the question of which countries should use each system.

Soviet statisticians responded to this question and the growing acceptance of the SNA with a conditional norm. They reasoned that underlying economic structure should determine the statistical system—statistics should be a mirror of the economy—and hence capitalist countries should have one system, the SNA, whereas centrally planned economies should employ the MPS. In this way, the subjects of the norm on national accounting systems were limited by specific conditions, namely the structure of the economy.

In table 7.1, I have summarized the norms on the SNA over time. The columns highlight the approximate time periods, types of norms, the holders of norms, the specific institutions in question, the subjects of the norms, and the types of conditions, if any.

The first row summarizes the Soviet conditional norm of different statistical systems for different types of economies. This conditional norm allowed Soviet and Russian statisticians to make sense of the two statistical systems without having to rank them against each other. Soviet statisticians could then actively participate in UN work on the SNA and accept the SNA as a legitimate system for market economies, while simultaneously continuing their commitment to the MPS in the USSR and other planned economies, thus reconciling what would otherwise be conflicting practices within their shared identity as national

Table 7.1 SNA norms over time

TIME PERIOD	TYPE OF NORM	HOLDERS OF NORM	APPROPRIATE ACTION	SUBJECTS OF NORM	TYPE OF CONDITION
~1970s to 1990s	Conditional	CMEA and Soviet/ Russian statisticians	Statistical system: SNA or MPS	Capitalist vs. socialist states	Economic structure
~1990s to present	Unconditional	National statisticians at international level	1993 SNA and 2008 SNA	All states	None

statisticians. A logical corollary to this conditional norm, which developed unexpectedly over time, was that as economic systems change, so should statistical systems. So if the USSR/Russia changes from a planned economy to a market economy, then the statistical system should change from the MPS to the SNA. Thus the introduction of market reforms meant the end of the legitimating condition for the Soviet statistical system, the MPS.

The second row in table 7.1 outlines the current unconditional SNA norm. With the development of the SNA, the end of the MPS, and increasing coordination among a number of countries regarding national accounts, there is now consensus among national statisticians worldwide that the SNA is the only appropriate system for national accounts. We can call this agreement on the appropriateness of the SNA a norm in the sense of a behavioral prescription for a given identity group, national statisticians. It is also an unconditional norm in that no state is exempted from it. This norm has reached near-hegemonic status at present: contestation is limited to debates about details of the system, rather than the system itself. Revisions to the 1993 SNA, including the 2008 update, are indicative of this type of contestation.[1]

But is there evidence of a conditional norm linking the appropriateness of the MPS and the SNA to economic structural conditions, which then drove postcommunist countries' decision to adopt and implement the SNA? Providing direct evidence of motivations behind norm development is always a difficult task, especially when the actions in question occurred several decades ago. Interviewing participants after the fact is susceptible to bias based on later events, and analysis of historical texts has to be considered in the context of Soviet censorship and the Cold War. No matter what evidence we look at, it is unlikely that any Soviet statistician would explicitly say that he or she supported a conditional norm legitimating the MPS for planned economies and the SNA for capitalist countries because it allowed him or her to support the Soviet state while maintaining legitimacy in international circles. Instead of such direct statements of the norm, I try to triangulate using existing sources, focusing on two types of evidence: the timing of the decision to adopt the SNA, and the stated reasons for the move. *Vestnik statistiki*, Goskomstat's journal, is the primary source.

First I show that the debate in the USSR regarding the appropriateness of the SNA shifted relatively quickly from the late 1980s to the early 1990s, corresponding to changes in the economy from central planning to a market-based economy. I trace a shift from the recognition of two systems based on different

1. While the SNA norm is unconditional, it is not *universal;* it is a norm only among a specific identity group, the international community of national statisticians.

economic structures to a discussion of integration of the two systems, then to the belief that the SNA was the only appropriate system.

The second type of evidence is an analysis of specific arguments for the adoption of the SNA. Although various reasons were given, the content analysis of *Vestnik statistiki* articles shows that the move to a market economy and the need for comparable data that complies with international standards were by far the most common.

The evidence in this chapter is based on systematic content analysis of articles in *Vestnik statistiki* supplemented by interviews and materials from other texts. *Vestnik statistiki* is not digitized for the years in this study. It was a monthly publication with approximately ten to fifteen articles per issue. My analysis entailed reading though each issue to find articles related to the MPS, the SNA, or statistics in other countries. In total there were approximately 350 articles on these topics from 1949 to 1993, with the bulk of the articles coming from the post-1968 period (which was around the time of the formalization of the MPS). This chapter contains analysis of articles specifically on the topic of use of the MPS or SNA at Goskomstat USSR/Russia and in the CMEA states; there were approximately thirty articles in this subset.

From Two Equal Systems to the SNA Alone

At its core, the argument of this book centers on the normative connection between national accounts and the economy: the belief that national statistics should reflect economic structure. For Marxists the argument that a country's underlying economic structure should determine other institutions was hardly a stretch—such lines of reasoning legitimated many political and economic institutional differences in the USSR. In itself, the use of Marxist categories of analysis for statistics is not unreasonable or surprising. As the intellectual history of the SNA shows, modern national accounts are a product of ideas about what the economy is and how it can be analyzed as much as a result of technical innovations.

The economy in any national accounting system is not objectively given; rather, it is defined by a production boundary that is anchored in a particular time and place and subject to ideas and interest—that is, socially constructed. However, the production boundary, and hence the economy, in a national accounting system is not simply made up or exogenously given. Rather, any national accounting system attempts to capture the economy, but there is debate and contestation over how best to do that, and these debates are influenced by social identities.

As a way to understand the evolving view of the relationship between the economy and national accounts in the USSR, it is useful to begin with an example of Stalinist-era discourse about national accounts and economic structure. In an article in *Vestnik statistiki,* P. Moskvin (1950) defined the concept of national income in the USSR, using it to show how socialism was much more productive than capitalism. He also considered methodological differences in the way that the USSR and capitalist states calculated national income.

Moskvin defines national income according to Marxist-Leninist precepts, an approach that continues though the Soviet period. Moskvin writes that national income is "part of the value of social product" (1950, 52). He links the concept to Marx's definition and cites a 1949 German version of *Das Kapital* (vol. 3, p. 854), writing, "Gross income is that portion of value and that portion of the gross product measured by it, which remains after deducting that portion of value and that portion of the product of total production measured by it, which compensates the constant capital invested and consumed in production." The national income thus is the newly created value in a certain period or the sum of the net product of different sectors of economy. The net income of a given sector is the difference between the gross product and material production costs, the most important among which are raw materials and fuel, among other things (Moskvin 1950, 52).

Moreover, Moskvin points out that "the national income of the USSR fundamentally, principally differs from the national income of the capitalist countries" (1950, 53). Here he is not talking about methodology, which is the focus of articles in the late 1960s and 1970s. Rather, he says that private ownership of the means of production and the exploitation of the working class gives the distribution of national income an antagonistic character, with the bigger part being seized by the exploiters. The difference between a capitalist economy and a socialist economy, where there is no exploitation, implies, as Moskvin argues, the ability of the socialist system to secure higher growth rates.

Returning to methodology, Moskvin wrote that based on Marxist definitions, national income could be calculated in four ways. In contrast, bourgeois statisticians calculated national income as a simple sum of all individual incomes and the nondistributed income of stock companies. In his view, this methodology exaggerates national income because much of it includes transfer payments. It also distorts reality because it includes the net value of goods and services, incorporating sectors of the economy that do not produce material goods. Finally, not only do bourgeois economists rely on unscientific methods, but they also resort to outright falsification, underestimating the income of capitalists and exaggerating the income of workers (Moskvin 1950, 57).

In contrast to later articles, the explication here is very general. The later articles usually repeat the ideological precepts outlined in this article before delving into specific questions that are narrowly professional in scope. One important point in Moskvin's article is the critique of the inclusion of services and nonmaterial production in national income in capitalist countries. Soviet statisticians repeated this objection to the SNA for decades. Moskvin's article also illustrates what would be a fundamental distinction for Soviet statisticians, the divide between capitalist and socialist economies.

Articles in the 1960s draw this distinction between socialist and capitalist countries even in their titles: for example, "A Critique of the System of National Accounts in Capitalist Countries" (Rozovskii 1962) and "The System of National Accounts in Capitalist Countries" (Maslov 1965). The 1962 article criticizes the SNA (based on a 1958 version published by the OEEC and the UN's *Yearbook of National Accounts Statistics* from 1961), citing the usual shortcomings such as the failure of SNA categories to reflect class antagonisms in capitalist economies, but there is also more selective and narrow technical nitpicking, suggesting a fair degree of engagement with the details of the SNA. Rozovskii cites quite a few foreign publications and points out that the United States has calculated national income since 1932 (based on 1929 data) and that England, Canada, Germany, and other countries made similar attempts. He tells his readers that the International Association for Research in Income and Wealth (IARIW), with a membership of forty states, was established in 1947 and that in 1953 the statistical organs of UN developed a system of national accounting, which is very close to the systems of the main capitalist states (1962, 30–31). Hence the article indicates awareness of what is happening at the international level.

The 1965 article by Maslov is less critical of the SNA than Rozovskii's and more descriptive (and double the length, at sixteen pages). The article begins with a brief history of what would become the MPS system, noting the important role that it played in central planning. After a discussion of differences between capitalist and socialist economies, Maslov says, "the increased attention of bourgeois economists to the practical issues of the analysis of economic relations has led to the creation of schematic models that represent not an insignificant interest" (1965, 44). Most of the article is neutral in tone, but there are criticisms such as that the concept of "factors of production" conflates profits and wages. Nevertheless, the conclusion of the article is noteworthy. Maslov states:

> All this is to say that national accounts, built on the basis of vulgar economic sciences, can hardly produce objective coverage of the economic situation in a country. At the same time, it is impossible not

> to acknowledge that the very principle of double-entry accounting as applied to the entire economy and the gradual integration of those entries, the ultimate amalgamation of which are the national accounts of production, allocation, and consumption, undeniably is an interesting idea, the practical implementation of which could be useful for the Soviet economy, on the condition, of course, that the national accounting system be reworked on truly scientific bases that match the distinctive features of our economy. (1965, 50)

In this conclusion Maslov brings up several interesting points. He recites the familiar critique of capitalist statistics but then makes clear that he finds the SNA interesting and shows awareness of some of the features that distinguish it from previous national accounting schemes, such as the use of double-entry bookkeeping and Keynesian categories. Finally, he suggests that the USSR could also use a more comprehensive national accounting system, but that such a system would have to be adapted to fit the economic conditions of the Soviet Union.

Numerous articles in *Vestnik statistiki* from the 1960s up to the perestroika era repeat the link between economic structure and statistical analysis. For example, in an article linking the communist revolution with the development of statistics S. Stanev (1968), the head of Bulgaria's national statistical office (NSO), claimed that the October Revolution changed the fundamental principles of statistical inquiry. In commenting on the development and publication of the 1968 SNA by the UN (VS 1968), the editors of *Vestnik statistiki* wrote that the SNA was a method based on capitalist understandings of political and economic processes and therefore flawed. Among its most important flaws were its failure to distinguish between material production and services and its focus on costs and prices at the expense of labor questions. The article further stated that the differences between the SNA and MPS were "deep and fundamental," with the SNA based on the capitalist "factors of production" theory and the MPS on the correct Marxist-Leninist vision of economic processes. It noted that although many important steps were being taken to make data from the two systems comparable, the differences between the systems remained significant. Other articles similarly argued that the SNA both characterized economic structure and derived from it (Ivanov and Riabushkin 1971).

The 1971 publication of the MPS methodology by the UN was extensively covered in *Vestnik statistiki* articles. In a discussion of the sixteenth session of the UN Statistical Commission (VS 1971), *Vestnik statistiki* reported that the USSR had wanted the MPS and SNA publications to be distributed together as a single set of recommendations for national accounts. Western countries objected to joint distribution but agreed to separate publication of the MPS documents.

Although at the time this was reported as a setback indicating a lack of recognition of the equality of the two systems, later articles treated the UN publication of MPS documents as evidence of the equality of the two systems.

The role of developing countries was somewhat contested. It was a topic of debate in the revision of the 1968 SNA and in the USSR. In some developing counties, state-owned sectors constituted a part of the economy. In these cases, it was suggested that the MPS could be used, even if those countries also used the SNA (VS 1971). Later, though, a book review on the SNA in developing countries criticized the use of the SNA by such economies and called for Marxist-Leninist-based instructions for changing the statistical systems of developing countries (Nesterov 1988).

In the 1970s discussion still involved ideological differences between the SNA and MPS, in which capitalists' interests determined the SNA methodology, which overestimated the capitalist states' income, while Marxist theories provided the only true and scientific basis for statistics (Simchera 1976; Driuchin 1977). A clear connection was made between the MPS and socialist economies (Lukin 1977; Leshchev and Antsiferova 1978). Later, however, ideological criticism by and large dropped out of the articles, to be replaced by a more neutral claim about the use of the SNA by capitalist countries and the MPS by socialist ones (Ivanov and Ryzhkov 1981; Tsyrlin 1981).

The Structural Basis for the MPS versus the SNA since Perestroika

If we fast-forward to the early Gorbachev era (before the perestroika reforms), we see that the MPS and the SNA are well established as two equal systems. In 1985 *Vestnik statistiki* reported on the thirty-third session of the UN Statistical Commission in New York (VS 1985). The journal stressed that the session focused on both the SNA, which is used in capitalist countries, and the MPS, which is used in socialist countries. It reported that there were various plans for further interaction between the systems, including the update to the SNA, which would involve coordination with the MPS and other international standards, and successful comparison projects between France and Hungary and between Bulgaria and Finland. On changes to the SNA, the journal stated that what was needed was not a radical modification of the SNA but the delimitation of its categories in accordance with other statistical standards and the MPS.

Although this report seems to support the idea of furthering cooperation between equal systems, it does not promote *integration* into a single system. Differences in economic structure determine the use of the two systems. The same view of the structural basis for the MPS versus the SNA also appears in methodology articles. For example, Nesterov (1985) discusses the methodological differences of systems of accounting for household capital between capitalist and socialist states.

A watershed in discussion of the SNA in the USSR came in June 1988, when *Vestnik statistiki* published methodology for calculating GNP in socialist countries (VS 1988). Up until that point, no one had mentioned using the SNA per se in socialist countries, although there had been some experimental comparisons as part of the International Comparison Program (ICP). *Vestnik statistiki* was not, however, promoting a move to the SNA. Instead it suggested a shift to the use of GNP, based on MPS data, as an aggregate indicator instead of the MPS's national income indicator.[2] GNP calculation would supplement existing methods; there is not a hint of abandoning the MPS or even integrating the two systems.

An article by Ivanov et al. (1988) provided further detail on the place of GNP in the MPS system. The article began by noting that the MPS would "play an important role in the future" along with GNP calculation. But the authors also explained that the UN methodology could not be used directly because it had been created for calculating economic activity in capitalist countries and had to be adapted to calculate GNP in the USSR (Ivanov et al. 1988, 32). They then presented and discussed tables for converting national income to GNP. An important point in this and the previous GNP articles was the statement that it would be useful to provide information on both "productive" and "nonproductive spheres"—that is, to include services. The acknowledgment of the legitimacy of services in macroeconomic aggregates was a major departure from the past (Ivanov et al. 1988, 38).

In general, if we consider the first half of the perestroika period, from 1985 to 1988, we see that although acceptance of GNP marks a major change in 1988, there is still no discussion of integration of the MPS or SNA or abandonment of the MPS, and the use of the two systems remains based on differences in the economy. This view was confirmed in later discussion of the use of the two systems. For example, in a 1996 article, Ivanov and Homenko wrote that the MPS and the SNA were designed for different types of economies and different purposes. The MPS "was designed for macro analysis and management of the centrally planned economy, and its underlying concept and accounting structure differ from those of the SNA" (Ivanov and Homenko 1996, 323).

A related argument was that structural economic differences had produced two legitimate systems for national accounts. Goskomstat Vice-Chairman Aleksei Ponomarenko writes in a national accounts textbook, "until the breakup

2. See (Kostinsky and Belkindas 1990) for a review of this article.

of the Soviet Union, the world had two widely used macroeconomic statistical systems. The Material Product System was used by countries with planned economies. The System of National Accounts (SNA) was used by countries with market economies. Both systems existed in parallel and for a long time both were recommended by the UN" (2002, 38).

Interviews from 2004 with Goskomstat officials support this view of two statistical systems based on differences in the structure of the economy. As Chairman Sokolin (2004) put it, "As a field, statistics is standardized according to international rules. The USSR was a member of international organizations in the realm of statistics but at the same time it insisted that the MPS was the best. The MPS did suit our planned economy. In the 1980s the UN Statistical Commission recognized that both systems (MPS and SNA) had a right to exist."[3] Another official said, "SNA calculations are similar to MPS calculations. The advantage of the SNA is that it provides a better reflection of a market economy" (GKS19 2003).

Integration of the MPS and SNA

The idea of two coexisting systems was upset in 1989, only a year after the introduction of GNP by Goskomstat USSR. Here the record of *Vestnik statistiki* reveals the unstable politics and economic policies of the time and highlights the timing of the move to the SNA, in particular how quickly the understanding of the relationship between the MPS and SNA shifted.

If we examine *Vestnik statistiki* in 1989–91, it is clear that the end of the MPS was not expected (nor was the end of the USSR). This period is vital because it illustrates an alternative possibility for changes to Soviet statistics in light of perestroika—that is, a counterfactual example of what we might have expected without the end of the USSR and the abrupt end to central planning. In this period there is discussion of further integration of the MPS and the SNA, but no suggestion of giving up the MPS altogether. This is a scenario of gradual institutional change.

In May 1989 Ivanov published an article titled, "Review of the UN system of national accounts." In comparison with previous discussions of the SNA, it is a much more positive assessment, and Ivanov even mentions that the SNA was sometimes criticized unfairly in the past.[4] The article notes the recent surge in Soviet interest in the SNA (due to the adoption of the GNP indicator, etc.) and

3. The MPS was published by the UN in 1971, so one could argue that UN recognition dates from that time. However, I think that Sokolin is using the term "1980s" to refer to the pre-perestroika era as a whole.

4. For an earlier treatment of the SNA, see Rozovskii 1962.

details the characteristics and goals of the SNA in comparison to the MPS. It also discusses the ongoing revisions of the SNA (in which Ivanov was participating, and which would eventually lead to the 1993 SNA). Although the article did not specifically call for "integration" of the two systems, it did define the goal as "to bring the two statistical systems closer together" and proposed that a system of macroeconomic indicators based on both systems would be the best outcome (Ivanov 1989).

Only a few months later, in September 1989, Ivanov and Riabushkin wrote "The Integration of the MPS and SNA." The authors praised the MPS as a legitimate system and noted that over several decades it had been greatly improved and recognized as an internationally recommended system. However, they argued that perestroika entailed major changes in the structure of the Soviet economy, and statistics had to adapt by using GNP, which they had already begun to do (Ivanov and Riabushkin 1989, 20–21). They described the process as cumbersome because they were calculating GNP based on data adapted from the MPS. To make things easier, they suggested a new data-gathering mechanism that could be used both for the MPS and for calculating GNP. They noted that the creation of this system would be gradual (Ivanov and Riabushkin 1989, 23). Their argument did not imply abandoning the MPS and regarding the SNA, they suggested only calculation of GNP rather than implementation of the SNA per se. They proposed a hybrid system: a matrix that would have information that was common to both systems as well as addenda that would describe the differences. They stated that this would be a program of integration of "two equal systems" (Ivanov and Riabushkin 1989, 27), but they later said that that the MPS should be used primarily (Ivanov and Riabushkin 1989, 31). The Ivanov and Riabushkin proposal for an integrated system was the first published proposal for integration of the two systems in Goskomstat's official journal. It continued the positive treatment of the SNA in Ivanov's May article but went a step further, emphasizing the similarity and compatibility of the two systems, albeit with the caveat that the SNA must be adapted to the specifics of the Soviet economy.

It is clear in this period that Goskomstat USSR had begun to address some of the thorniest issues that separated Soviet statistics from those of the West. By 1988 they had agreed that services and other "nonmaterial" production might usefully be included in national accounts, and in 1989 the issue of prices was also being reconsidered. An article in October 1989 by Klimenko, without mentioning moving to the SNA or abandoning the MPS, made the case that understanding the principles of price statistics in the SNA could be instrumental for improving Soviet price statistics. In addition, Ivanov and Riabushkin revisited some critiques of the SNA from the Soviet period to rebut those accounts, in effect saying that the whole issue of nonmaterial production in the SNA was sometimes "misinterpreted" by Soviet experts (Ivanov and Riabushkin 1991a). This was a remarkable renunciation of a long-standing position on services in national accounts.

From 1989 through 1991, articles in *Vestnik statistiki* continued to call for integration of the MPS and the SNA in the Soviet Union; and the focus was on the SNA per se, rather than certain elements such as GNP. There was no hint of dropping the MPS and replacing it with the SNA; in fact, most of the articles emphasized that the MPS would not be abandoned. In reporting on the December 1989 meeting of the Inter-Secretariat's Expert Group, held in conjunction with the final revisions to the 1993 SNA, Ivanov and Riabushkin supported the call for integration of the MPS and SNA as a single system, but they also said that "of course, the MPS will still play a substantial role" (1990, 63). They noted that at the international level an agreement had been reached to integrate the two systems and that the Soviet delegation supported the idea of integrating the systems while preserving unique aspects of each (1990, 64). They further emphasized that no matter how far acceptance of the two systems extends, the MPS must be kept as an independent system of macroeconomic indicators, because it was in practice necessary for understanding the economy, and hence integration should take place gradually.

This article also reported on the use of the MPS by other CMEA states, saying that states with centrally planned economies could be delineated into three groups depending on the speed of introduction of various aspects of the SNA or integration of the SNA and the MPS. Furthermore they noted that a recent CMEA meeting had decided that the methodology of calculating GNP in planned economies should be based primarily on the SNA (Ivanov and Riabushkin 1990, 63). This illustrates some divergence within the CMEA and between the USSR and CMEA. Nevertheless, an article from November 1990 described plans for the USSR to participate in another round of the International Comparison Program and suggested comparisons based on GDP only (as opposed to comparing GDP and the MPS's Net Material Product indicator) (VS 1990).

In 1990 and up to mid-1991 articles in *Vestnik statistiki* became increasingly detailed in their discussion of the SNA. There were comprehensive overviews of the SNA and GDP (Pogosov and Riabushkin 1990; Ivanov and Riabushkin 1991a). At the same time, some articles identified practical difficulties in integrating the two systems. Zarubin and Pogosov (1991) express frustration at having to compare indicators in such a convoluted way, via the MPS, SNA, and ICP. They note that direct comparison would be preferable but make no suggestion to switch exclusively to the SNA.

From June to October 1991 *Vestnik statistiki* published five long articles detailing accounts in the SNA (VS 1991a, 1991b, 1991c, 1991d, 1991e). The first was an overview of all accounts, and subsequent issues focused on one or two specific accounts.[5] The introductory article in this series suggested that the first stage of the introduction of the SNA in Soviet statistics began in 1988 with the calculations of GNP, but that a second stage should introduce the accounts of the SNA (based on the European System of Integrated Economic Accounts because the 1993 SNA was not yet completed), which explained the need to discuss these accounts in the journal (VS 1991a, 17). The discussion of the SNA in this series included recommendations to all union republics and could be taken as a draft methodological document for implementing the SNA in the USSR, but it still specifically cited integration as the goal: "implementation of the SNA into the statistical practice of the USSR at the current stage will proceed by integrating the SNA and the MPS, based on a system of macroeconomic indicators that could provide data on the country's economic development using the concepts of both the MPS and SNA" (VS 1991a, 19). The article also stated that the reason for the integration and use of both systems was the transitional condition of the economy. That is, if the MPS was for a planned economy, and the SNA was for a market economy, then an economy that had elements of both planning and markets should use both systems.

This transition option continued to appear in published articles until approximately mid-1992. Medvedev (1992), in an article primarily devoted to a technical description of calculations of growth in the MPS and SNA, suggested that Russia would eventually abandon central planning but in the interim the economy remained under a planning model, so some use of the MPS was necessary. He writes: "In the transition period state statistics continue to function within the parameters of the sectoral and functional statistics that serviced the centrally planned economy. It is clear that the national accounting system that reflects the state of the market economy must be different and that a new accounting system cannot be introduced instantly" (1992, 25).

The Move to the SNA

The first issue of *Vestnik statistiki* in January 1992 contained an article by Ivanov and Homenko suggesting an impending move to the SNA in the USSR (Ivanov and Homenko 1992).[6] It did not mention the MPS at all. The point of the article

5. On the production account, see VS 1991b; on formation of income and distribution of income accounts, see VS 1991c; on the use of income and capital accounts, see VS 1991d; and on goods and services and external economic relations accounts, see VS 1991e.

6. This reveals a publication lag: by January 1992 the USSR had ceased to exist. Most likely the article reflects plans from the fall of 1991.

was to explain the revision of the SNA (the draft version of the 1993 SNA was nearly complete) as well as variation in national accounts among European countries. The authors reported that the draft methodology for the SNA in the USSR, published in June–October 1991 in *Vestnik statistiki,* was based on the European System of Integrated Economic Accounts, which was itself a variant of the 1968 SNA, that was adapted to meet the conditions of European states. And, because each European state's national accounting system varied slightly, they argued that it made sense for the USSR to consider the variation in these practices (Ivanov and Homenko 1992, 16).

The USSR officially ceased to exist on December 25, 1991, and Goskomstat USSR vanished with it, leaving much of its infrastructure and staff to Goskomstat Russia. The articles in *Vestnik statistiki* in 1992, however, suggest that the transition from Goskomstat USSR to Goskomstat Russia took some time, and that the direction of the organization was somewhat unclear. Aside from two articles published in January, which still referenced the USSR, no new articles appeared on the SNA or MPS until Medvedev's June article discussed above, which continued to call for an integrated approach to the two systems.

In July 1992 *Vestnik statistiki* published for the first time an article that reflected a decision to implement the SNA alone (VS 1992a). The decision, however, came not from Russia but from Statkom CIS, which had chosen on March 5, 1992, to implement the SNA. To quote the article, "these recommendations should be regarded as the first stage in the realization of the program of the adoption of the SNA in the statistical practice of CIS states" (VS 1992a, 3). Most of the article consisted of a detailed timetable for the transition in 1992–93. The goal was to develop a methodology for calculating a system of macroeconomic indicators that were new and oriented toward a market economy (VS 1992a, 11–12). Following this article, in July, recommendations to CIS states for the calculation of GDP by final use were published (VS 1992b). What is interesting about these unsigned articles is that they issue recommendations to the former Soviet states, as if they came from Goskomstat USSR. Yet it was not clear what authority Statkom CIS had and whether *Vestnik statistiki* represented Goskomstat Russia or Statkom CIS. As it turns out, the situation was clarified in the next issue.

The lead article of the September 1992 issue of *Vestnik statistiki* was titled "Trust in Statistics" and written by Pavel Guzhvin, the acting chairman of Goskomstat *Russia* (reflecting the change from the USSR to Russia) (Guzhvin 1992a). This was a detailed and lengthy description of the steps Russia needed to take in making the transition to the SNA. It summarized the institutional basis for the move to the SNA (Guzhvin 1992a, 16–17), including the state program approved on January 14, 1992, and the progress of the working group in the Supreme

Soviet. Guzhvin explicitly stated that "the basis of the whole task will be the replacement of the MPS with the SNA" (1992a, 17), which he hoped to complete in only four years. The article also criticized Goskomstat USSR for being subject to political pressure and for engaging in distortion of data (Guzhvin 1992a, 7). Guzhvin argued that political pressure had ended, statistics from Goskomstat Russia could be trusted, and the SNA was to be the basis for that trust.

An interview with First Vice-Chairman of Goskomstat Russia A. P. Zakharov in February 1993 provided a detailed update on the plan to implement the SNA and the political support and institutional context for this program (VS 1993a). Zakharov dated the actual work on SNA implementation to the summer of 1991, which corresponds with the publication of the five-part series in *Vestnik statistiki.* The Guzhvin and Zakharov articles make clear that by 1992 Russia was in the process of implementing the SNA. The question of what kind of national accounts system Russia should have had been settled.

In table 7.2, I have summarized the arguments for variants in the national accounts systems in the USSR and Russia, from the articles discussed above.

The table shows that there was a change over time from support for the MPS and SNA as two separate and coexisting systems to support for only the SNA. This change happened relatively quickly, between 1988 and 1992. Initial proposals to calculate GNP in 1988 gave way to suggestions for a hybrid system in 1989–91. By late 1992 support for the MPS had fallen by the wayside, and Goskomstat was committed to implementing only the SNA.

If we briefly recall the trajectory of economic reform during and immediately after perestroika, we see that some of the crucial steps in the move from central planning to a market economy also took place in 1988–92. The critical laws introducing limited market mechanisms were in 1987–88 (Law on Cooperatives and Law on State Enterprises). The pace of economic and political reform, including the destruction of the Communist Party and concomitant end of central planning, increased from 1989 until the USSR collapsed in 1991. In January 1992 Russia liberalized prices on most goods, which was a major break with the past in terms of economic policy but also in terms of economic statistics, because the absence of market prices had posed a formidable challenge to the compatibility of Soviet and Western statistics. In sum, considering the timing of economic reform in the USSR and Russia, we can conclude that the shift in support for the SNA rather closely tracks these structural changes in the economy.

As momentous as the decision to move to the SNA was, the hard work for Goskomstat Russia was just beginning in 1992. The complexity of the task was illustrated by the number of technical articles on components of the SNA published by *Vestnik statistiki* in 1992–93. Several articles addressed the methodological aspects of calculating national wealth (Nesterov 1992a, 1993b, 1993a; Zharova 1993a). There was discussion of how to calculate services and intangible

Table 7.2 What system of national accounts should be used in the USSR and Russia? Articles from *Vestnik statistiki*, 1962–93

YEAR	MPS AND SNA AS TWO SEPARATE SYSTEMS	USE OF SOME SNA ELEMENTS	INTEGRATION OF TWO SYSTEMS	SNA ALONE SHOULD BE USED
1960–87	(Rozovskii 1962)			
	(Maslov 1965)			
	(Nesterov 1985)			
	(VS 1985)			
1988		(VS 1988)		
		(Ivanov et al. 1988)		
1989			(Ivanov 1989)	
			(Ivanov and Riabushkin 1989)	
1990			(Ivanov and Riabushkin 1990)	
			(Pogosov and Riabushkin 1990)	
1991			(Ivanov and Riabushkin 1991a)	
			(Zarubin and Pogosov 1991)	
			(VS 1991a)	
			(Medvedev 1992)	
1992				(VS 1992a)
				(VS 1992b)
				(Guzhvin 1992a)
				(Guzhvin 1992b)
				(Nesterov 1992a)
				(Nesterov 1992b)
1993				(VS 1993a)
				(Nesterov 1993a)
				(Nesterov 1993b)
				(Zharova 1993a)
				(Ponomarenko 1993)
				(Riabushkin 1993)
				(Zharova 1993b)
				(VS 1993b)

assets (Nesterov and Larionova 1992; Semchenko 1992) and how to handle the household sector (VS 1993d, 1993e). Nesterov (1992b) pointed out that the SNA would require the use (and hence implementation) of approximately 150 international standards.

Assessments of progress in Russia's implementation of the SNA in the first years also show that it was a complicated and difficult task. None of the articles, though, suggests a retreat from the SNA or a return to the MPS system. Zharova (1993b) reported on the progress of the SNA implementation in the first quarter of 1993 and was positive in many ways, listing various tasks that had been fulfilled and cooperation with the OECD and other international organizations, but the article also stated that the state program on the implementation of the SNA was held up by a lack of funds in March 1993, resulting in delays in the implementation schedule. This concern about financing was repeated in June 1993, even noting that contracts with subcontractors could not be fulfilled (VS 1993b). Ponomarenko (1993) outlined several difficulties including problems with how services were being included, but he nevertheless was entirely positive on the SNA as a goal.[7]

The closest thing to a criticism of the SNA itself was an article by Riabushkin (1993). He wrote that the implementation of the SNA in Russia was difficult because of the unstable economic situation, incomplete institutional reform at the national level regarding political and economic reforms, regional variation in governance structures, and different levels of economic development across regions (1993, 29–30). He suggested "adaptation" of the SNA to fit particular economic circumstances, using the United States and Germany as models and that in Russia's case some aspects of the MPS might be useful given the transition economy. He writes: "Today, it is evident that during the transition period, the parallel functioning of the implemented accounts of the SNA and traditional and nontraditional categories of the MPS...is possible. They do not have equivalents in the national accounting of foreign developed countries. But this does not exclude the possibility that, after a corresponding modernization and adaptation, they also might be used after the deep implementation of SNA in statistical practice" (1993, 30). The suggestion of the use of any MPS methodology at this point in time seems rather radical, but Riabushkin is quick to point out that (1) SNA practice varies across states (e.g., the U.S. and German models); (2) before any such tinkering, the SNA must first be implemented "deeply"; (3) anything from the MPS would have to be modernized and adapted before being used; and (4) international standards should be the guide for any such innovation. On this last point he explains: "Of course, it would be a mistake to invent something unique in the process of transition to world standards. It is necessary to adopt those standards that were selected and reviewed by international statistical organizations over many years and those in practice of national statistical agencies that

7. For another assessment of SNA progress as of September 1993, see VS 1993c.

are appropriate for us, and of course, not only in the United States and Germany" (1993, 31). As this article suggests, by 1993 even the hint of using elements from the MPS system had to be clarified to emphasize that there was no question of the commitment to implementing the SNA according to international standards.

In summary, consideration of *Vestnik statistiki* articles from 1985 to 1993 yields a clear conclusion about the commitment to systems of national accounting over time in the USSR and the Russian Federation: that the change in thinking regarding the appropriateness of different systems happened fairly quickly between 1988 and 1992. Whereas before 1988 there seemed to be a solid commitment to continuing the MPS in socialist states, that commitment was challenged in 1989–91, and the MPS was totally abandoned by 1992. Even in the face of difficulties in actual implementation, the post-1992 articles suggest continued and strengthened commitment to the SNA, and a striking aspect of this support is how rapidly it developed.

A Conditional Norm: Analysis of Arguments Supporting the SNA and Its Components

In this section we return to the core question of this book: what explains the enthusiasm for the SNA at Goskomstat in the early 1990s? Here I analyze the reasons put forth by actors involved in the introduction of the SNA and its components. I present evidence from three types of sources: content analysis of *Vestnik statistiki,* arguments from other text-based sources (i.e., journals and textbooks) by Goskomstat statisticians, and interviews with Goskomstat officials.

The primary argument that I make based on these sources is that a conditional norm specifying the use of the SNA for market-based economies and the MPS for centrally planned economies was at work; that is, actors repeatedly explained the need for the SNA (or parts of it) in the USSR and Russia by the change in the structure of the economy, which necessitated new types of data and a new statistical system. In addition, two other arguments for the move to the SNA were the need for international comparability of data and the need to meet international standards. These arguments are sensible in light of the earlier discussion of the content of identity at Goskomstat. The analysis here shows that the conditional norm specifying the appropriate circumstances for the SNA was consistent over time. What changed were the circumstances in the USSR.

In response to increasing international support for the SNA, Soviet statisticians attempted to maintain their standing internationally by linking the SNA to the structure of the economy. Their demarcation of circumstances in which the SNA was appropriate marked the creation of a conditional norm.

The delineation of spheres of appropriateness for the SNA also solved an internal problem for Goskomstat, the conflict between supporting the Soviet state and supporting science and the norms of the community of international statisticians. By agreeing that the SNA should be used in capitalist countries, whereas the Soviet system was appropriate for socialist countries, Goskomstat statisticians could be both Soviet and international at the same time.

Analysis of Support for the SNA in *Vestnik statistiki*

In this section I examine in greater detail the twenty-four articles from table 7.2 that contained an explicit statement in favor of institutional change (i.e., those from the final three columns). I begin the analysis with 1988 because there was no support for using the SNA or GNP in the USSR before that; I end the analysis with 1993, because at that point the debate over systems was over.

The analysis of explanations in support of the SNA in the USSR and Russia is presented in table 7.3.

The first column lists the proposed changes and approximate years. As in table 7.2, they are grouped into three categories: calculation of GNP; integration of the MPS and the SNA; and implementation of the SNA alone. The next column lists all twenty-four articles. The two most common reasons for the changes are given in the final two columns. The first concerns the comparability of economic data across countries and the need to follow international standards. The second is the change in economic structure or the shift from central planning to a market economy.

What we can easily see from table 7.3 is that every article references one or both of these arguments: fifteen of the twenty-four state that international compatibility of data and standards necessitate change, while twenty cite a change in economic structure and the introduction of market reforms. In many ways these two sets of arguments work together. The conditional norm links a change in economic structure to the SNA. Without the conditional norm, a change in structure might be associated with any one of a range of institutional arrangements. The conditional norm mandates, in the presence of a market economy, abandonment of the MPS. Because the SNA is a set of international standards that allows for comparability of economic information, the goal of increasing the comparability of data and meeting international standards entails, in the absence of the MPS, a move to the SNA.

Another set of arguments for institutional change that I do not list on table 7.3 but which appears in many of the articles is that implementation

Table 7.3 Explanations for changes to the statistical system of the USSR and Russia: articles from *Vestnik statistiki,* 1988–93

PROPOSED CHANGE	ARTICLES	REASON FOR CHANGES: INTERNATIONAL COMPARABILITY AND STANDARDS	REASON FOR CHANGES: CHANGE IN ECONOMIC STRUCTURE TOWARD MARKETS
GNP calculations (1988)	(VS 1988)	✓	✓
	(Ivanov et al. 1988)	✓	✓
Integration of two systems (1989–92)	(Ivanov 1989)	✓	
	(Ivanov and Riabushkin 1989)	✓	✓
	(Ivanov and Riabushkin 1990)	✓	✓
	(Pogosov and Riabushkin 1990)		✓
	(Ivanov and Riabushkin 1991a)		✓
	(Zarubin and Pogosov 1991)	✓	✓
	(VS 1991a)	✓	
	(Medvedev 1992)		✓
Implementation of SNA only (1992 on)	(VS 1992a)	✓	✓
	(VS 1992b)	✓	✓
	(Guzhvin 1992a)		✓
	(Guzhvin 1992b)	✓	
	(Nesterov 1992a)		✓
	(Nesterov 1992b)		✓
	(VS 1993a)	✓	✓
	(Nesterov 1993a)		✓
	(Nesterov 1993b)	✓	✓
	(Zharova 1993a)		✓
	(Ponomarenko 1993)	✓	✓
	(Riabushkin 1993)	✓	✓
	(Zharova 1993b)		✓
	(VS 1993b)	✓	
Total number of articles	24	15 63%	20 83%

of the SNA would improve the quality of economic information (usually by making it more complete) and analysis of the economy, which would benefit policy making. These arguments derive from the argument regarding structural change, since there would otherwise be no need for new types of data or analysis. In addition, it would be surprising if any advocate of a change in national accounting practices did not suggest that the proposed change would improve the quality of the data. For these reasons I do not analyze this set of arguments in a separate section, but rather include them in the discussion of the other arguments for change.

Below I present examples from the texts, beginning with arguments related to international standards and compatibility, then examining arguments linking economic structural changes with the move to the SNA.

Comparability of Data and International Standards

The first *Vestnik statistiki* article on GNP methodology for the USSR stated as one of the main reasons for introducing GNP that it would make possible direct comparisons of economic growth levels between the USSR and other countries (VS 1988). The article also framed GNP data as adding to the overall understanding of the economy and strengthening international ties. Ivanov and Riabushkin's 1990 article also made the case for integrating the MPS and the SNA as equal systems by arguing that integration would allow for internationally comparable macroeconomic indicators and improve domestic analysis of the economy.

Zarubin and Pogosov (1991) detailed the relationship among the indicators of the SNA, the MPS and the International Comparison Program. The article included a large table summarizing the relationships and highlighted the joint work of Goskomstat USSR and the UN on integrating the SNA and the MPS. In this case the integration of the two systems in the USSR was framed as an extension of international efforts toward comparability among standards.

In the first set of recommendations for implementation of the SNA, rather than integration of the MPS and the SNA, the Statkom CIS articles in July and August 1992 (VS 1992a, 1992b) cite the need for comparable economic data, and the July article also reported that the SNA was recommended by the UN and used in over 120 countries. Comparability of the data within the newly independent CIS was particularly important due to the extensive but erstwhile integration of the new states' economies. After mid-1992, when the decision to move to the SNA in Russia had been formalized and implementation was underway, comparability and the importance of international standards remained a commonly cited reason for the change (Nesterov 1992b).

Structural Economic Change toward a Market Economy

The arguments explaining the move to the SNA in terms of structural changes to the economy invoke the same explanation used in the pre-perestroika discourse: the suitability of the SNA for capitalist economies and the MPS for centrally planned economies. According to that view, when the economy changed, the country's statistical system also had to change. In an argument for integration of the MPS and the SNA in the context of a comprehensive overview of the SNA,

Pogosov and Riabushkin (1990) posited that the MPS was important for understanding the economy as the object of administrative methods of governing and centralized, structured planning, but that the SNA, as a macrostatistical model, was oriented toward a market economy. Given the market reforms, an approach combining the MPS and the SNA would be necessary. *Vestnik statistiki* explained the need for integration with the SNA in a similar way: "such an approach is dictated by current conditions and needs of the transition period from a centrally planned to a market economy" (VS 1991a, 19).

Another aspect of the suitability of the SNA to market economies is its potential to improve economic policy making. Ivanov and Riabushkin write, "the adoption of the SNA in the statistical practice of East European states is very important in the context of the forthcoming general adaptation of statistics of those countries to new economic conditions, because the SNA is central in the economy as an instrument of its coordination" (1991a, 21). Here the authors note that the SNA can be used as a tool in the coordination of market economies, based on a Keynesian approach. In reviewing the decision to move to the SNA in Russia and the progress on implementation by the spring of 1993, Zharova (1993b) explained that the state program on the transition to the SNA was one of the necessary elements in the development of a market economy. Riabushkin called the SNA "the macroeconomic model for a market economy" and a reflection of the way that a market economy works (1993, 30–31). He noted that strategic decisions and policy analysis were not possible without the appropriate macroeconomic indicators, which in a market economy come from the SNA.

Many articles mentioned both structural changes in the economy and the need for comparable data based on international standards. In the follow-up article to the introduction of GNP in the USSR, Ivanov et al. explained that the Soviet Union needed to calculate GNP because of general restructuring of the management of the national economy and the need for better data suited to the new conditions (1988, 32). But they also noted the necessity of further international exchanges of information. The next year Ivanov and Riabushkin argued that the context of radical economic reform required improved macroeconomic aggregate indicators, such as those provided by the SNA, and that these new indicators would allow for international comparisons (1989, 31).

The Statkom CIS recommendations of 1992 noted that the new SNA-based indicators would better reflect the economic processes of the market and allow for international comparisons and the use of international standards, which would lead to a better understanding of the economy and better ways to solve the current economic problems (VS 1992a). Similar arguments were presented throughout 1992–93 (Nesterov 1993b; Ponomarenko 1993; VS 1993a).

Evidence for a Conditional Norm in Other Texts

Evidence for the conditional norm among statisticians can be found in other sources such as *Voprosy ekonomiki* (Questions of economics), one of the leading economic journals. In an article titled "Russian Statistics Today and Tomorrow," Pavel Guzhvin states that "with the switch to a market economy [statistical] principles should be changed"(1993, 5).

Youri Ivanov and his coauthors published their arguments in other publications besides *Vestnik statistiki* and their reasoning on the need for changes to the statistical system in the USSR/Russia is very consistent. In *Voprosy ekonomiki,* Ivanov and Riabushkin note that the MPS was developed during the era of central planning when concepts such as "prices, interest, loans, and so on had only a secondary role in management of the economy" (1991b, 4). In the same article they argue, "it is clear that the MPS cannot be an effective instrument for analysis, forecasting, and planning the economy when the country is moving toward a market" (1991b, 3–4) and "the necessity of integrating the MPS and the SNA has to do with the fact that the economy is transitioning toward a market and must adapt to the world economic system, allowing the USSR to more actively participate in the activities of international economic organizations" (1991b, 4).

Ivanov (1993), again in *Voprosy ekonomiki,* invokes the same line of reasoning to explain the switch to the SNA. He states that the MPS was meant to describe a planned economy and therefore could not capture certain important aspects of a market economy—for example, analysis of foreign trade and financial services (1993, 24). He then sums up the advantages of the SNA: "the transition to the SNA will solve a number of issues: it will provide a market-economy-oriented system of macroeconomic data, which is necessary for developing economic policies by state officials; it will help establish economic cooperation within the CIS; it will solve the problem of reporting data to international economic organizations; and it will increase the general level of statistical and economic work" (1993, 31). Here Ivanov brings in not only the conditional norm linking the economy to the statistical system but also the need for higher-quality economic data, necessary for policy analysis, and the need for making Russian economic statistics accessible to international organizations. In a later article he again stresses the change in the economy as the primary reason for the transformation of Soviet statistics (Ivanov 2001), and makes virtually the same argument in an article summarizing ten years of the SNA in the CIS (Ivanov 2004a).

Individuals outside Goskomstat also make this connection between the economy and the appropriateness of a particular statistical system. In *Voprosy ekonomiki,* Iurii Stepanov of the Central Bank of Russia writes that "directly using the existing economic indicators, developed under the previous system of central planning, is insufficient, because in the new conditions that can lead to serious misrepresentation and underestimation of many factors that define the development of Russian economy in the transition period" (1993, 32). The idea has now permeated textbooks on regional statistics as well: "In Russia practical interest in the SNA appeared in the 1980s in connection with the transformation from the planned to a market economy" (Riabtsev and Chudilina 2001, 191).

The conditional norm held by Goskomstat statisticians is more than a structural explanation for move to the SNA. It legitimates Goskomstat's past work on the MPS in addition to prescribing change in the conditions of a move to markets. Those outside Goskomstat did not share this norm and that is evident in other articles published in *Voprosy ekonomiki.* In an article titled "The Market and Statistics," M. Nazarov (1991), an economist, makes the link between the economy and the statistical system but has no positive words for the MPS or Goskomstat USSR. He does not suggest that the MPS is appropriate for central planning. Instead, he points out that at the first Congress of People's Deputies in May–June 1989, Goskomstat was called "one of the state organizations, whose activities were allowed to manipulate public opinion with false numbers that misrepresented reality" (1991, 12) and recounts Goskomstat Chairman Kirichenko's admission that GNP calculations for 1985–87 were adjusted after the fact several times. He states clearly that Soviet methodology is deficient and should be totally replaced, criticizes Goskomstat as a politicized organization, and even calls for the creation of a new institute of statistics under the Russian Academy of Sciences. He attributes the serious economic problems of the time (high inflation, a drop in living standards, etc.) to significant mistakes by the Party and Gorbachev's government but also assigns Goskomstat USSR some of the blame.

Even so, Nazarov prominently mentions the market reforms as a key reason for adopting a new statistical system. He writes, "transition to the market fundamentally changes the sources of data" and that changes in price statistics will be "of great importance in the market conditions" (1991, 13–14). Although not yet calling for the SNA per se, he holds that "it is necessary to bring the system of indicators into accordance with internationally accepted approaches and standards, which will allow for direct international comparisons" (1991, 15) and that "at present, we have to approach the statistics of capitalist countries differently. Everything useful should be used in our own practice." (1991, 15–16). Nazarov clearly makes the link between the structure of the economy and the statistical system but without legitimating the MPS.

For Goskomstat statisticians, in contrast, the conditional norm allowed the change in economic structure to explain the move to the SNA in Russia, providing a face-saving way out of admitting any problems with past Soviet statistics.

For example, in an article on transition countries' implementation of the SNA Ivanov and Homenko acknowledge the need for new price statistics in Russia and Eastern Europe but did not admit problems with the price statistics of the Soviet period. Instead, they say only, "the methods that were used in this area in the recent past in conditions of the CPEs [centrally planned economies] are not acceptable under new circumstances" (1996, 336). New market conditions demand different prices statistics, but presumably in the absence of those "new circumstances" the previous type would be acceptable.

Consistent with the reliance on economic structure as the determining factor in the use of statistical systems and with the high regard for Soviet-era statistics, in the same article Ivanov and Homenko note that "the revised 1993 SNA is, in principle, applicable to any type of economy" (1996, 326) before listing several characteristics of transition economies that present problems for the SNA.[8] They imply that in conditions of transition, some elements of the MPS could still be used by postcommunist countries that have moved to the SNA: "the work on the introduction of the SNA in countries in transition should take into account the recent experience with the MPS; the MPS balances contain a lot of data necessary for compilation of national accounts, and in a number of cases only limited rearrangement of these data might be needed" (1996, 324).

Although I have not done a systematic analysis of arguments outside the USSR/Russia regarding the reasons for the move to the SNA, there is some evidence that the conditional norm was shared by statisticians in CMEA NSOs. It is clear from the writings of the Hungarian expert on national accounts, János Árvay (1973), that he thinks that economic structure is the key basis on which statistical decisions should be made, and that changes in structure require changes in statistics. In discussing how Hungary navigated the use of both the SNA and the MPS, Árvay notes that Hungary adopted SNA methodology on income distribution because "the income categories of the SNA could be directly connected with the concepts and regulations pertaining to the new economic management system introduced in 1968 [in Hungary]" (1994, 232).

Árvay defends the MPS as a system for centrally planned economies at several points and cautions against excessive expectations for the SNA during the transition period: "Many economists and statisticians in Eastern and Central Europe consider the SNA as a magic tool and expect from its introduction significantly more than it will realistically provide in the first years. This is particularly valid in the transition period when the institutional framework of a market economy has not yet been established; prices do not properly reflect supply and demand and

8. These included the "sectorization" of the economy, subsidies, bank output, social services provided by firms, privatization, and "holding gains or losses" (Ivanov and Homenko 1996, 326–33).

the structure of the economy is still greatly distorted, etc." (1994, 233). Although Árvay did not recommend the continued use of the MPS, he did make clear that the MPS was an internationally recommended system which had certain merits for centrally planned economies and that its development and demise were integral to the eventual formulation of the 1993 SNA.

The Conditional Norm at the International Level

The conditional norm that specified the appropriateness of the MPS versus the SNA was tolerated but not held as a norm among fellow national statisticians at the international level. Several factors operated here.

Above all, statisticians in the West did not think of the SNA as perfectly reflective of a "market economy" or capitalism, especially given the variety of economic institutions and statistical systems in the West before the 1990s. The contested history of the SNA suggests that statisticians in the West recognized that there are different ways to define, categorize, and measure any economy. Hence there was not the same level of support for the Marxist view that the economy should determine the statistical system. But there was awareness that politics and other factors impinge on statistics systems and NSOs. Thus Westerners could recommend the MPS as an international system without subscribing to Goskomstat's conditional norm.

Discussions of the transition to the SNA revealed certain differences between CMEA statisticians and their international colleagues. For example, Anne Harrison notes at a conference on this topic held in Minsk in April 1993 that, despite concerns about applicability of the 1993 SNA to planned economies, "it was discovered that in fact there are only half a dozen areas where special interpretation may be needed for centrally planned economies" (1996, 340). She goes on, "Typically, the SNA did give a solution, though these solutions were not always the same as in the MPS and therefore, for lack of familiarity, did not always seem easily acceptable (1996, 340).[9]

Harrison comments in greater detail on two crucial issues regarding the transition from the MPS to the SNA: inflation and the informal economy. On inflation she questions the fit of the SNA: "In 1992 inflation in the countries of the former Soviet Union was on the order of 1,200 percent, and concerns arise about

9. In one case, consumer subsidies, Harrison notes that the 1993 SNA in general does not address this issue adequately, and hence there was a special provision made for transition countries. Ironically, however, this issue was not included in the general 1993 SNA revision because CMEA representatives at the expert group meetings opposed it (based on the difficulty of drawing a line between government expenditure and consumer subsidies). See Harrison 1996, 340.

what current price figures mean in such circumstances. Should constant price data still be derived by deflation, or would it be better to derive estimates using volume measures directly?" (1996, 341). In this case the solution was not obvious and the use of volume measures, although a holdover from the Soviet past, may have been the right choice.

On the measurement of informal activity, Harrison is more directly critical of Soviet era practices: "The tradition in countries in transition was to measure activity meticulously with the care of a bookkeeper. The need to take into account small-scale informal activity that is mushrooming at an undreamed-of rate points to the need for the statistical offices to move away from past practices and to become statisticians instead of bookkeepers" (1996, 341). This rare criticism by someone working on national accounts at the international level of NSOs in Eastern Europe and the FSU touches on the issue of sampling, a topic that had separated Western and CMEA statisticians for decades. Here, as elsewhere in the Western literature, we see that, although the Goskomstat conditional norm was not explicitly rejected, neither were underlying structural economic conditions considered determinative of statistical systems by national statisticians at the international level.

Interviews: The SNA as a Conditional Norm at Goskomstat

I asked several Goskomstat officials how they personally became convinced that Russia needed to adopt the SNA. Chairman Vladimir Sokolin (2004) said, "In general, I was among the people who argued that it was important to introduce a whole new statistical system rather than to focus on specific [limited adaptations]. Former Goskomstat Chairman Iurkov was also for the modernization of the whole system." He then noted that during perestroika there were discussions about limited versus systemic changes within Goskomstat, with other Russian social scientists, and with foreigners. In the end, he said, "this is how we deepened our understanding of the fact that Soviet statistics, although they were quality statistics, were not suited to the new economic system" (Sokolin 2004). It is notable that Sokolin stressed his view that Soviet statistics were "quality statistics."

Andrei Kosarev, who was the head of national accounts at Goskomstat from 1995–1997, and who also directed the Center for Economic Analysis, which conducted some of the first independent estimates of GDP for 1990–1994, emphasized economic change as the main reason for the move to the SNA.[10] He said, "In the Soviet Union we knew about the System of National Accounts at a theoretical

10. Kosarev later served as one of twenty country experts responsible for the development of the 2008 SNA.

level. At the time, some economists declared that we needed the SNA because the rest of the world has it—that is something I disagree with. Sure, that is one reason, but it is not the fundamental reason.... I realized that a new system was needed given the new economy" (Kosarev 2004).

A number of Goskomstat officials did not put much thought into the move to the SNA. They claimed it was a natural outcome of the change in the structure of the economy. Irina Masakova (2004) noted: "Life itself suggested it as everything was changing. *Statistics is a mirror of the economy.* It was obvious that it was important to change, so there were no discussions about it. Everything was synchronous with the economy" (emphasis added).

Many other officials, especially lower-level ones, repeated this sentiment. One said: "I do not remember. This understanding was born naturally" (GKS40 2004). According to another, "reality simply brought us there" (GKS44 2004). Others were categorical in attributing the change to the change in the economy: "The transition was caused, first and foremost, by the economic changes" (GKS50 2004).

One official noted that unlike in the past, there was now a fundamental similarity across statistical systems, due to the existence of market economies across countries: "Russian statistics adapted to international principles. We became certain that the understanding of statistics in different countries is similar. Today statistics not only provide information but have also adapted to the market economy" (GKS49 2004). As economies became similar, so should statistical systems, and this norm of international commensurability across all statistical systems—the SNA—was appropriate for a postcommunist world.

In the interviews, of course, some differences were expressed. Not every official responded to the question about the reasons for the move to SNA in exactly the same way. Some officials offered a combination of reasons, including structural economic change as well as the efforts of employees, international assistance, and economic changes. One said, "As far as my department goes, the main explanations were: (1) changes in the economy, (2) the enthusiasm of our specialists, and (3) support and statistical experience of international organizations" (GKS12 2004). Another said: "A little bit of everything. Particularly important were the support of international organizations (without which it would have been difficult), ideas, and our enthusiastic specialists" (GKS35 2004). A third credited the economic changes and a desire to become part of the international community as the main drivers: "internal demand was probably the central reason here, even though this demand could have been born from an external push. Indeed, if we wanted to be part of the international community, we needed new information—hence the internal demand. That is, the economy began to change, and the need for new indicators appeared" (GKS40 2004). Here we again see the relationship between the need for international comparability of data and economic reform that characterized so many *Vestnik statistiki* articles. The need to be part of the "international community," however, speaks to an identity-based motivation.

In this chapter I have outlined the evidence for the existence of a conditional norm delineating the appropriateness of the SNA versus the MPS. Soviet statisticians were the primary "holders" of this norm, which limited the SNA to capitalist states or those with market economies and suggested that the MPS was the appropriate national accounting system for centrally planned economies.

When communism fell, this conditional norm triggered interest in the shift to the SNA among Goskomstat statisticians. Ironically, the same norm that made it possible for Goskomstat statisticians to reconcile for decades their use of the Soviet statistical system with their commitment to international statistical standards turned out to be a recipe for change.

The chapter illustrates two key aspects of the shift. First, there was genuine support for the SNA in Goskomstat at the beginning of the 1990s; the SNA was not simply imposed from outside. Second, support for implementation of the SNA at Goskomstat grew very quickly from 1988 to 1992. Before 1988 no one considered moving to the SNA as a possibility; after 1992 retention of the previous system seemed equally unthinkable.

Furthermore, the sources I analyze reveal that the need for international comparability and standards as well as market reforms were the key reasons given for the move to the SNA at Goskomstat. Although the shared identity of national statisticians proves to have been critical to the transformation of Soviet statistics, it is a change in the conditions specified by shared norms, rather than a change in norms or identity per se, that explains the rapid abandonment of the MPS in favor of the SNA in the USSR and Russia.

CONCLUSION

The story of institutional change at Goskomstat defies common perceptions of the intransigence of bureaucrats. By going inside the state and examining in depth what has happened at Goskomstat since the end of the USSR, we see that an apparently static, hierarchical, Soviet-type organization has actually been internally abuzz with change, spearheaded by people who are moved not by their meager salaries but by the idea of making Russian statistics legitimate and respected around the world. This is a story of the power of professional identities and norms and of the ingenuity of local actors who adapt those norms to suit their circumstances.

In this final chapter I review the primary findings from this study of the move by postcommunist countries to the System of National Accounts (SNA) and highlight key implications of the analysis for our understanding of bureaucracy, the state, the SNA, and institutional change. I explore what the move to the SNA means for Goskomstat as a bureaucratic organization: is this a case of bureaucratic "reform," and are the institutional changes at Goskomstat stable? I also consider what the analysis of institutional change at Goskomstat contributes to studies of state building and state capacity more generally. Given that implementation of the 2008 SNA is getting underway, I address the question of what Goskomstat's experience suggests for future implementation efforts. Finally, I propose how the concept of conditional norms—the central theoretical argument of this book—can contribute to understandings of institutional change more broadly.

Russia's Move to the System of National Accounts

The SNA is the basis for all national economic statistics because it structures virtually all economic information within and across countries. Even though the SNA per se is not particularly well known outside national accounting circles, the results of the SNA framework, aggregate macroeconomic indicators such as GDP, are easily recognized. One purpose of this book has been to pull back the curtain on tidy concepts like GDP and reveal the less orderly process by which a single system for national accounting in the world has been achieved.

Central to this development, I argue, was the move by postcommunist countries in the 1990s to give up their alternative system and embrace the SNA. The actions of postcommunist countries were far from the only important events in the development of the SNA as a hegemonic institution, but the events of the 1990s in the Soviet bloc were significant in turning the SNA into an international norm.

The adoption of the SNA by postcommunist countries was surprising in terms of both the magnitude and the direction of change. These countries abruptly abandoned the Material Product System (MPS) in 1989–90 and have since excelled on nearly every indicator of SNA implementation. This book offers an explanation located at both the international and domestic level for why that happened.

Analysis of the historical development of the SNA exposes certain factors that turned out to be critical for later implementation of the system. First and foremost, the SNA was not a top-down externally imposed institution. It developed in a context of significant variation in national practices and the actions of international organizations, and there was continuous, multilateral interaction between the national and international levels. In iterative rounds since its beginnings shortly after WWII, each version of the SNA underwent revisions soon after its formal approval. This was a process characterized by contestation and mutual constitution between national statistical offices and international rules. Implementation of the SNA has to be seen in this light.

Rather than treat the SNA as an exogenous, alien set of rules for which carrots and sticks guide compliance, we should consider how national statisticians view their own role in SNA development and how the system fits into the context of existing national statistical practices. At Goskomstat, Soviet interactions with East European and international statisticians were critical to Russia's later implementation of the SNA. International standards were not forced on Goskomstat in the 1990s; rather, there was *internal* interest in the SNA in postcommunist countries. This book explains the source of that interest.

There are several possible explanations for Russia's move to the SNA. Structural explanations are a start, given the changes in postcommunist economies, but the SNA was not just an efficient, aggregate reflection of economic structure—there are many mirrors of the economy. Actors had choices, so, support for the hard and costly work of implementing the SNA as the single coordinated statistical system for national accounts required more than compatible economic conditions. Structural variables such as material resources at the state and organizational level were severely limited, but implementation efforts at postcommunist NSOs were aided by their stock of human capital and technical support from international organizations. This resource support for implementation, however, does not explain the rapid change in internal interest in the SNA by postcommunist NSOs.

Politics or material incentives also failed to explain the shift in interests: Goskomstat operated with a high degree of autonomy in a weak and impoverished state, and its actions were not dictated by the government or other outside actors or by the material interests of statisticians. And, although fundamental change in Russia's economic structure did take place, the introduction of markets did not expand Goskomstat's resources: if anything, it reduced the material incentives to the agency for rapid and comprehensive institutional change.

International norms and organizational identities offer other potential explanations for the change in internal interest in the SNA in Russia. But because it was postcommunist countries' acceptance of the SNA that solidified the SNA as an international norm, the norm followed rather than caused those states to switch to the SNA.

Identity at Goskomstat and among national statisticians internationally was an important factor in the postcommunist turn to the SNA, but not in the way that we traditionally think of identity as a variable in institutional change. Although the organizational identity of Goskomstat did evolve in some areas, there was also much continuity. Rather than identity change, contestation in identity content at Goskomstat gave rise to a conditional norm delineating the appropriateness of the SNA and MPS as national accounting systems for different types of economies—the SNA for market economies and the MPS for planned economies. This conditional norm became the key factor driving Russia's move to the SNA.

Implications for Goskomstat as an Organization

One question not raised earlier in the book is what the dramatic change in the framework for national statistics means for "reform" at Goskomstat. How does the move to the SNA affect our assessments of Goskomstat as a bureaucratic organization, and what is the likelihood that institutional changes related to the SNA are permanent?

Reform at Goskomstat

The term "reform" is normatively charged and should be distinguished from analyses of specific institutional changes. Nevertheless, Goskomstat's move to the SNA raises the question of whether Goskomstat has been reformed. To answer this question, although there is no single metric for assessing reform of a bureaucracy, we can assess the organization in terms of the *content, reliability,* and *accessibility* of its data—typical ways in which national statistical offices are assessed—since its adoption of the SNA. In all three areas there have been significant, mostly positive changes at Goskomstat. The content of Russian economic statistics changed radically from the Soviet MPS to the SNA; this change was positive in that it increased the coverage of various areas of the economy and has allowed for greater international commensurability of Russian economic data.

The reliability of economic statistics at Goskomstat has also improved in the post-Soviet period. One reason for this is the strengthening of the legal framework in which Goskomstat operates in comparison to the Soviet period. In addition, politicization of economic statistics today is nowhere near the level it was in Soviet times; the SNA provides an institutional framework that leaves far less room for government discretion and hence politicization. To a great extent, Goskomstat has become an independent bureaucratic organization, although areas where this institutional autonomy could be strengthened remain.

Organizational capacity is often a critical variable for the reliability of data. While Goskomstat had a relatively high level of human capital, the level of material resources at the organization were lowest during the phase of greatest institutional change, the early 1990s. As the financial condition of the Russian state has recovered since 1999, Goskomstat's organizational capacity has improved. Its ability to carry out the goals it sets for itself has grown significantly, even though in some ways it still has less capacity than it did in the Soviet era.

Professional values at the organization have followed an uneven path. In the Soviet period employees felt allegiance both to statistics as a science and to the Soviet state. To some extent, these values have moved more toward the professionalism of international statisticians, although the conflicting allegiance to the state remains to some degree. At this juncture, public trust has not really been established between Goskomstat and its respondents in society at large; as in Soviet times, the level of trust today remains low.

In accessibility, measured in terms of data dissemination and transparency, there have been very significant and positive changes from the Soviet to the post-Soviet period. The sheer volume of data released by Goskomstat today is many times higher than in the Soviet period. In general, data are released in a timely manner and in a variety of formats. Moreover, although some serious transparency issues remain, the level of transparency now is vastly better than in the Soviet period. Although not every specific data anomaly has been explained, the days of foreign analysts independently attempting to decode purposefully misleading books is largely over. Now, most of the methodology is publicly available, and Goskomstat officials are by and large willing to explain their work. Even among the organization's critics, there is a scholarly consensus that accessibility of data at Goskomstat has improved dramatically.

Thus, measured in terms of content, reliability, and accessibility, "reform" of Goskomstat as a bureaucracy during the 1990s was fairly successful. The content of Russian statistics is now in line with international practice. The most egregious problems of reliability, especially politicization, have been addressed, and data accessibility is increasingly close to the highest international standards.

Future Prospects for Goskomstat

But is institutional change at Goskomstat permanent? Given the general retreat from democracy in Russia under Presidents Putin and Medvedev, one has to wonder whether Goskomstat can maintain its post-Soviet autonomy and international professionalism in an environment of growing executive power. Some institutional changes, once initiated, become self-reinforcing mechanisms. For example, once the decision to regularly publish methodological notes was made, and the content and categories of analysis at Goskomstat became more transparent, it became more difficult to hide information through "descriptive distortions" or other mechanisms involving methodological secrecy, and outside analysts attained greater ability to check the accuracy of Goskomstat's data. The change to the SNA entailed scrapping an entire set of categories of analysis, and the costs of moving back to some alternative to the SNA (which does not really exist anymore) would be enormous. In this way, the move to the SNA was a critical juncture, rendering a reversal very unlikely.

Furthermore, a comprehensive law on statistics was passed in the fall of 2007 (Federal'nyi zakon 2007), which set out the legal basis for statistical work in Russia. This law is consistent with international recommendations, including provisions regarding privacy of data and methodology. It also states that the statistical system should be based on "official statistical methodology corresponding to international standards and principles of official statistics, as well as to legislation of the Russian Federation" and should include "openness and accessibility of such methodology" (Federal'nyi zakon 2007). So at this point the legal basis for the use of the SNA and other international methodologies is fairly stable.

I have argued above that the primary explanation for institutional change in economic statistics in Russia was a conditional norm regarding the appropriateness of particular statistical systems, which was at work in the context of organizational identities, political interests, and economic resources. In this account, the crucial variable is the understandings regarding the appropriateness of the SNA. Currently, there is widespread internal support within Goskomstat for the SNA and for standards of content, reliability, and access that are consistent with international practice. However, if the Russian political establishment were to retreat from the standards of the international community, as it did in Soviet times, Goskomstat employees might again face conflicting goals. Under those circumstances, we might see the development of new conditional norms, but at present there is a great deal of consensus on the appropriateness of the SNA.

In terms of organizational autonomy and resources at Goskomstat, however, there is some cause for concern. In the summer of 2008, for the first time since it emerged from the institutional shadow of Gosplan in 1948, Goskomstat was put under the authority of a ministry, the newly created Ministry of Economic Development, rather than having independent status within the executive branch. At the time this change did not seem consequential, but the financial crisis that began in the fall of 2008 appears to have strained the relationship between Goskomstat and the government. In April 2009 Goskomstat stopped publishing monthly unemployment figures based on ILO methodology and announced it would publish quarterly reports instead (Kulikov and Skliarov 2009). Goskomstat Chairman Vladimir Sokolin said that the Goskomstat monthly reports were inaccurate and costly, but the real reason seems to have been that the Goskomstat reports conflicted with those of the Health and Social Development Ministry, which did not use ILO methodology. Perhaps not coincidentally, the Goskomstat numbers were also three times higher than the Health and Social Development Ministry figures, which portrayed unemployment as falling.

Another troubling sign came in the summer of 2009, when the government announced that the 2010 census would be delayed until 2013, which would have been a violation of the 2002 law on the census that calls for a census every ten years (Pravitel'stvo Rossiiskoi Federatsii 2002, art. 3, par. 1). The decision was reversed without explanation in late October, but the incident raises questions about Goskomstat's autonomy in the current political environment. When the decision was announced, Goskomstat had already begun preparations for the 2010 census, and there was much speculation that, because the pre-trials suggested that the Russian population of Russia might have fallen below 140 million (2 million fewer than the government was reporting at the time), a census in 2010 would reveal a dramatic drop in population. This would be politically embarrassing and could present a negative picture of the economy in terms of the available workforce. The ostensible reason for the postponement was lack of financing, but no one took this argument seriously—not least because the census is expected to cost between 11 to 17 billion rubles (374 to 578 million US dollars), which is only about 0.2 percent of Russian budget expenditures for 2010. It did not escape notice that a presidential election is scheduled for 2012, making the 2013 date politically suspect.

Then, in October 2009, Vladimir Sokolin abruptly retired as head of Goskomstat and gave sharply negative interviews to the magazine *Itogi* (a Russian equivalent of *Newsweek*) and *Vedomosti*, a widely respected financial newspaper (published in conjunction with the *Financial Times*), in which he directly criticized economists in the government and the Ministry of Economic Development. It was widely speculated that Sokolin was bothered by the interference of the Ministry of Economic Development and was disappointed by the postponement of the 2010 census. However, Aleksandr Surinov, a longtime deputy of Sokolin's, was named director of Goskomstat. Surinov has written methodological textbooks on statistics and was a proponent of the SNA and the law on statistics. His appointment is thus not a bad sign, although it is still unclear what impact, if any, the change of leadership will have on the organization.

Implications for State Building and State Capacity

Goskomstat's move to the SNA was an instance of building state capacity. The Russian state, as well as citizens and international actors, arguably now have more comprehensible information about the Russian economy than ever before. While state capacity is lauded as the basis for all kinds of positive outcomes—security, economic development, public health, and so on—this book suggests several lessons, including where to look and what kind of explanations to look for in efforts to build state capacity.

Capacity at both the state and international levels is fragmented—that is, not uniform across agencies internationally or within states. To understand the development of state capacity, then, the case of Goskomstat highlights the need to disaggregate the state and look at organizational variation within states and across time, and to look as well at cross-national variation in organizational outcomes. This is time-consuming research, but it yields a more accurate understanding of state capacity, including the important phenomenon of islands of state capacity within seemingly dysfunctional states, or vice versa.[1]

Another point about state capacity revealed by the experience of Goskomstat is that public attitudes toward government agencies are a poor indicator of the state of reform. Very little of what has happened at Goskomstat since the 1990s has registered with the public or even with experts. Most people in Russia continue to cite Soviet-era problems with statistics, know little of Goskomstat's move to the SNA, or even what the SNA is. Economists familiar with the SNA are among the strongest critics of Goskomstat because they hold it to the highest international standards and only grudgingly admit there has been substantial, positive institutional change, even though that fact is now well established in a range of international assessments of Russian statistics. Moreover, Goskomstat's experience is not unique—despite successful state reform in Russia related to tax policy, the legal system, and other state bureaucracies, widespread perceptions of a dysfunctional, corrupt state persist.[2]

As a result, to understand institutional change or state reform in Russia, we still have to investigate agency by agency; and we may expect to find that, given different institutional legacies, organizational norms, resources, specific actors' interests, and so on, the trajectory of institutional change or reform will differ. This is potentially true for all states. Hence we should be skeptical of generalizations about state capacity within states and of expert or public opinion about the progress of state reform. Unfortunately, many existing cross-national indicators of state capacity rely precisely on these assumptions of uniformity of capacity within states and the ability of expert opinion to accurately reflect reform. This study suggests we have to do more.

Beyond the question of where to look in analyzing state building and capacity, this book suggests what to look for—the causal factors that we should be considering. In particular, we need to take into account more explicitly international factors, such as norms and resources from international organizations. Although it may be self-evident that Goskomstat's move to the SNA—an international standard—requires attention to international factors, much of the literature

1. One important example of this is the ability of some states to develop highly demanding nuclear weapons programs in the midst of an otherwise weak state capacity environment. See Hymans 2008, 2010.

2. On this point, see Pryadilnikov 2009. Pryadilnikov finds substantial variation in reform of the Russian state bureaucracy. Kathryn Hendley (2007) has documented significant variation in courts and how well the legal system works.

on state building and state capacity, especially in comparative politics, remains focused on domestic rather than international factors.[3]

Another implication of this study for existing explanations of state building and capacity is the need to look beyond the material interests of actors to understand institutional change and bureaucratic reform. Although materially motivated struggles among elite interests have, no doubt, been a large part of the process of postcommunist state building, my analysis of Goskomstat's experience suggests that research on state building can benefit from attention to the norms that allow actors in particular times and places to define the appropriateness of specific institutional arrangements. Actors within Goskomstat were integral to the achievement of institutional change, but the origins of actors' changing interests turned out to be the result of conditional norms in the context of organizational identities and structural economic changes.

A cautionary implication of this study is that norm-based change may not be easy to replicate in other organizations. The seeds of change at Goskomstat were planted in the 1950s with the establishment of links to the international community of statisticians and the growth of a shared identity that gave meaning to group boundaries and norms. Without that shared identity, a conditional norm would probably not have arisen and the norms of the international community would have held little sway over Goskomstat statisticians. Identity building tends to be a long-term process, even if conditional norms can lead to rapid institutional transformation when conditions change.

Hence, in understanding the development of state capacity, the move to the SNA by postcommunist countries directs us to examine cross-national variation at the level of domestic state organizations, and to bring international factors and organizational-level norms and identities to our analyses of state building and institutional change.

Implications for Future Implementation of the SNA

As a practical organizational template for economic data the SNA is only as good as its implementation. As we know, implementation of the 1993 SNA varied quite a bit across countries. Implementation of the 2008 SNA is just beginning. It is worth considering what this analysis of the development and implementation of

3. Juliet Johnson's work on the reform of central banks in postcommunist states is a notable exception (2010).

the 1993 SNA by postcommunist countries suggests for future implementation efforts.

It is clear that ISWGNA—the organization behind the SNA—takes the issue of implementation very seriously. Even before the 2008 SNA was formally adopted, there was already a major conference devoted to it and a report with a series of concrete recommendations for implementation.[4] In the report ISWGNA identified six impediments to implementation (2008, 2). Three of the impediments were structural factors at the level of national statistical offices (NSOs)—low organizational capacity in terms of human resources, the need to improve infrastructure for data collection, and statistical and computational capacity. Two factors involved the actions of international organizations—the need for coordination across regional and international agencies and the need for more pragmatic training programs, including making manuals and other materials more accessible. One factor focused on the demand for high-quality economic statistics, citing the need to promote the quality and policy relevance of national accounts data.

To overcome these impediments, ISWGNA recommends a three-pronged implementation strategy (2008, 4). The first part concerns "strategic planning" to develop national statistical capacity by incorporating SNA implementation with overall development objectives in a country. This makes sense: the SNA is itself a metric for assessing NSO reform, and the improvement of NSO capacity and output should result in not only SNA implementation but also the production of higher-quality information for use by national policy makers and citizens. This has already happened in postcommunist countries. As they have implemented the SNA, there is no question that the quality and quantity of data available to governments, firms, and citizens have dramatically increased.

The second part of the implementation strategy focuses on coordination, monitoring, and reporting. Coordination addresses the timing and sequencing of NSO activity, monitoring implies assessment of how NSOs are doing, and reporting suggests active communication with international and regional organizations. At their core, coordination, monitoring, and reporting entail engagement between NSOs and international organizations. This can take the form of the IMF's Data Quality Assessment Framework. But it also connects to other international recommendations for statistical offices, such as the United Nations

4. See UN Statistical Commission 2008, 9–13; ISWGNA 2008. The conference was jointly organized by the Statistical Office of the European Communities and United Nations Statistics Division and was called the "International Conference on International Outreach and Coordination in National Accounts for Sustainable Growth and Development." It was held on May 6–8, 2008, in Luxembourg.

Economic Commission for Europe's recently revised *Classification of Statistical Activities*, which is a framework for annual reporting on the work of NSOs.

The third part of the implementation strategy involves improving national statistical systems. As discussed above, reform or improvement of the work of NSOs is in many ways related to SNA implementation, and a program for implementation of the SNA is a program for improvement of NSOs. However, whereas ISWGNA focused its 1993 SNA implementation efforts on what international organizations should do for NSOs, with the 2008 SNA implementation program it also explicitly cites the need to create "demand" from NSOs for implementation—an effort ISWGNA calls "advocacy" (2008, 7).

The implementation strategy for the 1993 SNA was based on four "modalities": meetings and workshops, technical cooperation, manuals and handbooks, and sponsorship of research on the implementation of the SNA (UN Statistical Commission 2008, 10). For 2008, the ISWGNA report notes:

> It is recognized that the well-tested four modalities used in the past are insufficient for a fully successful implementation of the SNA as they only address the support provided to countries for implementation. To be fully successful, the implementation strategy should also take into account the responsibilities of the countries to take ownership of the implementation process by including it in the development of their national statistical systems. Therefore, an additional element, advocacy, is added to the existing modalities with the aim to stimulate the demand for national accounts data and encourage the use of the accounts. (2008, 7–8)

Essentially, advocacy means getting actors at the national level to support the goal of developing high-quality economic statistics themselves.

Although the terminology is different, one can read this emphasis on advocacy as a recognition that national and organizational actors and interests affect SNA implementation. Whereas the focus of the implementation strategy in the past was on structural factors and information transfer, as if all interests were aligned toward the SNA to begin with, ISWGNA now seems to recognize that implementation also depends on getting national statisticians and policy makers *interested* in implementing the SNA.

The creation of interest in the implementation of the SNA has been the subject of this book; in particular, I have considered why national statisticians in postcommunist countries like Russia were willing to abandon the MPS and embrace the SNA. I find that the course of institutional change, and especially the national implementation of international institutions, is not so easily guided or managed by international actors alone. The history of SNA development is a case of mutual constitution where national interests and identities have an impact on the development of international institutions and norms and vice versa. My research supports the current ISWGNA strategy to focus on the creation of demand for SNA implementation at the national level. The postcommunist experience with the SNA may provide useful lessons.

The question of how to get bureaucrats to change course cannot be answered without directly examining the motivations of bureaucrats themselves, and the case of Goskomstat's move to the SNA suggests that identities and norms, rather than structural factors or material incentives alone, are critical variables for institutional change. The development of professional identities and of the conditional norm that delineated the appropriateness of the SNA, however, was not a short-term process at Goskomstat. Building a sense of group legitimacy among international actors as well as a desire by national statisticians in communist states to be accepted in international circles took decades. Nevertheless, this case suggests that professional identities and norms can be very powerful and may offer a way to build organizational capacity in conditions of limited material resources. Material incentives and information transfer will not be enough. Professional development in the form of conferences, meetings, journals, and other community-building measures—some of which are already underway in the existing four "modalities" for implementation of the SNA—may eventually bear fruit in the form of shared professional identities, norms, and shared interest in SNA implementation. In sum, the case of postcommunist countries' move to the SNA suggests a focus on identities and norms, including conditional norms, can both explain and contribute to institutional change and SNA implementation.

One cautionary note, however, is that this analysis does not suggest that norms, including conditional norms, are associated only with positive institutional outcomes. The conditional norm associated with the move to the SNA in the 1990s is the same one that supported the Soviet statistical system and the MPS for several decades. Moreover, by rationalizing the Soviet system both in the past and in the present, this norm enables Goskomstat as an organization to avoid any self-criticism or reflection on the failings of Soviet statistics. Although this norm was crucial to the change in economic statistics and the move to the SNA, it did not entail significant change in the identity of the organization overall. Indeed, one of the significant aspects of conditional norms is that they are consistent with maintaining legitimacy in groups and hence stability in identities and organizational culture.

Goskomstat's move to the SNA, however, has resulted in much closer engagement with international statisticians, and in the long run this engagement may have a significant effect on identity change. Russia's experience thus suggests that identities and conditional norms did make a significant difference in moving to the SNA, and that international organizations would do well to consider the role of professional identities and norms in future implementation strategies.

Conditional Norms and Institutional Change

The concept of conditional norms brings to the table a specific definition of norms, which builds on the existing scholarly consensus but advances conceptual clarity. Not only are norms behavioral prescriptions within a given identity group, but they also have holders—identity group members—and subjects—the type of actor to which the norm should apply. When a norm applies equally to all subjects, it is unconditional. When subjects are limited to certain types of actors, we can say the norm is conditional, and the specific limitations on the type of subjects to which the norm applies serve as important indicators of where and when the norm will be in effect. It is therefore useful to consider whether norms are conditional and to investigate the malleability of conditions if we seek to recognize the possibilities of norm-based change. Moreover, by understanding conditions, we gain a more precise understanding of the logic of norms, including their limitations and the contexts in which they work.

Investigating norms in terms of holders and subjects directs our attention to actors, who create and amend as well as carry out norm-based action. Rather than a diffuse sense of norms being somehow "out there" or generally in effect, to speak of holders of norms compels us to specify the identity group and actual people that embrace the norm as a part of their shared identity. The concept of norm subjects acknowledges the reality that many norms are targeted toward particular actors, denoted by certain conditions. Hence conditionality focuses analysis on understanding the actors who hold norms and the actors subject to norms.

When we focus our analysis of norms on actors, we necessarily have to work at the level of people on the ground. If the question is one of institutional change in a state bureaucratic organization, that means going into the bureaucracy to investigate identity content, including norms. If the analysis concerned firm-level support for particular institutions, it would require investigation of employee identity and norms. By focusing on practices and beliefs of identity groups at the organizational level, rather than in "the state" or "society" writ large, we are in a far better position to tackle the complex question of actors' interests, including how these interests relate to institutional change. Analysis of the implementation of the SNA—an international norm—took me to Goskomstat offices all over

Russia and to an examination of the historical relationship between Soviet and international statisticians.

The concept of conditional norms builds on pragmatism in setting out a constructivist approach that takes agency and mutual constitution seriously. To understand how identity-derived rules can work in a world of innovation and contingency is a difficult balancing act. But the acknowledgment that rules or norms are outcomes—set up by real people, followed under certain conditions, amended in some instances—and that rules can also affect the actors who engage with them is a necessary first step in an accurate analysis of the role of rules in social action. In the context of international institutions this process of mutual constitution has two aspects: the interaction between international rules and domestic actors; and the interaction between rules or norms and the identities from which those norms are derived.

Conditional norms are a way to highlight the interactive relationship between international standards and domestic actors. The development of the SNA was an international outcome that depended on harmonization of a wide variety of national practices, which in turn often drove developments at the international level. The MPS and the SNA developed in concert with each other. In this process, national statisticians constantly had choices to make, including whether to go along or to push for change based on their own practices. The formulation of a conditional Soviet norm allowed Goskomstat officials to be at the same time pro-Soviet and pro-international community of statisticians: they could pursue the development of the MPS at home and in other similar economies, such as in Eastern Europe, while supporting SNA development at the UN and in other capitalist economies.

The conditional norm that delineated the appropriateness of the SNA was also a manifestation of mutual constitution, an identity-based outcome as much as a rule that shaped behavior. The specific conditions—types of economic structure—were clearly based on Marxist understandings of the relationship between economic structure and institutions. They were thus part of the identity of Soviet statisticians. But the conditional norm was also a strategic response to growing international acceptance of the SNA: it allowed Soviet statisticians to preserve their system, the MPS, while maintaining legitimacy in international circles. Hence it was a function of both identity and strategic action.

The analysis here offers a novel approach to the role of norms in institutional change. Conditional norms can promote two kinds of change. First, the development of conditional norms may result in new norms and related institutional choices. Second, once the conditional norm has been established, behavioral change may be due to changes in the conditions rather than in the norms themselves. Whereas norms tend to be developed over long periods of time, meaning they are neither easy to create nor easy to change, a sudden alteration in conditions can produce rapid change. At Goskomstat the conditional norm about the appropriateness of statistical systems took on, over time, a life of its own, making the move to the SNA, when structural economic conditions changed, seem like the natural response. This analysis does not preclude changes in identities and the attendant norms that constitute those identities as sources of institutional change. Instead, it offers an additional mechanism for norm-based institutional change.

Finally, by positing a range of variables, from identities to structural economic factors, as possible contingent conditions of norms, the concept of conditional norms provides a new way of understanding the interrelationship of such variables in institutional change. Most important, in this view, the economy operates not through its effect on material incentives but through its role as a catalyst for norm-based change; economic conditions are linked to bureaucrats' interests through norms, rather than material incentives. Thus we see that there is a clear connection between structural conditions and agency, in that a change in structure is ideationally connected to understandings of appropriate action through the norm. Similarly, actors and their interests matter in this analysis of institutional change, but those interests are not necessarily reducible to material benefit or power—instead, identities shape individual and group interests and action through norms.

Appendix

SNA milestone assessment guide

LEVEL	DESCRIPTION	CONTENT
1	Basic indicators of gross domestic product (GDP)	Final expenditures on GDP at current and constant prices; GDP by industry at current and constant prices[a]
2	Gross national income and other primary indicators	External account of primary incomes and current transfers; capital and financial accounts for the rest of the world
3	Institutional sector accounts: first steps	Production accounts for all institutional sectors; generation of income, allocation of primary income, secondary distribution of income, use of income, capital and financial accounts for general government
4	Institutional sector accounts: intermediate steps	Generation of income, allocation of primary income, secondary distribution of income, use of income, capital accounts for all institutional sectors other than general government
5	Institutional sector accounts: last of the transaction accounts	Financial accounts for all institutional sectors other than general government
6	Other flow accounts and balance sheets	Other changes in assets accounts for all institutional sectors; balance sheets

Source: Adapted from UN Statistical Commission 2004b.

Notes: For the 1992–97 assessment (UN Statistical Commission 1999), there were amendments by UN regional and country experts to the initial milestone assessments. In notes accompanying the data, adjustments were made up or down on the 0–6 values, based on experts' knowledge of the quality and quantity of data submitted by specific countries. If there is measurement error in this dataset, there is no indication that any one region's data are biased in comparison to other regions/states of the world. The same applies to use of the regional notes, which actually are important to raising the scores of some regional averages: there is no indication of bias by particular regional experts.

On the number of countries included in the analysis: In 1998 there were 185 UN member states. In 1999, three states (Kiribati, Nauru, Tonga) joined the UN; in 2000 one (Tuvalu) joined, and in 2002 two more (Switzerland and Timor-Leste) joined. UN assessments published until 2000 (based on data up to 1998) include 185. UN reports published in 2001 include 189 countries, and reports published after 2002 include 191.

[a] The assessment of 2000, presented to the Statistical Commission at its thirty-second session in 2001, so relaxed this definition as to require only current *or* constant prices for each of the GDP compilation approaches, not both.

References

Abdelal, Rawi, Yoshiko M. Herrera, Alastair Iain Johnston, and Rose McDermott. 2006. "Identity as a Variable." *Perspectives on Politics* 4, no. 4: 695–711.

——, eds. 2009. *Measuring Identity: A Guide for Social Scientists.* New York: Cambridge University Press.

Aberbach, Joel, Robert Putnam, and Bert Rockman. 1981. *Bureaucrats and Politicians in Western Democracies.* Cambridge, Mass.: Harvard University Press.

Allison, Graham T. 1971. *Essence of Decision: Explaining the Cuban Missile Crisis.* Boston: Little, Brown.

Alonso, William, and Paul Starr, eds. 1987. *The Politics of Numbers.* New York: Russell Sage.

Alvesson, Mats. 2002. *Understanding Organizational Culture.* Thousand Oaks, Calif.: Sage Publications.

Antsiferova, L. 1983. "Novoe napravlenie v mezhdunarodnykh sopostavleniiakh stran—chlenov SEV" [A new direction in international comparisons of CMEA states]. *Vestnik statistiki,* no. 1: 41–49.

Antsiferova, L., and G. Zarubin. 1984. "K provedeniiu mezhdunarodnykh sopostavlenii vazhneishikh ekonomicheskikh pokazatelei stran-chlenov SEV po dannym za 1983 g." [On conducting international comparisons of the most important economic indices of CMEA member states based on 1983 data]. *Vestnik statistiki,* no. 2: 47–56.

Apelt, Siegfried K., and Andreas Kahnert. 1992. "Bilateral and Multilateral Cooperation in Statistics for the Improvement of Systems of National Statistics." In *Statistics in the Democratic Process at the End of the 20th Century: Anniversary Publication for the 40th Plenary Session of the Conference of European Statisticians,* ed. E. Hölder, C. Malaguerra, and G. Vukovich, 95–100. Wiesbaden, Germany: Federal Statistics Office.

Appel, Hilary. 2000. "The Ideological Determinants of Liberal Economic Reform: The Case of Privatization." *World Politics* 52, no. 4: 520–49.

Armstrong, John A. 1965. "Sources of Administrative Behavior: Some Soviet and Western European Comparisons." *American Political Science Review* 59, no. 3: 643–55.

Árvay, János. 1973. *National Production, National Income, National Wealth.* Budapest: Publishing House of Economy and Law.

——. 1994. "The Material Product System (MPS): A Retrospective." In *The Accounts of Nations,* ed. Z. Kenessey, 218–36. Amsterdam: IOS Press.

Bailes, Kendall E. 1978. *Technology and Society under Lenin and Stalin: Origins of the Soviet Technical Intelligentsia, 1917–1941.* Princeton, N.J.: Princeton University Press.

Baran, Paul A. 1947. "Appraisals of Russian Economic Statistics: National Income and Product of the U.S.S.R. in 1940." *Review of Economic Statistics* 29, no. 4: 226–34.

Barnett, Michael, and Martha Finnemore. 2004. *Rules for the World: International Organizations in Global Politics.* Ithaca, N.Y.: Cornell University Press.

Bauer, Raymond A., Alex Inkeles, and Clyde Kluckhohn. 1959. *How the Soviet System Works: Cultural, Psychological, and Social Themes.* Cambridge, Mass.: Harvard University Press.

Belkin, Viktor. 1992. "O dostovernosti informatsii" [On the reliability of information]. *Svobodnaia mysl'*, no. 10: 97–104.
Belkindas, Misha. 2001. Interview with author. Washington, D.C., December 4.
Belkindas, Misha, and Olga V. Ivanova, eds. 1995. *Foreign Trade Statistics in the USSR and Successor States.* Washington, D.C.: World Bank.
Belov, N. 1987. "Zadachi statistiki v kontekste reformy upravleniia ekonomikoi" [The tasks of statistics in the context of the reform of economic management]. *Vestnik statistiki,* no. 7: 8–19.
Bendor, Jonathan. 1995. "A Model of Muddling Through." *American Political Science Review* 89, no. 4: 819–40.
Berger, M. 1989. "Ne tol'ko tsifry priiatnye vo vsekh otnosheniiakh" [Interview with Vadim Kirichenko: It is not only numbers that are pleasant in all respects]. *Izvestiia,* no. 213, July 31: 2.
Bergson, Abram. 1947. "Appraisals of Russian Economic Statistics: A Problem in Soviet Statistics." *Review of Economic Statistics* 29, no. 4: 234–42.
——. 1953a. *Soviet National Income and Product in 1937.* New York: Columbia University Press.
——. 1953b. "Reliability and Usability of Soviet Statistics: A Summary Appraisal." *American Statistician* 7, no. 3: 13–16.
——. 1961. *The Real National Income of Soviet Russia since 1928.* Cambridge, Mass.: Harvard University Press.
——. 1991. "The USSR before the Fall: How Poor and Why." *Journal of Economic Perspectives* 5, no. 4: 29–44.
Berk, Gerald, and Dennis Galvan. 2009. "How People Experience and Change Institutions: A Field Guide to Creative Syncretism." *Theory and Society* 38, no. 6: 543–80.
Berman, Sheri. 1998. *The Social Democratic Moment: Ideas and Politics in the Making of Inter-war Europe.* Cambridge, Mass.: Harvard University Press.
——. 2001. "Ideas, Norms, and Culture in Political Analysis." *Comparative Politics* 33, no. 2: 231–50.
Blades, Derek, and Anne Harrison. 1992. "Statistics in Central and Eastern Europe: Past, Present, and Future." In *Statistics in the Democratic Process at the End of the 20th Century: Anniversary Publication for the 40th Plenary Session of the Conference of European Statisticians,* ed. E. Hölder, C. Malaguerra, and G. Vukovich, 101–6. Wiesbaden, Germany: Federal Statistics Office.
Blais, André, and Stéphane Dion, eds. 1991. *The Budget-Maximizing Bureaucrat.* Pittsburgh: University of Pittsburgh Press.
Bleich, Erik. 2002. "Integrating Ideas into Policy-Making Analysis: Frames and Race Policies in Britain and France." *Comparative Political Studies* 35, no. 9: 1054–76.
Blyth, Mark M. 2003. "Structures Do Not Come with an Instruction Sheet: Interests, Ideas, and Progress in Political Science." *Perspectives on Politics* 1, no. 4: 695–706.
——. 1997. "'Any More Bright Ideas?' The Ideational Turn of Comparative Political Economy." *Comparative Politics* 29, no. 2: 229–50.
Bockman, Johanna, and Gil Eyal. 2002. "Eastern Europe as a Laboratory for Economic Knowledge: The Transnational Root of Neoliberalism." *American Journal of Sociology* 108, no. 2: 310–52.
Boli, John, and George M. Thomas, eds. 1999. *Constructing World Culture: International Nongovernmental Organizations Since 1875.* Stanford, Calif.: Stanford University Press.
Bos, Frits. 1994. "Constancy and Change in the United Nations Manuals on National Accounting (1947, 1953, 1968, and 1993)." In *The Accounts of Nations,* ed. Z. Kenessey, 198–217. Amsterdam: IOS Press.

Bourdieu, Pierre. 1990. *In Other Words: Essays Towards a Reflexive Sociology.* Translated by M. Adamson. Stanford, Calif.: Stanford University Press.
——. 1992 [1977]. *Outline of a Theory of Practice.* Translated by R. Nice. New York: Cambridge University Press.
Brubaker, Rogers, Mara Loveman, and Peter Stamatov. 2004. "Ethnicity as Cognition." *Theory and Society* 33, no. 1: 31–64.
Brym, Robert J., and Vladimir Gimpelson. 2004. "The Size, Communications, and Dynamics of the Russian State Bureaucracy in the 1990s." *Slavic Review* 63, no. 1: 90–112.
Carpenter, Daniel P. 1996. "Adaptive Signal Processing, Hierarchy, and Budgetary Control in Federal Regulation." *American Political Science Review* 90, no. 2: 283–302.
——. 2001. *The Forging of Bureaucratic Autonomy.* Princeton, N.J.: Princeton University Press.
Checkel, Jeffrey T. 1997. *Ideas and International Political Change: Soviet/Russian Behavior and the End of the Cold War.* New Haven: Yale University Press.
——. 1998. "The Constructivist Turn in International Relations Theory." *World Politics* 50, no. 2: 324–48.
——. 2001. "Why Comply? Social Learning and European Identity Change." *International Organization* 55, no. 3: 553–88.
——. 2005. "International Institutions and Socialization in Europe." *International Organization* 59, no. 4: 801–26.
Chong, Dennis 1996. "Rational Choice Theory's Mysterious Rivals." In *The Rational Choice Controversy: Economic Models of Politics Reconsidered,* ed. J. Friedman, 37–58. New Haven: Yale University Press.
CIA. 1990. "Measuring Soviet GNP: Problems and Solutions: A Conference Report." SOV 90-10038, September. Washington, D.C.: Directorate of Intelligence, United States Central Intelligence Agency.
Clark, Colin. 1939. *A Critique of Russian Statistics.* London: Macmillan.
——. 1940. *The Conditions of Economic Progress.* London: Macmillan.
——. 1947. "Appraisals of Russian Economic Statistics: Russian Income and Production Statistics." *Review of Economic Statistics* 29, no. 4: 215–17.
Conference of European Statisticians. 1958. "Report of the Sixth Plenary Session." CES/94.
Cortell, Andrew P., and James W. Davis, Jr. 1996. "How Do International Institutions Matter? The Domestic Impact of International Rules and Norms." *International Studies Quarterly* 40, no. 4: 451–78.
——. 2000. "Understanding the Domestic Impact of International Norms: A Research Agenda." *International Studies Review* 2, no. 1: 65–87.
Crozier, Michel. 1967. *The Bureaucratic Phenomenon.* Chicago: University of Chicago Press.
CWC. 2006. *Convention on the Prohibition of the Development, Production, Stockpiling, and Use of Chemical Weapons and on Their Destruction, 13 January 1993.* www.icrc.org/ihl.nsf/INTRO/553?OpenDocument (accessed January 24, 2006).
Demchenko, Irina. 1992. "Nel'zia upravliat' stranoi, ne imeia nadezhnoi informatsii" [You cannot run the country without reliable information]. *Izvestiia,* no. 192, August 26: 1–2.
Denzau, Arthur T., and Douglass C. North. 1994. "Shared Mental Models: Ideologies and Institutions." *Kyklos* 47, no. 1: 3–31.
Derlien, Hans Ulrich. 1993. "German Unification and Bureaucratic Transformation." *International Political Science Review* 14, no. 4: 319–34.
Desrosières, Alain. 1991. "How to Make Things Which Hold Together: Social Science, Statistics and the State." In *Discourses on Society: The Shaping of the Social*

Science Disciplines, ed. P. Wagner, B. Wittrock, and R. Whitley. Boston: Kluwer Academic Publishers.

——. 1998. *The Politics of Large Numbers: A History of Statistical Reasoning.* Cambridge, Mass.: Harvard University Press.

Dewey, John. 2002 [1922]. *Human Nature and Conduct: An Introduction to Social Psychology.* Mineola, N.Y.: Dover.

D'iakonov, Yu. L., and T. S. Bushueva, eds. 1992. *Fashistskii mech kovalsia v SSSR* [The fascist sword was forged in the USSR]. Moscow: Sovetskaia Rossiia.

DiIulio, John J. 1987. *Governing Prisons: A Comparative Study of Correctional Management.* New York: Free Press.

DiMaggio, Paul J., and Walter W. Powell. 1991. "The Iron Cage Revisited: Institutional Isomorphism and Collective Rationality in Organizational Fields." In *The New Institutionalism in Organizational Analysis,* ed. W. W. Powell and P. J. DiMaggio, 63–82. Chicago: University of Chicago Press.

Donda, A. 1970. "Segodnia i zavtra statistiki Germanskoi Demokraticheskoi Respubliki" [The statistics of the German Democratic Republic today and tomorrow]. *Vestnik statistiki,* no. 6: 29–38.

Dorling, Daniel, and Stephen Simpson, eds. 1999. *Statistics in Society: The Arithmetic of Politics.* New York: Arnold.

Driuchin, A. 1977. "K itogam mezhdunarodnogo seminara 'Statisticheskie sluzhby cherez desiat' let'" [Summary of the international seminar "Statistical services in ten years"]. *Vestnik statistiki,* no. 2: 42–51.

Easter, Gerald M. 2002. "Politics of Revenue Extraction in Post-Communist States: Poland and Russia Compared." *Politics and Society* 30, no. 4: 599–627.

Eden, Lynn. 2004. *Whole World on Fire: Organizations, Knowledge, and Nuclear Weapons Devastation.* Ithaca, N.Y.: Cornell University Press.

Ekiert, Grzegorz, and Stephen E. Hanson, eds. 2003. *Capitalism and Democracy in Central and Eastern Europe: Assessing the Legacy of Communist Rule.* New York: Cambridge University Press.

Elkins, Zachary, and Beth Simmons. 2005. "On Waves, Clusters, and Diffusion: A Conceptual Framework." *Annals of the American Academy of Political and Social Science* 598, no. 1: 33–51.

Elster, Jon. 1989. "Social Norms and Economic Theory." *Journal of Economic Perspectives* 3, no. 4: 99–117.

England, Richard W., and Jonathan M. Harris. 1997. "Alternatives to Gross National Product: A Critical Survey." In *Human Wellbeing and Economic Goals,* ed. F. Ackerman, D. Kiron, N. Goodwin, J. Harris, and K. P. Gallagher. Vol. 3 [online edition]. Chicago: Island Press.

Ericson, Richard E. 1990. "The Soviet Statistical Debate: Khanin vs. TsSU." In *The Impoverished Superpower: Perestroika and the Soviet Military Burden,* ed. H. S. Rowen and C. Wolf, 63–92. San Francisco: ICS Press.

Eurostat, Statistical Office of the European Community. 1970. "European System of Integrated Economic Accounts (ESA)." Luxemburg: Office for Official Publications of the European Communities.

Evangelista, Matthew. 1999. *Unarmed Forces: The Transnational Movement to End the Cold War.* Ithaca, N.Y.: Cornell University Press.

Farmer, Kenneth C. 1992. *The Soviet Administrative Elite.* New York: Praeger.

Fearon, James D., and David D. Laitin. 2003. "Ethnicity, Insurgency, and Civil War." *American Political Science Review* 97, no. 1: 75–90.

Federal'nyi zakon: Ob ofitsial'nom statisticheskom uchete i sisteme gosudarstvennoi statistiki v Rossiiskoi Federatsii [Federal Law: On official statistical accounting and the system of state statistics in the Russian Federation]. 2007. Putin, V., President, Russian Federation. No. 282-FZ.

Finnemore, Martha. 1993. "International Organizations as Teachers of Norms: The United Nations Educational, Scientific, and Cultural Organization and Science Policy." *International Organization* 47, no. 3: 565–97.

——. 1996a. *National Interests in International Society.* Ithaca, N.Y.: Cornell University Press.

——. 1996b. "Norms, Culture and World Politics: Insights from Sociology's Institutionalism." *International Organization* 50, no. 2: 325–47.

Franchet, Yves. 1992. "International Statistical Norms and Standards—The Basis for Consistent and Efficient National Statistical Standards." In *Statistics in the Democratic Process at the End of the 20th Century: Anniversary Publication for the 40th Plenary Session of the Conference of European Statisticians,* ed. E. Hölder, C. Malaguerra, and G. Vukovich, 85–94. Wiesbaden, Germany: Federal Statistics Office.

Frieden, Jeffry. 1991. *Debt, Development, and Democracy.* Princeton, N.J.: Princeton University Press.

Frieden, Jeffry, and Ronald Rogowski. 1996. "The Impact of the International Economy on National Policies: An Analytic Overview." In *Internationalization and Domestic Politics,* ed. R. Keohane and H. V. Milner, 25–47. New York: Cambridge University Press.

Furst, G. M. W. 1964. "Changing Tasks in Official Statistics: An Attempt at a General Survey." Paper read at International Statistical Institute, 1963, at Ottawa, Canada.

Galvan, Dennis, and Rudra Sil, eds. 2007. *Reconfiguring Institutions across Time and Space: Syncretic Responses to Challenges of Political and Economic Transformation.* New York: Palgrave/Macmillan.

Ganev, Venelin. 2007. *Preying on the State: The Transformation of Bulgaria after 1989.* Ithaca, N.Y.: Cornell University Press.

Geddes, Barbara. 1994. *Politician's Dilemma: Building State Capacity in Latin America.* Berkeley: University of California Press.

Gerschenkron, Alexander. 1947. "Appraisals of Russian Economic Statistics: The Soviet Indices of Industrial Production." *Review of Economic Statistics* 29, no. 4: 217–26.

——. 1978. "Samuelson in Soviet Russia: A Report." *Journal of Economic Literature* 16, no. 2: 560–73.

GKS4, Goskomstat Official #4. 2003. Interview with author. Russia, fall.

GKS12, Goskomstat Official #12. 2004. Interview with author. Russia, summer.

GKS19, Goskomstat Official #19. 2003. Interview with author. Russia, fall.

GKS29, Goskomstat Official #29. 2003. Interview with author. Russia, fall.

GKS35, Goskomstat Official #35. 2004. Interview with author. Russia, summer.

GKS40, Goskomstat Official #40. 2004. Interview with author. Russia, summer.

GKS43, Goskomstat Official #43. 2003. Interview with author. Russia, fall.

GKS44, Goskomstat Official #44. 2004. Interview with author. Russia, summer.

GKS49, Goskomstat Official #49. 2004. Interview with author. Russia, summer.

GKS50, Goskomstat Official #50. 2004. Interview with author. Russia, summer.

Goldman, Marshall I. 1994. *Lost Opportunity: What Has Made Economic Reform in Russia So Difficult?.* New York: W. W. Norton.

Goldsmith, Arthur A. 2001. "Foreign Aid and Statehood in Africa." *International Organization* 55, no. 1: 123–48.

Gordon, Michael. 1998. "Statisticians Accused of Aiding Tax Evasion." *New York Times,* June 10: A3.

Goskomstat Russia and World Bank. 1995. *Russian Federation: Report on National Accounts,*. October ed. Moscow and Washington, D.C.: Goskomstat Rossii and World Bank.

Goskomstat Russia, Gosudarstvennyi komitet Rossiiskoi Federatsii po statistike. 1996a. *Metodologicheskie polozheniia po statistike, vypusk 1* [Methodological guidelines on statistics, volume 1], ed. I. A. Iurkov. Moscow: Goskomstat Rossii.

——. 1996b. *Rossiiskaia gosudarstvennaia statistika: 1802–1996* [Russian state statistics 1802–1996]. Moscow: Goskomstat Rossii.

——. 1997. *Osnovnye indikatory kadrovogo potentsiala organov gosudarstvennoi vlasti v Rossii* [Key indicators of human resource potential of organs of state power in Russia]. Moscow: Goskomstat Rossii.

——. 1998. *Metodologicheskie polozheniia po statistike, vypusk 2* [Methodological guidelines on statistics, volume 2], ed. I. A. Iurkov. Moscow: Goskomstat Rossii.

——. 2000. *Metodologicheskie polozheniia po statistike, vypusk 3* [Methodological guidelines on statistics, volume 3], ed. V. L. Sokolin. Moscow: Goskomstat Rossii.

——. 2003. *Metodologicheskie polozheniia po statistike, vypusk 4* [Methodological guidelines on statistics, volume 4], ed. V. L. Sokolin. Moscow: Goskomstat Rossii.

——. 2004. *Organizatsiia gosudarstvennoi statistiki v Rossiiskoi Federatsii* [Organization of state statistics in the Russian Federation], ed. V. L. Sokolin. Moscow: Goskomstat Rossii.

Goskomstat SSSR, Gosudarstvennyi komitet SSSR po statistike. 1987. *Narodnoe khoziaistvo SSSR v 1987 godu* [Economy of the USSR in 1987]. Moscow: Goskomstat SSSR.

——. 1988. *Metodika ischisleniia valovogo natsional'nogo produkta SSSR* [Method of calculating the gross national product of the USSR]. Moscow: Goskomstat SSSR.

——. 1989. *Narodnoe khoziaistvo SSSR v 1989 godu* [Economy of the USSR in 1989]. Moscow: Goskomstat SSSR.

Gourevitch, Peter. 1978. "The Second Image Reversed: The International Sources of Domestic Politics." *International Organization* 32, no. 4: 881–912.

Graham, Loren R. 1993. *Science in Russia and the Soviet Union: A Short History.* New York: Cambridge University Press.

——, ed. 1990. *Science and the Soviet Social Order.* Cambridge, Mass.: Harvard University Press.

Grossman, Gregory. 1960. *Soviet Statistics of Physical Output of Industrial Commodities; Their Compilation and Quality. A Study by the National Bureau of Economic Research.* Princeton, N.J.: Princeton University Press.

Grzymala-Busse, Anna, and Pauline Jones Luong. 2002. "Reconceptualizing the State: Lessons from Post-Communism." *Politics and Society* 30, no. 4: 529–54.

Gurowitz, Amy. 1999. "Mobilizing International Norms: Domestic Actors, Immigrants, and the Japanese State." *World Politics* 51, no. 3: 413–45.

Guzhvin, Pavel F. 1992a. "Doverie k statistike" [Trust in statistics]. *Vestnik statistiki,* no. 9: 3–21.

——. 1992b. "Zagranitsa nam pomozhet?" [Will foreigners help us?]. *Vestnik statistiki,* no. 10: 3–14.

——. 1993. "Rossiiskaia statistika segodnia i zavtra" [Russian statistics today and tomorrow]. *Voprosy ekonomiki,* no. 5: 4–13.

Haas, Peter M. 1989. "Do Regimes Matter? Epistemic Communities and Mediterranean Pollution Control." *International Organization* 43, no. 3: 377–403.

——. 1992. "Introduction: Epistemic Communities and International Policy Coordination." *International Organization* 46, no. 1: 1–35.

Hague Declaration. 2006. *First Peace Conference of The Hague, Declaration (IV, 2) concerning Asphyxiating Gases, 29 July 1899.* www.icrc.org/ihl.nsf/INTRO/165?OpenDocument (accessed January 24, 2006).

Hall, Peter A. 1993. "Policy Paradigms, Social Learning, and the State: The Case of Economic Policymaking in Britain." *Comparative Politics* 25, no. 3: 275–96.

Hardin, Russell. 1995. *One for All: The Logic of Group Conflict.* Princeton, N.J.: Princeton University Press.

Harris, Seymour E. 1947. "Appraisals of Russian Economic Statistics: Introduction." *Review of Economic Statistics* 29, no. 4: 213–14.

Harrison, Anne. 1994. "The SNA: 1968–1993 and Beyond." In *The Accounts of Nations,* ed. Z. Kenessey, 169–97. Amsterdam: IOS Press.

——. 1996. "Discussion of Chapter 10 (Adaptation of the SNA for Transition Economies by Y. Ivanov and T. Homenko)." In *The New System of National Accounts,* ed. J. W. Kendrick, 339–41. Boston: Kluwer Academic Publishers.

Hausner, Jerzy. 2001. "Security through Diversity: Conditions for Successful Reform of the Pension System in Poland." In *Reforming the State: Fiscal and Welfare Reform in Post-Socialist Countries,* ed. J. Kornai, S. Haggard, and R. R. Kaufman, 210–34. Cambridge: Cambridge University Press.

Heclo, Hugh. 1974. *Modern Social Politics in Britain and Sweden.* New Haven: Yale University Press.

——. 1977. *A Government of Strangers: Executive Politics in Washington.* Washington, D.C.: Brookings Institution.

Heleniak, Timothy E., and Albert Motivans. 1991. "A Note on *Glasnost'* and the Soviet Statistical System." *Soviet Studies* 43, no. 3: 473–90.

Helmke, Gretchen, and Steven Levitsky. 2004. "Informal Institutions and Comparative Politics: A Research Agenda." *Perspectives on Politics* 2, no. 4: 725–40.

Hendley, Kathryn, ed. 2007. *Remaking the Role of Law: Commercial Law Reform in Russia and the CIS.* Huntington, N.Y.: Juris.

Herrera, Yoshiko. 2001. "Russian Economic Reform 1991–1998." In *Challenges to Democratic Transition In Russia,* ed. Z. B. and R. Moser, 135–73. New York: Cambridge University Press.

——. 2004. "The 2002 Russian Census: Institutional Reform at Goskomstat." *Post-Soviet Affairs* 20, no. 4: 350–86.

Herrigel, Gary. 2005. "Institutionalists at the Limits of Institutionalism: A Constructivist Critique of Two Edited Volumes from Wolfgang Streeck and Kozo Yamamura." *Socio-Economic Review* 3, no. 3: 559–67.

——. 2010. *Manufacturing Possibilities: Creative Action and Industrial Recomposition in Germany, the US, and Japan.* Oxford: Oxford University Press.

Herzfeld, Michael. 1992. *The Social Production of Indifference: Exploring the Symbolic Roots of Western Bureaucracy.* New York: St. Martin's.

Hill, T. P. 1971. *The Measurement of Real Product: A Theoretical and Empirical Analysis of the Growth Rates for Different Industries and Countries.* Paris: OECD.

Holquist, Peter. 1997. "'Information Is the Alpha and Omega of Our Work': Bolshevik Surveillance in Its Pan-European Context." *Journal of Modern History* 69, no. 3: 415–50.

Hopf, Ted. 2002. *Social Construction of International Politics: Identities and Foreign Policies, Moscow 1955 and 1999.* Ithaca, N.Y.: Cornell University Press.

Huber, John D., and Nolan McCarty. 2004. "Bureaucratic Capacity, Delegation, and Political Reform." *American Political Science Review* 98, no. 3: 481–94.

Hunter, Wendy, and David S. Brown. 2000. "World Bank Directives, Domestic Interests, and the Politics of Human Capital Investment in Latin America." *Comparative Political Studies* 33, no. 1: 113–43.

Husein, Hasan M. 1964. "Changing Tasks in Official Statistics in a Developing Country." Paper read at International Statistical Institute, 1963, at Ottawa, Canada.

Hymans, Jacques E. C. 2008. "Assessing North Korean Nuclear Intentions and Capacities: A New Approach." *Journal of East Asian Studies* 8, no. 2: 259–92.

——. 2010. "Implementing Nuclear Ambitions: The Political Foundations of Technical Achievement." Unpublished manuscript.

IMF, International Monetary Fund. 2004. "Russian Federation: Report on the Observance of Standards and Codes—Data Module, Response by Authorities, and Detailed Assessment Using Data Quality Assessment Framework." IMF Country Report, 04/134, May. IMF.

——. 2009a. "IMF Executive Board Approves US$20.58 Billion Arrangement for Poland under the Flexible Credit Line." *IMF Press Release,* No. 09/153, May 6. www.imf.org/external/np/sec/pr/2009/pr09153.htm (accessed April 30, 2010).

——. 2009b. *Introduction to the Data Quality Reference Site.* http://dsbb.imf.org/pages/dqrs/introduction.aspx (accessed August 6, 2010).

——. 2009c. *Reports on the Observance of Standards and Codes: Data Modules.* http://dsbb.imf.org/Applications/web/dqrs/dqrsroscs/ (accessed July 2, 2009).

——. 2009d. *SDDS: Subscription Information.* http://dsbb.imf.org/Applications/web/sddssubscriptiondates/ (accessed July 2, 2009).

——. 2009e. *Special Data Dissemination Standard.* http://dsbb.imf.org/Applications/web/sddshome/ (accessed May 3, 2010).

ISWGNA, Inter-Secretariat Working Group on National Accounts. 1993. "System of National Accounts 1993." Studies in Methods, Series F, no. 2, rev. 4, ST/ESA/STAT/SER.F/2/Rev.4. Brussels: Commission of the European Communities.

——. 2007. "The Full Set of Consolidated Recommendations: The Recommendations Made by the Advisory Expert Group for the Update of the System of National Accounts, 1993." Background document for UN Statistical Commission, Thirty-eighth Session, February 27–March 2, 2007.

——. 2008. "Implementation Strategy for the System of National Accounts, 2008." Background document for the UN Statistical Commission, Fortieth Session, February 24–27, 2009.

——. 2009. *System of National Accounts 2008.* http://unstats.un.org/unsd/nationalaccount/SNA2008.pdf (accessed October 12, 2009).

Ivanov, Youri. 1972. "Nekotorye voprosy mezhdunarodnykh sravnenii natsional'nogo dokhoda" [Some issues for international comparisons of national income]. *Vestnik statistiki,* no. 8: 48–55.

——. 1987. "Possibilities and Problems of Reconciliation of the SNA and the MPS." *Review of Income and Wealth* 33, no. 1: 1–18.

——. 1989. "Peresmotr sistemy natsional'nykh schetov OON" [Review of the UN system of national accounts]. *Vestnik statistiki,* no. 5: 42–47.

——. 1993. "Perspektivy perekhoda na sistemu natsional'nykh schetov v stranakh SNG" [Prospects of transition of the CIS countries to the system of national accounts]. *Voprosy ekonomiki,* no. 5: 22–31.

——. 2001. "Primenenie mezhdunarodnykh standartov v rossiiskoi statistike" [Adoption of international standards in Russian statistics]. *Voprosy ekonomiki,* no. 3: 69–81.

——. 2004a. "Desiatiletie sistemy natsional'nykh schetov v stranakh SNG: itogi i problemy" [Tenth anniversary of the system of national accounts in the CIS countries: results and problems]. *Voprosy ekonomiki,* no. 3: 128–40.

——. 2004b. Interview with author. Moscow, July 1.

Ivanov, Youri, and T. Homenko. 1992. "Osobennosti sistem natsional'nykh schetov v stranakh Evropeiskogo Ekonomicheskogo Soobshchestva" [Distinctive features of the system of national accounts in the countries of the European Economic Community]. *Vestnik statistiki,* no. 1: 16–23.

——. 1996. "Adaptation of the SNA for Transition Economies." In *The New System of National Accounts,* ed. J. W. Kendrick, 317–38. Boston: Kluwer Academic Publishers.

Ivanov, Youri, and B. Riabushkin. 1971. "Novoe v standartnoi sisteme natsional'nykh schetov" [Innovations in the standards of the system of national accounts]. *Vestnik statistiki,* no. 1: 31–37.

——. 1989. "Integratsiia balansa narodnogo khoziaistva i sistemy natsional'nykh schetov" [Integration of the MPS and SNA]. *Vestnik statistiki,* no. 9: 20–31.

——. 1990. "Voprosy sblizheniia i uviazki SNS i BNKh" [Issues in the convergence and linkage of the SNA and MPS]. *Vestnik statistiki,* no. 3: 62–65.

——. 1991a. "Sistema natsional'nykh schetov: mify i real'nost'" [System of national accounts: myths and reality]. *Vestnik statistiki,* no. 1: 16–21.

——. 1991b. "Problemy razvitiia makroekonomicheskoi statistiki v SSSR" [Problems of development of macroeconomic statistics in the USSR]. *Voprosy ekonomiki,* no. 4: 3–10.

Ivanov, Youri, B. Riabushkin, and M. Eidel'man. 1988. "Ischislenie valovogo natsional'nogo produkta SSSR" [Calculating gross national product of the USSR]. *Vestnik statistiki,* no. 7: 32–39.

Ivanov, Youri, and I. Ryzhov. 1978. "A New Stage in the Activities of the Council for Mutual Economic Assistance in the Field of International Comparisons of National Product." *Review of Income and Wealth* 24, no. 2: 177–84.

——. 1981. "Sovershenstvovanie metodologii sopostavleniia pokazatelei Sistemy natsional'nykh schetov i Balansa narodnogo khoziaistva" [Improvement of the methodology of comparisons between the system of national accounts and the material product system]. *Vestnik statistiki,* no. 2: 38–42.

——. 1983. "Obzor osnovnykh napravlenii razvitiia mezhdunarodnoi statistiki natsional'nogo dokhoda" [Overview of major directions in the development of international statistics on national income]. *Vestnik statistiki,* no. 9: 40–46.

Jackson, Dudley. 2000. *The New National Accounts: An Introduction to the System of National Accounts 1993 and the European System of Accounts 1995.* Northampton, Mass.: Edward Elgar.

Jenkins-Smith, Hank C., and Paul A. Sabatier. 1993. "The Dynamics of Policy-Oriented Learning." In *Policy Change and Learning: An Advocacy Coalition Approach,* ed. P. A. Sabatier and H. C. Jenkins-Smith, 41–56. Boulder, Colo.: Westview.

Jepperson, Ronald L., Alexander Wendt, and Peter J. Katzenstein. 1996. "Norms, Identity, and Culture in National Security." In *The Culture of National Security: Norms and Identity in World Politics,* ed. P. J. Katzenstein, 33–75. New York: Columbia University Press.

Johnson, Juliet. 2003. "'Past' Dependence or Path Contingency? Institutional Design in Postcommunist Financial Systems." In *Capitalism and Democracy in Central and Eastern Europe: Assessing the Legacy of Communist Rule,* ed. G. Ekiert and S. Hanson, 289–316. Cambridge: Cambridge University Press.

——. 2010. "Priests of Prosperity: The Transnational Central Banking Community and Post-Communist Transformation." Unpublished manuscript.

Johnston, Alastair Iain. 2001. "Treating International Institutions as Social Environments." *International Studies Quarterly* 45, no. 4: 487–515.

Jupille, Joseph, James A. Caporaso, and Jeffrey T. Checkel. 2003. "Integrating Institutions: Rationalism, Constructivism, and the Study of the European Union." *Comparative Political Studies* 36, no. 1/2: 7–40.

Karklins, Rasma. 2005. *The System Made Me Do It: Corruption in Post-Communist Societies.* Armonk, N.Y.: M. E. Sharpe.

Katzenstein, Peter J., ed. 1996. *The Culture of National Security: Norms and Identity in World Politics.* New York: Columbia University Press.

Kaufman, Herbert. 1960. *The Forest Ranger: A Study in Administrative Behavior.* Baltimore: Johns Hopkins University Press.

Kavalets, V. 1969. "Statistika Pol'skoi Narodnoi Respubliki v 1969" [Statistics of the Polish People's Republic in 1969]. *Vestnik statistiki,* no. 4: 37–44.

Keck, Margaret E., and Kathryn Sikkink. 1998. *Activists beyond Borders: Advocacy Networks in International Politics.* Ithaca, N.Y.: Cornell University Press.

Kendrick, John W., ed. 1996. *The New System of National Accounts.* Boston: Kluwer Academic Publishers.

Kenessey, Zoltan. 1994a. "The Genesis of National Accounts: An Overview." In *The Accounts of Nations,* ed. Z. Kenessey, 1–15. Amsterdam: IOS Press.

——, ed. 1994b. *The Accounts of Nations.* Amsterdam: IOS Press.

Keohane, Robert O., and Helen Milner, eds. 1996. *Internationalization and Domestic Politics.* New York: Cambridge University Press.

Keynes, John Maynard. 1936. *The General Theory of Employment, Interest and Money.* CambridgeK: Cambridge University Press.

——. 1940. *How to Pay for the War: A Radical Plan for the Chancellor of the Exchequer.* London: Macmillan.

Khanin, Grigorii. 1988. "Ekonomicheskii rost: al'ternativnaia otsenka" [Economic growth: An alternative evaluation]. *Kommunist,* no. 17: 83–90.

Khasbulatov, R. I. 1992. "Rasporiazhenie predsedatelia verkhovnogo soveta Rossiiskoi Federatsii: O perekhode Rossiiskoi Federatsii na priniatuiu v mezhdunarodnoi praktike sistemu ucheta i statistiki. 14 ianvaria 1992 goda N 2184rp-1" [Directive from the chairman of the supreme soviet of the Russian Federation: On the transition of the Russian Federation to adopt international practices in accounting and statistics]. N2184rp-1. January 14, 1992.

Kingdon, John. 1995. *Agendas, Alternatives, and Public Policy.* 2d ed. New York: Harper Collins College.

Kirichenko, Vadim N. 1990. "Vernut' doverie statistike" [Return trust to statistics]. *Kommunist,* no. 3: 22–33.

——. 1991. *Zhizn' diktuet: po-novomu stroit' statistiku* [Life dictates: A new way to build statistics]. Moscow: Goskomstat SSSR.

Kirichenko, Vadim N., and I. Pogosov. 1991. "Novye printsipy statistiki: pervye rezul'taty" [New principles of statistics, initial results]. *EKO: Ekonomika i organizatsiia promyshlennogo proizvodstva,* no. 10: 87–99.

Klimenko, B. 1989. "Tseny v sisteme natsional'nykh schetov" [Prices in the system of national accounts]. *Vestnik statistiki,* no. 10: 43–50.

Klotz, Audie. 1995. *Norms in International Relations: The Struggle Against Apartheid.* Ithaca, N.Y.: Cornell University Press.

Knott, Jack H., and Gary J. Miller. 1987. *Reforming Bureaucracy: The Politics of Institutional Choice.* Englewood Cliffs, N.J.: Prentice-Hall.

Koen, Vincent. 1996. "Russian Macroeconomic Data: Existence, Access, Interpretation." *Communist Economies and Economic Transformation* 8, no. 3: 321–33.

Konevskii, A. 1981. "XXI sessiia Statisticheskoi komissii OON" [XXI Session of the UN Statistical Commission]. *Vestnik statistiki,* no. 5: 54–58.

——. 1982. "IX sessiia Rabochei gruppy Statisticheskoi komissii OON" [IX Session of the UN Statistical Commission Working Group]. *Vestnik statistiki,* no. 3: 63–64.

——. 1983. "XXII sessiia Statisticheskoi komissii OON" [XXII Session of the UN Statistical Commission]. *Vestnik statistiki,* no. 7: 50–53.

——. 1987. "XXIV sessiia Statisticheskoi komissii OON" [XXIV Session of the UN Statistical Commission]. *Vestnik statistiki,* no. 5: 72–75.

Kornai, János, Stephan Haggard, and Robert R. Kaufman, eds. 2001. *Reforming the State: Fiscal and Welfare Reform in Post-Socialist Countries.* Cambridge: Cambridge University Press.

Korolev, Mikhail. 1987. "O korennoi perestroike raboty organov gosudarstvennoi statistiki" [On radical restructuring of the work of state statistical agencies]. *Vestnik statistiki,* no. 9: 3–17.

——. 1989. "Statistika li znat'?" [Does Statistics Know?]. *Pravda,* January 30: 2.

Kosarev, Andrei. 2004. Interview with author. Moscow, June 29.

Kostinsky, Barry, and Misha Belkindas. 1990. "Official Soviet Gross National Product Accounting." In *Measuring Soviet GNP: Problems and Solutions, SOV 90-10038,* ed. CIA, 193–92. Washington, D.C.: Directorate of Intelligence, United States Central Intelligence Agency.

Kotz, Samuel, and Eugene Seneta. 1990. "Lenin as a Statistician: A Non-Soviet View." *Journal of the Royal Statistical Society, Series A (Statistics in Society)* 153, no. 1: 73–94.

Kowert, Paul, and Jeffrey Legro. 1996. "Norms, Identity, and Their Limits: A Theoretical Reprise." In *The Culture of National Security: Norms and Identity in World Politics,* ed. P. J. Katzenstein, 451–97. New York: Columbia University Press.

Kreps, David M. 1990. "Corporate Culture and Economic Theory." In *Perspectives in Positive Political Economy,* ed. J. E. Alt and K. A. Shepsle, 90–143. New York: Cambridge University Press.

Kudinov, V. 1979. "Krepnet sotrudnichestvo statistikov stran-chlenov SEV" [Cooperation of CMEA statisticians strengthens]. *Vestnik statistiki,* no. 1: 16–19.

——. 1982. "Statistika v sovremennykh usloviiakh" [Statistics under current conditions]. *Vestnik statistiki,* no. 1: 44–49.

Kudrov, Valentin M. 1960. "Ob ofitsial'nykh raschetakh natisonal'nogo dokhoda SShA" [On official calculations of national income of the USA]. *Vestnik statistiki,* no. 6: 33–51.

——. 1970. "B. T. Riabushkin, 'Sistema natsional'nykh schetov v zarubezhnoi statistike' [Book Review: B. T. Riabushkin's "System of national accounts in foreign statistics"]. *Vestnik statistiki,* no. 2: 74–76.

——. 1993. "Nadezhny li raschety tempov rosta ekonomiki SSSR i Rossii?" [Are the calculations of economic growth rates for the USSR and Russia reliable?]. *Voprosy ekonomiki,* no. 10: 122–31.

——. 1994. "Rossiiskaia statistika i otsenka ekonomicheskoi situatsii v Rossii v 1992–1993 gg." [Russian statistics and evaluation of Russian economic conditions in 1992–1993]. Doklady Instituta Evropy, 5. Moskva: Rossiiskaia akademiia nauk.

——. 1995. "Sovetskii ekonomicheskii rost: ofitsial'nye dannye i al'ternativnye otsenki" [Soviet economic growth: official data and alternative estimates]. *Voprosy ekonomiki,* no. 10: 100–12.

——. 2004. Interview with author. Moscow, June 30.

Kulikov, Sergei, and Sergei Skliarov. 2009. "Strana statisticheskikh paradoksov" [The country of statistical paradoxes] *Nezavisimaia gazeta,* no. 97, May 20.

Kuzin'skii, S. 1979. "Nashi sovmestnye dostizheniia i tseli" [Our common achievements and goals]. *Vestnik statistiki,* no. 1: 19–24.

Laliberté, Lucie, Werner Grünewald, and Laurent Probst. 2004. "Data Quality: A Comparison of IMF's Data Quality Assessment Framework (DQAF) and Eurostat's Quality Definition." IMF, International Monetary Fund, Eurostat. http://dsbb.imf.org/vgn/images/pdfs/dqaf_eurostat.pdf (accessed April 30, 2010).

Lampert, Nicholas. 1979. *The Technical Intelligentsia and the Soviet State: A Study of Soviet Managers and Technicians, 1928–1935*. London: Macmillan.

Ledeneva, Alena V. 2006. *How Russia Really Works: The Informal Practices That Shaped Post-Soviet Politics and Business*. Ithaca, N.Y.: Cornell University Press.

Lequiller, François, and Derek Blades. 2006. *Understanding National Accounts*. Paris: OECD.

Leshchev, A. 1974. "Plodotvornoe sotrudnichestvo statistikov stran-chlenov SEV" [Fruitful cooperation of CMEA member states' statisticians]. *Vestnik statistiki*, no. 3: 11–16.

——. 1977. "Sotrudnichestvo stran-chlenov SEV v oblasti statistiki" [Cooperation of the CMEA states in the field of statistics]. *Vestnik statistiki*, no. 7: 25–31.

——. 1983. "K 20-letiiu Postoiannoi komissii SEV po sotrudnichestvu v oblasti statistiki" [Twentieth anniversary of the CMEA Standing commission on cooperation in the field of statistics]. *Vestnik statistiki*, no. 2: 30–36.

——. 1985. "Plodotvornoe sotrudnichestvo statistikov stran-chlenov SEV" [Fruitful cooperation of CMEA member states' statisticians]. *Vestnik statistiki*, no. 11: 39–46.

Leshchev, A., and L. Antsiferova. 1978. "Sotrudnichestvo stran-chlenov SEV v oblasti statistiki" [Cooperation of the CMEA member states in the field of statistics]. *Vestnik statistiki*, no. 3: 7–16.

Levi, Margaret. 2003. "Inducing Preferences within Organizations: The Case of Unions." *Center for Labor Studies, Occasional Paper Series, Working Paper*. Seattle, Wash.

Lieberman, Robert C. 2002. "Ideas, Institutions, and Political Order: Explaining Political Change." *American Political Science Review* 96, no. 4: 697–712.

Light, Paul C. 1997. *The Tides of Reform: Making Government Work, 1945–1995*. New Haven: Yale University Press.

Lindblom, Charles E. 1959. "The Science of 'Muddling Through.'" *Public Administration Review* 19, no. 2: 79–88.

Lukach, O., and L. Nesterov. 1969. "Statisticheskaia sluzhba OON" [UN Statistical Service]. *Vestnik statistiki*, no. 5: 38–47.

Lukin, L. 1977. "Mezhdunarodnye sviazi SEV v oblasti statistiki" [International links of the CMEA in the field of statistics]. *Vestnik statistiki*, no. 11: 70–78.

——. 1980. "Statistika v Organizatsii ob'edinennykh natsii" [Statistics in the United Nations]. *Vestnik statistiki*, no. 5: 44–53.

Maier, Mark, and Todd Easton. 1999. *The Data Game: Controversies in Social Science Statistics*. 3d ed. Armonk, N.Y.: M. E. Sharpe.

Mantzavinos, C., Douglass C. North, and Shariq Syed. 2004. "Learning, Institutions, and Economic Performance." *Perspectives on Politics* 2, no. 1: 75–84.

March, James G., ed. 1965. *Handbook of Organizations*. Chicago: Rand McNally.

March, James G., and Johan Olsen. 1989. *Rediscovering Institutions: The Organizational Basis of Politics*. New York: Free Press.

——. 1998. "The Institutional Dynamics of International Political Orders." *International Organization* 52, no. 4: 949–54.

March, James G., and Herbert A. Simon. 1993 [1958]. *Organizations*. 2d ed. Cambridge, Mass.: Blackwell.

Marcussen, Martin. 1999. "The Dynamics of EMU Ideas." *Cooperation and Conflict* 34, no. 4: 383–411.

Martin, Joanne. 2002. *Organizational Culture: Mapping the Terrain.* Thousand Oaks, Calif.: Sage Publications.

Masakova, Irina Dmitrievna. 2004. Interview with author. Moscow, June 29.

Maslov, O. 1975. "Krizis sovremennoi burzhuaznoi ekonometriki" [The crisis of contemporary bourgeois econometrics]. *Vestnik statistiki,* no. 7: 49–56.

Maslov, P. 1965. "Sistema natsional'nykh schetov v kapitalisticheskikh stranakh" [The system of national accounts in capitalist countries]. *Vestnik statistiki,* no. 9: 44–50.

Mattli, Walter, and Ngaire Woods. 2009. *The Politics of Global Regulation.* Princeton, N.J.: Princeton University Press.

McAdam, Doug, and Dieter Rucht. 1993. "The Cross-National Diffusion of Movement Ideas." *Annals of the American Academy (AAPSS),* no. 528: 56–74.

McDonald, Jason. 1993. "Transition to Utopia: A Reinterpretation of Economics, Ideas, and Politics in Hungary, 1984–1990." *East European Politics and Societies* 7, no. 2: 203–39.

McNamara, Kathleen R. 1998. *The Currency of Ideas: Monetary Politics in the European Union.* Ithaca, N.Y.: Cornell University Press.

Meade, James. 1988 [1940]. "Employment and Inflation." In *The Collected Works of James Meade,* vol. 1, chap. 7. London: Unwin Hyman.

Meade, James, and Richard Stone. 1941. "The Construction of Trade Tables of National Income, Expenditure, Savings, and Investment." *Economic Journal* 51, no. 202/203: 216–31.

Medvedev, V. 1992. "Razrabotka MOB v sisteme pokazatelei SNS" [Development of interbranch balances in the system of indicators of the SNA]. *Vestnik statistiki,* no. 6: 25–32.

Merton, Robert. 1952. "Bureaucratic Structure and Bureaucracy." In *Reader in Bureaucracy,* ed. R. Merton, 361–71. Glencoe, Ill.: Free Press.

Meyer, Marshall W. 1990. "The Growth of Public and Private Bureaucracies." In *Structures of Capital: The Social Organization of the Economy,* ed. S. Zukin and P. J. DiMaggio, 153–72. Cambridge: Cambridge University Press.

Mill, John Stuart. 1956 [1859]. *On Liberty.* New York: Macmillan.

Milner, Helen. 1988. *Resisting Protectionism.* Princeton, N.J.: Princeton University Press.

Mistry, Dinshaw. 2002. "Technological Containment: The MTCR and Missile Proliferation." *Security Studies* 11, no. 3: 91–122.

——. 2003. "Beyond the MTCR: Building a Comprehensive Regime to Contain Ballistic Missile Proliferation." *International Security* 27, no. 4: 119–49.

Mitchell, Wesley. 1939. *The National Bureau Enters Its Twentieth Year.* New York: Press of A. Colish.

Moe, Terry. 1987. "Interests, Institutions, and Positive Theory: The Politics of the NLRB." *Studies in American Political Development* 2: 236–302.

Morrow, James D. 2002. "The Laws of War, Common Conjectures, and Legal Systems in International Politics." *Journal of Legal Studies* 31 (Part 2): S41–S60.

Moskvin, P. 1949. "O metodakh ischisleniia obshchestvennogo produkta sotsialisticheskogo khoziaistva" [Methods of calculating the social product of a socialist economy] *Vestnik statistiki,* no. 5: 15–27.

——. 1950. "Chto takoe natsional'nyi dokhod i kakovy metody ego ischisleniia" [What is national income and what are the methods of calculating it] *Vestnik statistiki,* no. 1: 52–58.

Murphy, Craig N. 1994. *International Organization and Industrial Change: Global Governance since 1850.* New York: Oxford University Press.

National Accounts Research Unit, OEEC. 1951. *A Simplified System of National Accounts.* Paris: Organisation for European Economic Co-operation.

——. 1952. *A Standardised System of National Accounts.* Paris: Organisation for European Economic Co-operation.
Nazarov, M. 1991. "Rynok i statistika" [The market and statistics]. *Voprosy ekonomiki,* no. 4: 11–18.
Nelson, Joan M. 2001. "The Politics of Pension and Health-Care Reforms in Hungary and Poland." In *Reforming the State: Fiscal and Welfare Reform in Post-Socialist Countries,* ed. J. Kornai, S. Haggard, and R. R. Kaufman, 235–66. Cambridge: Cambridge University Press.
Nesterov, Leonid. 1985. "Domashnee imushchestvo v natsionalnom bogatstve" [Domestic assets in national wealth]. *Vestnik statistiki,* no. 5: 43–54.
——. 1988. "Vazhnaia rabota po statistike osvobodivshchisia stran" [Book Review: Important work on statistics of liberated countries]. *Vestnik statistiki,* no. 7: 66–67.
——. 1990. "Dostovernost' otsenok natsional'nogo bogatstva v statistike zarubezhnykh stran" [Reliability of estimations of national wealth in foreign countries' statistics]. *Vestnik statistiki,* no. 1: 36–40.
——. 1992a. "Natsional'noe bogatstvo v sistemakh statisticheskoi informatsii: metodologicheskie aspekty" [National wealth in systems of statistical information: methodological aspects]. *Vestnik statistiki,* no. 1: 23–30.
——. 1992b. "Mezhdunarodnye standarty ucheta i statistika Rossii" [International accounting standards and Russian statistics]. *Vestnik statistiki,* no. 12: 5–10.
——. 1993a. "Problemy sovershenstvovaniia statistiki natsional'nogo bogatstva" [Issues in improving national wealth statistics]. *Vestnik statistiki,* no. 1: 42–43.
——. 1993b. "Natsional'noe bogatstvo: sistemoobrazuiushchie pokazateli statisticheskoi informatsii" [National wealth: system-generating indicators of statistical information]. *Vestnik statistiki,* no. 3: 45–48.
Nesterov, Leonid. 1997. "National Wealth Estimation in the USSR and the Russian Federation." *Europe-Asia Studies* 49, no. 8: 1471–84.
Nesterov, Leonid, and E. Larionova. 1992. "Nematerial'nye sredstva, bukhgalterskii uchet i natsional'noe schetovodstvo" [Nonmaterial assets, accounting, and national accounts]. *Vestnik statistiki,* no. 7: 34–36.
Niitamo, O. E. 1982. "Sotrudnichestvo Finliandii i stran-chlenov SEV v oblasti statistiki" [Cooperation between Finland and the CMEA member states in the field of statistics]. *Vestnik statistiki,* no. 2: 42–46.
Niskanen, William. 1971. *Bureaucracy and Representative Government.* Chicago: Aldine/Atherton.
Noren, James H. 1993. "The FSU Economies: The First Year of Transition." *Post-Soviet Geography* 34, no. 7: 419–52.
——. 1994. "Statistical Reporting in the States of the Former USSR." *Post-Soviet Geography and Economics* 35, no. 1: 13–37.
North, Douglass C. 1990. *Institutions, Institutional Change and Economic Performance.* New York: Cambridge University Press.
NPT. 2006. *Treaty on the Non-Proliferation of Nuclear Weapons, 5 March 1970.* www.fas.org/nuke/control/npt/text/npt2.htm (accessed January 24, 2006).
Odell, John S. 1982. *U.S. International Monetary Policy: Markets, Power, and Ideas as Sources of Change.* Princeton, N.J.: Princeton University Press.
OECD, Organisation for Economic Co-operation and Development. *Organisation for European Economic Co-operation.* www.oecd.org/pages/0,3417,en_36734052_36761863_1_1_1_1_1,00.html (accessed July 24, 2009).
Orlov, B. P. 1988. "Illiuzii i real'nost' ekonomicheskoi informatsii" [Illusions and reality of economic information]. *EKO: Ekonomika i organizatsiia promyshlennogo proizvodstva,* no. 8: 3–20.

Ouchi, William G. 1980. "Markets, Bureaucracies, and Clans." *Administrative Science Quarterly* 25, no. 1: 129–41.
Padgett, John F. 1980. "Bounded Rationality in Budgetary Research." *American Political Science Review* 74, no. 2: 354–72.
——. 1981. "Hierarchy and Ecological Control in Federal Budgetary Decision Making." *American Journal of Sociology* 87, no. 1: 75–129.
Peters, B. Guy. 2001. *The Politics of Bureaucracy.* 5th ed. New York: Routledge.
——. 2003. "Administrative Traditions and the Anglo-American Democracies." In *Civil Service Systems in Anglo-American Countries,* ed. J. Halligan, 10–26. Cheltenham, UK: Edward Elgar.
Peters, B. Guy, and Jan Pierre, eds. 2001. *Politicians, Bureaucrats, and Administrative Reform.* New York: Routledge.
Peterson, Ivars. 1999. "Census Sampling Confusion: Controversy Dogs the Use of Statistical Methods to Adjust U.S. Population Figures." *Science News* 155, no. 10: 152.
Peterson, Stephen. 1997. "A Tale of Too Many Systems: The Role of Informatics in Reforming Tax Administration in Eastern Europe and the Former Soviet Union." Development Discussion Papers: Taxation Research Series, 600. Cambridge, Mass.: International Tax Program: Harvard Law School, Harvard Institute for International Development.
Pierson, Paul. 2000. "Increasing Returns, Path Dependence, and the Study of Politics." *American Political Science Review* 94, no. 2: 251–67.
Pitzer, John S. 1990. "Alternative Methods of Valuing Soviet Gross National Product." In *Measuring Soviet GNP: Problems and Solutions, SOV 90-10038,* ed. CIA, 1–28. Washington, D.C.: Directorate of Intelligence, United States Central Intelligence Agency.
Pogosov, Igor. 1993. "Ekonomicheskie reformy i informatsiia" [Economic reforms and information]. *Voprosy ekonomiki,* no. 5: 14–21.
Pogosov, Igor, and B. Riabushkin. 1990. "O vvedenii v praktiku sovetskoi statistiki sistemy natsional'nykh schetov" [On the introduction of the system of national acccounts to soviet statistics]. *Vestnik statistiki,* no. 7: 8–17.
Ponomarenko, Aleksei N. 1993. "Uchet uslug v natsional'nykh schetakh" [Accounting for services in national accounts]. *Vestnik statistiki,* no. 4: 32–38.
——. 2002. *Retrospektivnye natsional'nye scheta Rossii 1961–1990* [Retrospective national accounts in Russia 1961–1990]. Moscow: Finansy i statistika.
Poovey, Mary. 1998. *A History of the Modern Fact: Problems of Knowledge in the Sciences of Wealth and Society.* Chicago: University of Chicago Press.
Popov, P. I. 1926. *Balans narodnogo khoziaistva SSSR 1923–24 goda* [Balance of the national economy of the USSR, 1923–24], vol. 29. Moscow: TsSU.
Porter, Theodore M. 1995. *Trust in Numbers: The Pursuit of Objectivity in Science and Public Life.* Princeton, N.J.: Princeton University Press.
Pravda. 1989. "Pervaia sessiia Verkhovnogo Soveta SSSR" [First session of the USSR Supreme Soviet]. *Pravda,* no. 194, July 13: 1.
Pravitel'stvo Rossiiskoi Federatsii. 2002. "Ofitsial'nye materialy. Rossiiskaia Federatsiia. Federal'nyi zakon 25 ianvaria 2002 g. N 8-F3 o Vserossiiskoi perepisi naseleniia" [Official materials. Russian Federation. Federal law of January 25, 2002, N 8-F3 on the All-Russian census]. *Rossiiskaia gazeta,* no. 17, January 29: 5.
——. 2004. *Polozhenie o Federal'noi sluzhbe gosudarstvennoi statistiki* [Regulation on the Federal state statistics service], *No. 399, 30 July 2004.*
——. 2008. *Postanovlenie: O Federal'noi sluzhbe gosudarstvennoi statistiki* [Resolution on the Federal state statistics service], *No. 420 , 2 June 2008.*
Price, Richard. 1995. "A Genealogy of the Chemical Weapons Taboo." *International Organization* 49, no. 1: 73–103.

——. 1998. "Reversing the Gun Sights: Transnational Civil Society Targets Land Mines." *International Organization* 52, no. 3: 613–44.

Pryadilnikov, Mikhail V. 2009. "The State and Markets in Russia—Understanding Bureaucratic Performance through the Study of Implementation of Regulatory Reform: 2001–2008." Ph.D dissertation, Harvard University.

Reiter, Dan. 1996. *Crucible of Beliefs: Learning, Alliances, and World Wars.* Ithaca, N.Y.: Cornell University Press.

RFE/RL, Radio Free Europe/Radio Liberty. 2004. "Former Statistics Chief Sentenced." *RFE/RL Newsline* 8, no. 21, February 3.

Riabtsev, V.M., and G.I. Chudilina. 2001. *Regional'naia statistika: Uchebnik* [Regional statistics: Textbook]. Moscow: MID.

Riabushkin, B. 1993. "SNS i problemy ee adaptatsii k otechestvennym usloviiam" [SNA and problems of adapating it to domestic conditions]. *Vestnik statistiki,* no. 10: 26–31.

Rice, Stuart A. 1952. "Statistical Conceptions in the Soviet Union Examined from Generally Accepted Scientific Viewpoints." *Review of Economics and Statistics* 34, no. 1: 82–86.

——. 1953. "Reliability and Usability of Soviet Statistics: Introduction." *American Statistician* 7, no. 2: 8.

Risse, Thomas, and Kathryn Sikkink. 1999. "The Socialization of International Human Rights Norms into Domestic Practices: Introduction." In *The Power of Human Rights: International Norms and Domestic Change,* ed. T. Risse, S. C. Ropp and K. Sikkink. New York: Cambridge University Press.

Roberts, Cynthia, and Thomas Sherlock. 1999. "Bringing the Russian State Back In: Explanations of the Derailed Transition to Market Democracy." *Comparative Politics* 31, no. 4: 477–98.

Rogowski, Ronald. 1989. *Commerce and Coalitions: How Trade Affects Domestic Political Alignments.* Princeton, N.J.: Princeton University Press.

Rose, Richard. 1993. *Lesson-Drawing in Public Policy: A Guide to Learning across Time and Space.* Chatham, N.J.: Chatham House Publishers.

Rosstat, Federal'naia sluzhba gosudarstvennoi statistiki Rossiiskoi Federatsii. 2005. *Metodologicheskie polozheniia po statistike, vypusk 5* [Methodological guidelines on statistics, volume 5], ed. V. L. Sokolin. Moscow: Rosstat.

——. 2009a. Website for Rosstat, 'O Rosstate' [About Rosstat] page. www.gks.ru/wps/portal/!ut/p/.cmd/cs/.ce/7_0_A/.s/7_0_1RK/_th/J_0_CH/_s.7_0_A/7_0_FL/_s.7_0_A/7_0_1RK (accessed August 14, 2009).

——. 2009b. Website for Rosstat, Main page, English version. www.gks.ru/wps/portal/english [accessed August 14, 2009].

Rozovskii, L. 1962. "Kritika sistemy 'natsional'nogo schetvodstva' v kapitalisticheskikh stranakh" [Criticism of the "system of national accounts" in capitalist countries]. *Vestnik statistiki,* no. 2: 30–42.

Rutherford, Kenneth R. 2000. "The Evolving Arms Control Agenda: Implications of the Role of NGOs in Banning Antipersonnel Landmines." *World Politics* 53, no. 1: 74–114.

Sabatier, Paul A. 1987. "Knowledge, Policy-Oriented Learning, and Policy Change: An Advocacy Coalition Framework." *Knowledge: Creation, Diffusion, Utilization* 8, no. 4: 649–92.

Salsburg, David. 2001. *The Lady Tasting Tea: How Statistics Revolutionized Science in the Twentieth Century.* New York: W. H. Freeman.

Samuelson, P. (Soviet edition). 1964. *Ekonomika, vvodnyi kurs* [Economics, an introductory analysis], ed. A. V. Anikin, A. I. Shapiro, and R. M. Entov. Moscow: Progress.

Samuelson, Paul A. 1947. *Foundations of Economic Analysis.* Cambridge, Mass.: Harvard University Press.

Schein, Edgar H. 2004. *Organizational Culture and Leadership.* 3d ed. San Francisco: Jossey-Bass.

Schimmelfennig, Frank. 2001. "The Community Trap: Liberal Norms, Rhetorical Action, and the Eastern Enlargement of the European Union." *International Organization* 55, no. 1: 47–80.

——. 2002. "Introduction: The Impact of International Organizations on the Central and East European States—Conceptual and Theoretical Issues." In *Norms and Nannies: The Impact of International Organizations on the Central and East European States,* ed. R. H. Linden, 1–29. Lanham, Md.: Rowman and Littlefield.

——. 2003. "Strategic Action in a Community Environment: The Decision to Enlarge the European Union to the East." *Comparative Political Studies* 36, no. 1/2: 156–83.

Schimmelfennig, Frank, and Ulrich Sedelmeier. 2005a. "Introduction." In *The Europeanization of Central and Eastern Europe,* ed. F. Schimmelfennig and U. Sedelmeier, 1–28. Ithaca, N.Y.: Cornell University Press.

——, eds. 2005b. *The Europeanization of Central and Eastern Europe.* Ithaca, N.Y.: Cornell University Press.

Schroeder, Gertrude. 1995. "Reflections on Economic Sovietology." *Post-Soviet Affairs* 11, no. 3: 197–234.

——. 2001. Interview with author. McLean, Virginia, December 3.

Schwartz, Harry. 1953. "Reliability and Usability of Soviet Statistics: The Organization and Operation of the Soviet Statistical Apparatus." *American Statistician* 7, no. 2: 9–13.

Scott, James. 1999. *Seeing Like a State.* New Haven: Yale University Press.

Seliunin, Vasilii, and Grigorii Khanin. 1987. "Lukavaia tsifra" [Deceptive number]. *Novyi mir,* no. 2: 181–201.

Seltzer, William. 1995. "Five Decades of the Statistical Commission: Five Results from a Systematic Sample." Paper presented at the twenty-eighth session of the Statistical Commission, UN Headquarters, New York, 27 February–3 March 1995 to commemorate the fiftieth anniversary of international statistical work in the United Nations system.

Semchenko, N. 1992. "Voprosy garmonizatsii natsional'noi i mezhdunarodnoi otraslevykh klassifikatsii" [Issues of harmonization of national and international branch classifications]. *Vestnik statistiki,* no. 12: 15–18.

Seneta, E. 1985. "A Sketch of the History of Survey Sampling in Russia." *Journal of the Royal Statistical Society: Series A (General)* 148, no. 2: 118–25.

Shevchenko, V. 1989. "XXV sessiia Statisticheskoi komissii OON" [XXV Session of the UN Statistical Commission]. *Vestnik statistiki,* no. 5: 68–69.

Simchera, V. 1970. "V. L. Cholganskaia, 'Publikatsii OON i ee spetsializirovannykh uchrezhdenii'" [Book Review: V. L. Cholganskaia's "Publications of the UN and its specialized bodies"]. *Vestnik statistiki,* no. 3: 72–73.

——. 1976. "Sovremennoe sostoianie i tendentsii razvitiia burzhuaznoi statistiki" [The current state and development tendencies of bourgeois statistics]. *Vestnik statistiki,* no. 5: 63–76.

Simmons, Beth, Frank Dobbin, and Geoffrey Garrett. 2008. "Introduction: the Diffusion of Liberalization." In *The Global Diffusion of Markets and Democracy,* ed. B. Simmons, F. Dobbin, and G. Garrett, 1–63. New York: Cambridge University Press.

Simon, Herbert A. 1976 [1945]. *Administrative Behavior: A Study of Decision-Making Processes in Administrative Organization.* 3d ed. New York: Free Press.

Skocpol, Theda. 1992. *Protecting Soldiers and Mothers: The Political Origins of Social Policy in the United States.* Cambridge, Mass.: Belknap.

Smith, Adam. 1976 [1776]. *An Inquiry into the Nature and Causes of the Wealth of Nations.* Chicago: University of Chicago Press.

Smith, Roger K. 1987. "Explaining the Non-Proliferation Regime: Anomalies for Contemporary International Relations Theory." *International Organization* 41, no. 2: 253–81.

Sobol, V. A. 1960. *Ocherki po voprosam balansa narodnogo khoziaistva* [Essays on the material product system]. Moscow: TsSU.

Sokolin, Vladimir Leonidovich. 2004. Interview with author. Moscow, June 28.

Stanev, S. 1968. "Velikii Oktiabr' i razvitie statistiki v sotsialisticheskikh stranakh" [Great October and the development of statistics in socialist countries]. *Vestnik statistiki,* no. 2: 3–4.

Stark, David, and László Bruszt. 1998. *Postsocialist Pathways: Transforming Politics and Property in East Central Europe.* New York: Cambridge University Press.

Statkomitet SNG, Statisticheskii komitet Sodruzhestva nezavisimykh gosudarstv. 1992. "O seminare po metodologii ischisleniia osnovnykh pokazatelei sistemy natsional'nykh schetov" [About the seminar on the methodology of calculating the indicators of SNA]. *Informatsionnyi biulleten' Statkomiteta SNG* 1, no. 1: 13–20.

——. 1993. "O seminare po metodologii ischisleniia osnovnykh pokazatelei sistemy natsional'nykh schetov" [About the seminar on methodology of calculating the indicators of SNA]. *Informatsionnyi biulleten' Statkomiteta SNG* 1, no. 4: 5.

Stepanov, Iurii. 1993. "Makroanaliz i prognozirovanie v usloviiakh perekhoda na SNS" [Macroanalysis and forecasting in the period of transition to the SNA]. *Voprosy ekonomiki,* no. 5: 32–43.

Stigler, Stephen M. 1999. *Statistics on the Table: The History of Statistical Concepts and Methods.* Cambridge, Mass.: Harvard University Press.

Stiglitz, Joseph E., Amartya Sen, and Jean-Paul Fitoussi. 2009. "Report by the Commission on the Measurement of Economic Performance and Social Progress." www.stiglitz-sen-fitoussi.fr/documents/rapport_anglais.pdf (accessed October 22, 2009).

Stone, Richard. 1945. "Definition and Measurement of the National Income and Related Totals. Appendix to the Report of the Sub-Committee on National Income Statistics for the League of Nations Committee of Statistical Experts." Geneva: League of Nations.

Streeck, Wolfgang, and Kathleen Thelen. 2005a. "Introduction." In *Beyond Continuity: Institutional Change in Advanced Political Economies,* ed. W. Streeck and K. Thelen, 1–39. New York: Oxford University Press.

——, eds. 2005b. *Beyond Continuity: Institutional Change in Advanced Political Economies.* New York: Oxford University Press.

Studenski, Paul. 1958. *The Income of Nations.* New York: New York University Press.

Suleiman, Ezra N. 1974. *Politics, Power, and Bureaucracy in France: The Administrative Elite.* Princeton, N.J.: Princeton University Press.

Swartz, David. 1997. *Culture and Power: The Sociology of Pierre Bourdieu.* Chicago: University of Chicago Press.

Swidler, Ann. 1986. "Culture in Action: Symbols and Strategies." *American Sociological Review* 51, no. 2: 273–86.

Tabata, Shinichiro. 1994. "The Anatomy of Russian Foreign Trade Statistics." *Post-Soviet Geography* 35, no. 8: 433–54.

——. 1996. "Changes in the Structure and Distribution of Russian GDP in the 1990s." *Post-Soviet Geography and Economics* 37, no. 3: 129–44.

Tannenwald, Nina. 2005. "Stigmatizing the Bomb: Origins of the Nuclear Taboo." *International Security* 29, no. 4: 5–49.

Tanzi, Vito. 2001. "Creating Effective Tax Administrations: The Experience of Russia and Georgia." In *Reforming the State: Fiscal and Welfare Reform in Post-Socialist Countries,* ed. J. Kornai, S. Haggard, and R. R. Kaufman, 53–74. Cambridge: Cambridge University Press.

Thelen, Kathleen. 2003. "How Institutions Evolve: Insights from Comparative Historical Analysis." In *Comparative Historical Analysis in the Social Sciences,* ed. J. Mahoney and D. Rueschemeyer, 208–40. New York: Cambridge University Press.

Treaty of Rome. 2006. *Treaty Establishing the European Community as Amended by Subsequent Treaties, 25 March 1957.* www.hri.org/docs/Rome57/ (accessed January 24, 2006).

Treml, Vladimir. 1988. "*Perestroika* and Soviet Statistics." *Soviet Economy* 4, no. 1: 65–94.

——. 1989. "Dr. Vanous's 'Dark Side of Glasnost' Revisited." *Comparative Economic Studies* 31, no. 4: 95–109.

——. 1994. "Problems with Soviet Statistics: Past and Present." In *Defense Conversion, Economic Reform, and the Outlook for the Russian and Ukrainian Economies,* ed. H. S. Rowan, C. Wolf, Jr., and J. Zlotnick, 19–38. London: Macmillan.

——. 2001. "Ten Years of Change in Russian State Statistics." Unpublished manuscript.

——. 2004. E-mail correspondence with author, May 10.

TsK KPSS and Sovet Ministrov SSSR. 1987. "Postanovlenie TsK KPSS i Soveta Ministrov SSSR. 17 iiulia 1987 g. No 822. O merakh po korennomu uluchsheniiu dela statistiki v strane" [Resolution of the CPSU Central Committee and USSR Council of Ministers. July 17, 1987. No. 822. On measures for radical improvement of the work of statistics in the country]. In *O korennoi perestroike upravleniia ekonomikoi. Sbornik dokumentov* [On the radical restructuring of economic management. Collection of documents], 178–90. Moscow: Politizdat.

Tsyrlin, L. 1970. "Statisticheskii ezhegodnik OON za 1968" [Book Review: UN 1968 Statistical Yearbook]. *Vestnik statistiki,* no. 9: 73–76.

——. 1981. "K voprosu o sopostavlenii statisticheskikh pokazatelei ekonomiki SSSR i SShA" [On the Question of comparison of statistical indices of the USA and USSR economies]. *Vestnik statistiki,* no. 4: 32–40.

UN Statistical Commission. 1946. "Report of the Statistical Commission to the Economic and Social Council," vol. 1. *Journal of the Economic and Social Council,* no. 17, E39. New York: United Nations.

——. 1977. "Provisional International Guidelines on National and Sectoral Balance Sheet and Reconciliation Accounts of the System of National Accounts." M-60. New York: United Nations.

——. 1979. "Guidelines on Statistics of Tangible Assets." MN-68. New York: United Nations.

——. 1989. "Report on the Twenty-fifth Session, Supplement No. 3." E/1989/21, E/CN.3/1989/25. New York: United Nations Economic and Social Council.

——. 1994. "Fundamental Principles of Official Statistics of the United Nations Statistical Commission, Official Records of the Economic and Social Council, 1994, Supplement No. 9." New York: United Nations Economic and Social Council.

——. 1999. "Thirtieth Session, Milestone Assessment of the Implementation of the System of National Accounts, 1993 by Member States, Report of the Secretary-General." E/CN.3/1999/3. New York: United Nations Economic and Social Council.

——. 2000. "Thirty-first Session, Milestone Assessment of the Implementation of the System of National Accounts, 1993 by Member States, Report of the Secretary General." E/CN.3/2000/3. New York: United Nations Economic and Social Council.

——. 2001. "Thirty-second Session, Assessment of the Implementation of the System of National Accounts 1993, Report of the Secretary General." E/CN.3/2001/8. New York: United Nations Economic and Social Council.

——. 2002. "Thirty-third Session, Report of the Task Force on National Accounts, Note by the Secretary General." E/CN.3/2002/8. New York: United Nations Economic and Social Council.

——. 2004a. "Thirty-fifth Session, 2–5 March 2004, Implementation of the Fundamental Principles of Official Statistics." E/CN.3/2004/21. New York: United Nations Economic and Social Council.

——. 2004b. "Thirty-fifth Session, Report of the Intersecretariat Working Group on National Accounts, Note by the Secretary General." E/CN.3/2004/10. New York: United Nations Economic and Social Council.

——. 2005. "Thirty-sixth Session, Report of the Intersecretariat Working Group on National Accounts, Note by the Secretary General." E/CN.3/2005/4. New York: United Nations Economic and Social Council.

——. 2008. "Thirty-ninth Session, Report of the Intersecretariat Working Group on National Accounts, Note by the Secretary General." E/CN.3/2008/5. New York: United Nations Economic and Social Council.

UN Statistical Division. 2003. "National Accounts: A Practical Introduction." Studies in Methods, Series F, no. 85, ST/ESA/STAT/SER.F/85. New York: United Nations, Department of Economic and Social Affairs.

——. 2008. "GDP at Constant 1990 Prices in U.S. Dollars." *National Acccounts Main Aggregates Database.* Maintained by Economic Statistics Branch of the United Nations Statistics Division. http://unstats.un.org/unsd/snaama/dnllist.asp (accessed April 30, 2010).

UN Statistical Office. 1947. "Report of the Sub-Committee on National Income Statistics for the League of Nations Committee of Statistical Experts: Measurement of National Income and the Construction of Social Accounts." Studies and Reports on Statistical Methods, no. 7. Geneva: United Nations.

——. 1953. "A System of National Accounts and Supporting Tables." Studies in Methods, Series F, no. 2, Rev. 1, ST/STAT/ser.F/2. New York: United Nations.

——. 1968. "A System of National Accounts and Supporting Tables." Studies in Methods, Series F, no. 2, rev. 3, ST/STAT/ser.F/2/rev. 3. New York: United Nations.

——. 1971. "Basic Principles of the System of Balances of the National Economy." Studies in Methods, Series F, no. 17, ST/STAT/ser.F/17. New York: United Nations.

——. 1977. "Comparisons of the System of National Accounts and the System of Balances of the National Economy: Part One, Conceptual Relationships." Studies in Methods, Series F, no. 20, pt. 1, ST/ESA/STAT/SER.F/20. New York: United Nations.

——. 1981. "Comparisons of the System of National Accounts and the System of Balances of the National Economy." Studies in Methods, Series F, no. 20, pt. 2, ST/ESA/STAT/SER.F/20 (Part II). New York: United Nations.

——. 1989. "Basic Methodological Principles Governing the Compilation of the System of Statistical Balances of the National Economy," vols. 1 and 2. Studies in Methods, Series F, no. 17, rev. 1, ST/ESA/STAT/SER.F/17/rev.1. New York: United Nations.

UNECE, United Nations Economic Commission for Europe. 1982. "Review and Development of the United Nations System of National Accounts." Report of the Expert Group Meeting, CES/WP.22/66. New York: United Nations.

UNESCO, United Nations Educational, Scientific and Cultural Organization. 2003. *Education for All Global Monitoring Report 2003/4: Gender and Education for All, the Leap to Equality.* Paris: UNESCO. www.unesco.org/en/efareport/reports/20034-gender/ (accessed April 30, 2010).

Vanoli, André. 2005. *A History of National Accounting.* Translated by M. Pinot and G. H. Partmann. Amsterdam: IOS Press.

Vanous, Jan. 1987. "The Dark Side of 'Glasnost': Unbelievable National Income Statistics in the Gorbachev Era." *PlanEcon Report: Developments in the Economics of the Soviet Union and Eastern Europe* 3, no. 6, February 13: 1–16.

Vaughan, Diane. 1996. *The Challenger Launch Decision: Risky Technology, Culture, and Deviance at NASA.* Chicago: University of Chicago Press.

Verkhovnyi sovet Rossiiskoi Federatsii. 1992. "Postanovlenie Verkhovnogo soveta Rossiiskoi Federatsii: O gosudarstvennoi programme perekhoda Rossiiskoi Federatsii na priniatuiu v mezhdunarodnoi praktike sistemu ucheta i statistiki v sootvetstvii s trebovaniiami razvitiia rynochnoi ekonomiki" [Resolution of the Supreme Soviet of the Russian Federation: On the state program of transition of the Russian Federation to the system of accounting and statistics accepted in international practice, in correspondence with the requirements of a market economy]. *Rossiiskaia gazeta,* no. 242, November 6: 4.

Vlasov, V. A. 2001. "V perepisnoi komissii Goskomstata Rossii" [Inside the census commission of Goskomstat Russia]. *Voprosy statistiki,* no. 4: 60.

Volkov, A. 1997. "Kak stalo krivym zerkalo obshchestva: k 60-letniiu perepisi 1937 goda" [A crooked mirror of society: the 60th anniversary of the 1937 census]. *Voprosy statistiki,* no. 3: 14–21.

Volkov, A., and A. Samokhvalov. 1989. "Real'ny li balansy?" [Are balances realistic?]. *Kommunist,* no. 6: 22–23.

Volkov, V. 2000. "The Political Economy of Coercion, Economic Growth, and the Consolidation of the State." *Problems of Economic Transition* 43, no. 4: 24–40.

Volodarskii, L. 1978. "60 let sovetskoi gosudarstvennoi statistiki" [60th anniversary of soviet state statistics]. *Vestnik statistiki,* no. 7: 3–9.

VS, Vestnik statistiki. 1968. "XV sessiia Statisticheskoi komissii OON" [XV Session of the UN Statistical Commission]. *Vestnik statistiki,* no. 11: 85–88.

——. 1971. "XVI sessiia Statisticheskoi komissii OON" [XVI Session of the UN Statistical Commission]. *Vestnik statistiki,* no. 5: 66–69.

——. 1979. "XX sessiia Statisticheskoi komissii OON" [XX Session of the UN Statistical Commission]. *Vestnik statistiki,* no. 6: 60–63.

——. 1985. "XXIII sessiia Statisticheskoi komissii OON" [XXIII session of the UN Statistical Commission]. *Vestnik statistiki,* no. 6: 66–69.

——. 1987. "Uskorit' perestroiku deiatel'nosti i organizatsionnoi struktury statisticheskikh organov" [To speed up the restructuring of the activities and organizational structure of statistical organs]. *Vestnik statistiki,* no 12: 3–6.

——. 1988. "Metodika ischisleniia valovogo natsional'nogo produkta SSSR" [Methods of calculating gross national product of the USSR]. *Vestnik statistiki,* no. 6: 30–43.

——. 1990. "Mezhdunarodnye sopostavleniia v ramkakh OON" [International comparison in the framework of the UN]. *Vestnik statistiki,* no. 11: 29–36.

——. 1991a. "Metodologiia sostavleniia natsional'nykh schetov SSSR: svodnye scheta" [Methodology of the creation of national accounts in the USSR: summary accounts]. *Vestnik statistiki,* no. 6: 17–26.

——. 1991b. "Metodologiia sostavleniia natsional'nykh schetov SSSR: schet proizvodstva" [Methodology of the creation of national accounts in the USSR: production account]. *Vestnik statistiki,* no. 7: 30–39.

——. 1991c. "Metodologiia sostavleniia natsional'nykh schetov SSSR: schet obrazovaniia dokhodov i schet raspredeleniia dokhodov" [Methodology of the creation of national accounts in the USSR: formation of income and distribution of income accounts]. *Vestnik statistiki,* no. 8: 28–42.

——. 1991d. "Metodologiia sostavleniia natsional'nykh schetov SSSR: schet ispol'zovaniia dokhodov i schet kapital'nykh zatrat" [Methodology of the creation of national accounts in the USSR: use of income and capital accounts] *Vestnik statistiki,* no. 9: 12–21.

——. 1991e. "Metodologiia sostavleniia natsional'nykh schetov SSSR: schet produktov i uslug i scheta vneshnikh ekonomicheskikh sviazei" [Methodology of the creation of national accounts in the USSR: goods and services and external economic relations accounts]. *Vestnik statistiki,* no. 10: 20–29.

——. 1992a. "Programma metodologicheskikh rabot Statkomiteta SNG" [Program of methodological works of the Statistical Committee of CIS]. *Vestnik statistiki,* no. 7: 11–17.

——. 1992b. "Rekomendatsii po ischisleniiu valovogo vnutrennego produkta po napravleniiam konechnogo ispol'zovaniia" [Recommendations for calculation of gross domestic product according to output]. *Vestnik statistiki,* no. 8: 3–18.

——. 1993a. "Aktual'noe interv'iu" [Timely interview with A. P. Zakharov]. *Vestnik statistiki,* no. 2: 25–31.

——. 1993b. "Eshche odin shag" [Another step]. *Vestnik statistiki,* no. 6: 27–30.

——. 1993c. "Novoe v statisticheskoi otchetnosti" [News in statistical reporting]. *Vestnik statistiki,* no. 9: 25–29.

——. 1993d. "Metodika postroeniia schetov sektora domashnego khoziaistva" [Method of constructing household sector accounts], part 1. *Vestnik statistiki,* no. 11: 28–40.

——. 1993e. "Metodika postroeniia schetov sektora domashnego khoziaistva" [Method of constructing household sector accounts], part 2. *Vestnik statistiki,* no. 12: 21–26.

VS, Voprosy statistiki. 2001. "O sostoianii informatsionno-statisticheskoi bazy po sotsial'no-demograficheskim kharakteristikam naseleniia" [On the state of the statistical databases on the socio-demographic characteristics of the population]. *Voprosy statistiki,* no. 10: 69–70.

Walsh, James I. 2000. "When Do Ideas Matter? Explaining the Successes and Failures of Thatcherite Ideas." *Comparative Political Studies* 33, no. 4: 483–516.

Ward, Michael. 2004. *Quantifying the World: UN Ideas and Statistics.* Bloomington: Indiana University Press.

Waring, Marilyn. 2004. *Counting for Nothing: What Men Value and What Women Are Worth.* 2d ed. Toronto: University of Toronto Press.

Weingast, Barry R. 1995. "A Rational Choice Perspective on the Role of Ideas: Shared Belief Systems and State Sovereignty in International Cooperation." *Politics and Society* 23, no. 4: 449–64.

Williamson, Oliver. 1981. "The Economics of Organization: The Transactions Cost Approach." *American Journal of Sociology* 87, no. 3: 548–77.

Wilsford, David. 1985. "The *Conjoncture* of Ideas and Interests: A Note on Explanations of the French Revolutions." *Comparative Political Studies* 18, no. 3: 357–72.

Wilson, Andrew. 2005. *Virtual Politics: Faking Democracy in the Post-Soviet World.* New Haven: Yale University Press.

Woodruff, David M. 2000. "Rules for Followers: Institutional Theory and the New Politics of Economic Backwardness in Russia." *Politics and Society* 28, no. 4: 437–82.

World Bank. 1998. *Assessing Aid: What Works, What Doesn't, and Why.* Oxford: Oxford University Press.

——. 1999. "Project Appraisal Document on a Proposed Loan in an Amount of US$30 Million to the Russian Federation for the Development of the State

Statistical System (Stasys) Project." 19010-RU. Poverty Reduction and Economic Management Unit, Russia Country Management Unit, and Europe and Central Asia Region. http://web.worldbank.org/external/projects/main?pagePK=64283627&piPK=73230&theSitePK=305600&menuPK=305634&Projectid=P050487 (accessed April 30, 2010).

——. 2008. "Governance Matters 2008: Worldwide Governance Indicators 1996–2007." http://info.worldbank.org/governance/wgi/index.asp (accessed June 15, 2009).

——. 2010. "Bulletin Board on Statistical Capacity (BBSC)." http://go.worldbank.org/6EIB0ZUV00 (accessed May 3, 2010).

Yugow, A. 1947. "Appraisals of Russian Economic Statistics: Economic Statistics in the U.S.S.R." *Review of Economic Statistics* 29, no. 4: 242–46.

Zagladina, S. 1963. "Sovokupnyi obshchestvennyi produkt SShA i metodologiia ego ischisleniia" [Gross social product in the USA and methodology for its calculation]. *Vestnik statistiki,* no. 1: 38–47.

Zakaria, Fareed. 1994. "Culture Is Destiny: A Conversation with Lee Kuan Yew." *Foreign Affairs* 73, no. 2: 109–26.

Zarubin, G., and I. Pogosov. 1991. "Vzaimosviaz' pokazatelei BNKh, SNS, i PMS OON" [Relationship of indicators of the MPS, SNA, and the UN's ICP]. *Vestnik statistiki,* no. 5: 20–26.

Zarubin, G., and S. Sergeev. 1990. "Uchastie SSSR v rabote nad Proektom mezhdunarodnykh sopostavlenii OON" [Participation of the USSR in the UN International comparison program]. *Vestnik statistiki,* no. 8: 57–64.

Zharova, A. 1993a. "Zadachi sovershenstvovaniia statistiki natsional'nogo bogatstva" [Tasks for improving national wealth statistics]. *Vestnik statistiki,* no. 3: 43–45.

——. 1993b. "Realizatsiia gosudarstvennoi programmy" [Realization of the state program]. *Vestnik statistiki,* no. 4: 29–31.

Index